ZITHERS, MOSQUITOES

ESSAYS & REVIEWS
1982-2021

Jonathan Falla

STUPOR MUNDI

FIFE
2021

Sᴛᴜᴘᴏʀ Mᴜɴᴅɪ
Wonder of the World
KY14 6JF, Fife UK

www.stupormundibooks.wordpress.com
mundibooks@gmail.com

Set in Perpetua 12 pt
and designed by Kit McCarthy

*Stupor Mundi was the name often given to the Holy Roman
Emperor Frederick II of Hohenstaufen (d.1250). A man of great
talents and learning, he was a lawgiver and patron of the arts
and sciences, linguist and warrior whose Sixth Crusade retook
Jerusalem by negotiation rather than bloodshed. His court at
Palermo was described by Dante as 'the birthplace of Italian
poetry.'*

CONTENTS

ACKNOWLEDGEMENTS

Essays and reviews reprinted here have previously appeared in the following publications: *Cambridge Anthropology, Early Music News, The Economist, Economist Development Report, Eritrean Health News, The Guardian, The Health Exchange, Hospital Doctor, International Journal of Children's Rights, New Internationalist, New Statesman, Nursing Times, Open Mind, Orbit, Oxfam News, Recorded Sound, Scotland on Sunday, Scottish Review of Books, South, Times Literary Supplement, Writers Guild of GB Newsletter.*

INTRODUCTION

This volume of essays and reviews complements an earlier book, *Beyond the Roadblocks* (2017), and collects together the last remains of a disparate career in occasional writing. *Roadblocks* contained pieces of general interest; there are similar items here but also articles on more specialist subjects: music, tropical health and mental health, aid and disaster work. I had wanted to make it comprehensive; the two volumes together contain almost every short piece I've written over a period of some forty years, but a few items have eluded me. In one or two places, to avoid repetition I have combined articles on the same subject (for example on Nicaragua), but otherwise I have only made editorial changes for clarity or to correct an obvious error. Footnotes indicate the place and date of each publication.

Archives and documented change are what this collection is about. It includes some of the earliest pieces I wrote after leaving university and then returning from two years with Voluntary Service Overseas in Indonesia. 1982 was of course pre-digital, and finding material now often means visits to the National Library of Scotland, retrieving boxes of old weekly issues of *The New Statesman* or *Hospital Doctor,* spreading the pages on a library desk and photographing them with my phone to take home and retype. Or it means threading clumsy microfilms onto the spools of massive reading devices, and spinning through frame after frame in what can seem a near-hopeless quest as I realise that I have often recorded the dates of articles incorrectly, or have perhaps noted the date I submitted copy rather than the date of publication. I was much indebted to Library staff for their help.

Retrieving one's own work from archives is a sobering process.

I discovered that national papers will digitise the work of their staff writers, but often not that of outside contributors; we are disposable. Clearly much of the early material has only distant and indirect bearing on anything in the 2020s, and the interest is mostly historical; like any secondary source, these essays and their tone often say as much about the time and circumstances in which they were written as they do about the actual subject.

PUBLIC HEALTH AND WORLD AFFAIRS

From 1978, when I first went to Indonesia with Voluntary Service Overseas, I was involved off and on with aid and disaster work until 1991. My second posting was with Oxfam in Uganda during the Karamoja famine of 1981; I was in Burma from 1986-7 with a small agency called Health Unlimited assisting the Karen people; then in Darfur (Sudan) as medical programme coordinator for Save The Children in 1990-91; and lastly in Nepal as stand-in field director for SCF's medical provision to refugee camps. Between overseas postings, I trained as a general nurse in Oxford, as a tropical diseases nurse in London, and as a paediatric nurse in Aberdeen.

Out of this came the writing on public health and international affairs. A trip to Nicaragua and El Salvador in 1986 was the origin of several articles on war and its impact on civilians, and the fate of the Nicaraguan revolution of 1979 is reflected in accounts of how the CIA-funded 'Contra' insurgency that attempted to undermine the 'Triumph' dramatically affected public health.

The circumstances of publication have their interest too; several articles were written for journals that no longer exist, publications which expressed the busy activist outrage – and optimism – of the time. *Medicine in Society*, for example, was issued by Marxists in Medicine, an association of the Communist Party of Great Britain; I didn't know this when I wrote about Nicaragua for them, assuming that the journal was simply the work of earnest health developmentalists like myself. I discovered the link later, but realised also that the editors had in no way interfered with what I had written – unlike certain others: see below. (It is, incidentally, ironic to see my own shock at beds in the corridors in Nicaragua's hospitals at a time of civil war in 1986, given the state of Britain's NHS under the onslaught of Covid-19 in 2021.)

There was also the journal *Eritrean Health News*, a product of enthusiasm for another popular insurgency, this time the Eritrean People's Liberation Front rebelling against Ethiopia. Western support included practical measures such as the development of a tiny handheld plastic microscope for diagnosing malaria[1] – I had one, a gift from my sister – which was produced in the UK for the Eritreans. Today, with Eritrea supposedly free but with one of the most repressive governments in the world, it is difficult to imagine any such charitable feelings or any such publication as *Eritrean Health News*, with its 'Other countries' section evoking an imagined worldwide community of the indignant poor coming together and exchanging health care ideas.

Next came *South* magazine, produced with generous funding from the Bank of Credit and Commerce International (BCCI, a glamorous Anglo-Pakistani venture), and with editorial headquarters in smart offices in London's Haymarket. The magazine's name reflected a modish view of the southern

---

[1] The McArthur microscope, produced for the Eritrea Public Health Programme (EPHP). The design was in some respects refined by my present employer, the Open University.

hemisphere as the world's developmental front line, a view that went along with Peters projection maps. *South* was glossy compared to *Eritrean Health News*, and its very existence was another symptom of that same purposeful activism on the part of Western developmentalists of the 1980s and 1990s, full of determination to 'engage' with the Third World. Publication in its pages was something that I would have wanted to repeat – were it not that, in 1991, BCCI was revealed to be involved in massive international frauds and soon folded, taking *South* with it. It is difficult to imagine *South* being published today, even without the internet undermining print journals. Who would fund it? Who would read it? Who today is that interested? My recent web search for *South* found only magazines praising the cuisine and tourist highlights of the southern United States. *South* would have reported in detail on development projects in Afghanistan but, after the 2021 disaster, it would have been full of drear post mortems.

Another magazine I flirted with was *New Internationalist*, produced in Oxford with money from Oxfam and others. *NI* was educational in a broad sense, advocating for the world's poor in many admirable ways. It should have been just my publication, except that I found its relentless agenda unsubtle and difficult to adapt to. They commissioned an article from me to demonstrate how the poor of the earth are more generous to others than are the rich – but as I began to write, I realised I did not necessarily think this true, or at least I knew of no evidence; I recalled that charitable institutions such as Islam's *Zakat* (alms) originated as much in politics as in altruism. This (said the editors) was simply 'off message' and they declined to publish it, but at least paid me a kill fee.

NI asked me for a group of short essays on 'classic books': I chose works by Mary Seacole, Bernal Diaz, Karen Blixen, Mariano Azuela, Ivan Illich, and A.R.Wallace. An *NI* editor took exception to Wallace writing (in 1869): 'I have lived with communities of savages where each man (*sic*) scrupulously respects the rights of his (*sic*) fellows.' The editor inserted the *sic* brackets, at which I finally lost sympathy with *NI*. And yet I regret the parting; there was a time when any teacher with half an interest in world affairs would have left copies of *NI* lying around the classroom, but no more.

This shift of attention may be the result of self-serving insularity, but perhaps it has some benefits: at least we no longer assume so readily that we in the developed north can sort out the rest. I cannot imagine a repeat of Tony Blair's report on Africa, launched in Edinburgh in 2005 with very few Africans involved. These days, if there are any specialist publications that still explore Third World affairs, they're all online – and I doubt that anyone besides specialists looks at them. Even the term Third World is out of fashion, now being most often a term of insult as in, 'dreadful roads worthy of a Third World country.'

So, part of the interest in re-reading these essays is to see how fashion has treated both the topics and the people. Aung San Suu Kyi, whose book *Freedom from Fear* is reviewed admiringly here, was idolised for many years for her heroic resistance to military dictatorship in Burma. Then, when she came into a semblance of government, she was vilified in the West for the Army's dreadful treatment of the Muslim Rohingya people of Rakhine State, although whether she could have prevented it – walking a tightrope with the generals always poised to take back power – is unclear. As I write today, she is back in detention after the Army's latest coup. Will her reputation be restored by this?

Other intellectual fashions of the 1980s and before may now seem oddly nonsensical. In revisiting Ivan Illich's *Limits to Medicine* (1974), I cite Illich's argument that China does very well without the hi-tech medical equipment that is standard in the West; the simpler Chinese model was held up as desirable. Today, I suspect that Chinese hospitals – at least in the major cities – are as wedded to technology as anywhere else.

By the mid-1990s I was growing increasingly sceptical about many aspects of aid and development projects. My worries had received early expression in my 1981 play *Topokana Martyrs Day*, then in my novel *Poor Mercy* from a decade later. In this collections the reviews of *Moving Mountains* and of *World in Crisis* further explore such doubts.

Arts essays & reviews

One reason for preserving arts essays and reviews is that these too convey their time and circumstances, and contemporary morals and mores. In 2004 I greatly enjoyed the novel *Cooking with Fernet Branca* by James Hamilton Paterson, and thought it very funny. Many of the jokes, however, hint at pathetic fantasies of the sexual abuse of young boys. Would I be so amused now? Would I praise it in print so cheerfully? Would JHP even have written it?

Meanwhile, an ethnomusicologist may read here what the traditional music scene in Sunda (West Java) looked like in the late 1970s, in the first quarter century after Indonesian independence and before the influx of westernised (or Korean) rock and pop music really hit the country as it now has. From a quarter century later, there are three notes I wrote to accompany recordings of Renaissance French, Spanish, English and Scots music performed by Fires of Love, the Early Music quartet I worked with, and these pieces display degrees of knowledge and ignorance and performance attitudes which, in their unspectacular way, will have been changing just as internationalism has changed. The essay on *Love & Reconquest* mentions a revived fashion for Spanish culture which in 2021 is a given, but which a few decades earlier under the Franco dictatorship was decidedly a niche interest. The little piece called 'Rekindlings' describes a band on the road at a time when Early Music in Scotland was a niche too – which it still is. I seem to have a predilection for niches.

Remember me, my deir, the Scottish CD essay, talks of the myth of the Castalian Band, a group of court poets in Scotland supposedly emulating the French Pléiade, and it notes how that myth, dating from the 1960s, was demolished by more careful scholarship four decades later. This demolition was not altogether welcome in Scotland, where the idea of the Castalians had been viewed as a Renaissance feather in the country's cultural cap. It was only by chance – just as I embarked on writing the sleeve notes for the CD – that I learned how the Castalian idea had been discredited, and thus we in the ensemble narrowly avoided appearing foolish and ignorant. When Fires of Love performed that concert programme, audience members would accost me saying sadly that a fond illusion had been taken from them.

Other essays hint at other changes: the failure of London's Museum of Mankind, for instance (see 'War Drums'), which after some twenty seven years had to admit that the British public were not very interested in the outside world except as a holiday destination; the Museum closed not long before the

Commonwealth Institute shut also.

Many of my reviews were written for the *New Statesman* or *Scotland on Sunday*, both of which cut back on contributors as the printed news market shrank. The last reviewing I did for *Scotland on Sunday* was in fact a group effort; two of us met with the books editor as a panel to discuss a new novel. We got our travel expenses, but no fee. Soon the editor was out of a job too.

Another change in attitude was my own: in the decades of most of my book reviewing, I was a published book author and dramatist myself, with some modest success. I would now be reluctant to write a damning review, simply because I learned from experience how hurtful that can be for the author. But, ten or twenty years ago, encountering a badly written book made me cross – as several reviews here demonstrate. A Nicaraguan memoir – *The Country Under My Skin*, by Gioconda Belli – was given much more review space in other publications, largely because of the mildly interesting story it told of the Revolution. But to me it just seemed so poorly written that it didn't merit any such close attention; it was just a bad book.

This attitude hardly helped my own career. I was dismayed by the failure of editorial common sense with regard to *At the Edge of Empire* by Michael Gardiner which had allowed the author to state, among other absurdities, that the Imperial Japanese Navy had 'overrun Russia' at the beginning of the 20th century, a major historical event which had hitherto passed me by. Again, it was just a bad book. My aggressive review went down rather badly, however, because at the time I had the same publisher and editor.

My most uncomfortable relationship was with *The Economist* – indeed, I cannot now think how I got involved there at all, except that they seemed open to topics that interested me: little press poetry, Amazonia, and Nicaragua. But the editors' interference in my unsigned (and thus vulnerable) articles was a world apart from the respectful light touch of the Marxist editors of *Medicine in Society*.

Finally, I have included a handful of 'public' letters. Two of these concern nuclear disarmament (again, evocative of their period), and the rest are on a ragbag of topics for the *Times Literary Supplement*. I'm always delighted to have a letter published by the *TLS*, the more niche the better; my proudest contribution pondered whether the word 'shepe' in line 2 of *Piers Plowman* (written *c.*1380) refers to a sheep or a shepherd, given that the studio dog in BBC TV's *Blue Peter* was a Border collie called Shep. They printed that one.

Remembering, however, the old truism that the reason academic disputes are so vicious is that the stakes are so small, I now try to mind my manners.

THE WAR AND THE BRIGADES
HEALTH UNDER FIRE IN CENTRAL AMERICA

Introduction

The family of General Anastasio Somoza controlled Nicaragua for 44 years, their power being based on a strong military – the National Guard – and the wealth of a small oligarchy. Like much of Central America, Nicaragua had been dominated by the United States for decades, and had been occupied by US Marines from 1912-1933 to protect US interests – which the Somozas willingly represented.

The Somoza dictatorship had largely ignored public health, relying almost entirely on private healthcare on the US model for the wealthy, with minimal provision for the poor. Education was similarly lacking. General Somoza is quoted as saying, 'I don't want an educated population; I want oxen.' [2]

'Popular' resistance focused on rebel leader Augusto Sandino who fought a guerrilla campaign from 1927-33, finally being assassinated in 1934. Sandino was commemorated in the name and ideology of the renewed Sandinista rebellion of the 1960s and 1970s, triumphing in 1979. General Somoza fled the country, and was himself assassinated in Paraguay in 1980. The US government did not take kindly to Somoza's overthrow, lending its weight to the Contra, the counter-revolution waged by Nicaraguan exiles based in Honduras to the north and Costa Rica to the south, with CIA funding and training. The persistent Contra cross-border raiding was aimed at exhausting, terrifying and

---

[2] Holloway, T.H. (2011) *A Companion to Latin American History.* Oxford, Basil Blackwell p.408.

demoralising the Nicaraguan population. [3]

In 1986, as a qualified nurse and having just completed a six-month speciality training at the Hospital for Tropical Diseases in London, I spent some time in Central America. I had an informal brief from the new Nicaragua Health Fund to help them identify worthwhile projects to be supported with British money or expertise, and I spent much of my time visiting hospitals, clinics and healthcare projects in Nicaragua and El Salvador. The following is an edited composite of reports written on my return, and printed in various UK journals in 1986-7.

THE EPIDEMIOLOGY OF AGGRESSION [4]

As the Contra war continues to take its toll of the new public health services in revolutionary Nicaragua, the 'epidemiology of aggression' has become a key field of research. On April 2nd, Nicaragua's new Health Ministry (MINSA) launched a study of the effects of the war on Region VI,[5] an area particularly badly affected by counter-revolutionary attacks, both in order to confirm epidemiological suspicions and to provide factual evidence with which to publicise Nicaragua's plight in the face of United States support for the Contra forces.

The Sandinistas took charge in 1979 of a country with one of

[3] Fighting continued sporadically until the 1990 elections which the Sandinista candidate Daniel Ortega lost. The Contras might therefore be said to have partly succeeded.

[4] *Medicine in Society,* summer 1986.

[5] Region VI is Norte (Jinotega), touching the Honduras border.

15

the worst health profiles in Latin America, a life expectancy of 53, high infant mortality and large rural areas beyond the reach of any medical help. The Sandinistas declared healthcare free as of right for everyone, and, to deal with the situation, they formed a strategy of rapid building and staff training, of mass vaccination campaigns and drives to eliminate mosquito breeding grounds, and of the mobilisation of many thousands of young volunteer health workers, the *brigadistas de salud*, who for many observers came to represent all that was 'popular' about health in the new Nicaragua. Their efforts – which *inter alia* eliminated new polio cases and cut infant mortality by one-third – led the WHO to add Nicaragua to an elite group of nations selected for the development of primary health care models. Here, WHO considered, was a country that took Alma Ata seriously.[6]

Times have changed. The Contra war escalated seriously in 1983, and the direct physical damage is now well known: 22 health workers have been killed and many more kidnapped or threatened; hospitals and health posts have been destroyed, parts of the country made hopelessly unsafe for medical teams. The epidemiological results soon became apparent and the evidence of a tragic disruption of the early successes continues to mount. Some recent reports concern rises in malaria, TB, measles and dermatological conditions.

Malaria was not previously seen as a big problem in Nicaragua. The vast majority of cases are ascribed to *plasmodium vivax*; only on the Atlantic coast is *p.falciparum* regularly met. There is no serious resistance to chloroquine therapy (there have been one or

------

[6] The Alma Ata conference (Kazakhstan, 1978) was organised by WHO. The final Declaration was seen as a milestone, calling for worldwide commitment to 'health for all' in a broad holistic sense, achieved through primary health care. Developmentalists were all very aware of Alma Ata.

two suspicious reports, nothing more) and, given the availability of large numbers of *brigadistas* (amongst whose recent achievements had been to teach half the population to read in five short months in 1980), a serious attack on both the mosquito vector and the blood-borne parasite seemed feasible. That is what happened after 1981. Standing water breeding grounds were either filled or treated with 'Abate', and 1.9 million people simultaneously were given three days of prophylaxis. It is estimated that 92,000 cases of malaria were prevented, and for many months the incidence was dramatically reduced.

But, as the war threatened to intensify in late 1982, the basic training of the *brigadistas* was switched to first aid, and the struggling economy and infrastructure of Nicaragua was unable to support continued anti-malarial efforts. Vector control has virtually collapsed, and a press report on March 11th this year [1986] described the return of 'clouds' of mosquitoes to the outskirts of Managua itself.

The effects of this upsurge on, for example, the Zelaya Sur region of the Atlantic coast have been devastating.[7] The rural communities of Zelaya Sur are very remote – often many days travel by boat and forest path from any town – and are very exposed to Contra attacks. Any disruption of communications cuts off the hard-pressed local *brigadistas* from local support. Systematic training of *brigadistas* had begun in 1981 with 4-7 day courses at area centres; they'd been given drug supplies and, where necessary, canoes with outboard motors to bring them into regular contact with supervisors and to transport acute cases to hospital. By the end of 1984, however, six *brigadistas* and two

_____

[7] For information and guided visits in the Caribbean / Atlantic coast region, my particular thanks are due to Mary Ellsberg of Bluefields, Nicaragua.

17

nurses had been killed, three midwives and twenty *brigadistas* kidnapped and four doctors injured. Five health posts had been destroyed and the new 15-bed hospital at Tortuguero razed only weeks after it had been opened.

Clearly, a campaign to control malaria cannot survive under such pressure; nor can epidemiological surveys. In 1980 there had been some 85 *brigadistas* collaborating in Zelaya Sur, taking blood films and treating all febrile cases. By 1983 the team had risen to 233. The incidence of malaria then appeared to rise, as the remote, previously untreated areas were reached. The expectation was that the incidence would fall in 1984 as treatment became widespread. The Contra put a stop to that. By the end of 1984, the *brigadistas* had been reduced in number to 64, and the collection and examination of blood films was drastically curtailed. Incidence continued to rise: in one area, up to three times over the course of 1984. In 1985 the apparent incidence fell again – but this was simply because the high-risk outlying areas were no longer being visited.

In late 1985 and the first months of this year, the Sandinistas have re-established control over much of Zelaya Sur. Communities such as San Francisco on the Kukra River, long held by the Contra, have been freed, and medical teams have begun very tentatively to return to work. But the damage will be lasting. For example, of the fifty outboard motors on which the *brigadistas* had relied, by April this year not a single one remained operational.

Zelaya Sur had also been coping well with measles until the Contra came. There had been some 120 cases reported in 1980 but vaccination was going well and the incidence fell right off. But in late 1984/85 significant numbers of refugees from remote areas came to Bluefields, the regional capital. Many had not been vaccinated and the reappearance of measles has been traced to one small refugee girl. The groups above and below school vaccination age, the infants and later teens, began to succumb. In the second half of 1985 there were again 97 cases and the trend has continued into 1986.

Predictably, the return of fatal cases of measles is linked to malnutrition. It is impossible to be precise about the current nutritional status of remote Zelaya communities; suffice it to say that food barges, travelling upriver, require heavy Army protection and are sometimes turned back. But malnutrition affects the whole country and is as bad in the war zones of the north as it is in Zelaya Sur. On March 9th this year, Dr Romeo Oseguado claimed that 60% of the country's children are currently malnourished, more so now that many are war orphans.

The government response has been to establish infant feeding centres throughout Nicaragua. This has been made extremely difficult, however, by the large numbers of people who have abandoned the war zones and moved to empty land elsewhere, or have clustered around Managua and the central cities in illegal, unserviced marginal settlements. In 1984 there were 140,000 displaced people. The latest (March 1986) estimate from INSSBI, the social security office, is 250,000 – but, in the circumstances, accuracy is impossible. With the low standards of hygiene and sanitation and the overcrowding usual in such settlements, the consequences for health are obvious. The new 'epidemiology of aggression' study announced by MINSA in April cites rising TB incidence as of particular concern – TB having hitherto been a problem but not a major killer. The already stretched hospitals and health posts of Managua are further strained by the new influx. Meanwhile, just to make things truly miserable, it was reported in March that there was a marked rise in cases of scabies in Managua's barrios, apparently brought back from the countryside by returning coffee pickers and demobilised soldiers.

The soldiers are also associated with a more exotic feature of the epidemiology of aggression. Cutaneous Leishmaniasis (known as 'mountain leprosy') has long been present in the remoter, more luxuriantly vegetated regions of Nicaragua but in low prevalence. In 1983, however, as the war took off, the Sandinistas introduced general conscription. Large numbers of troops from the populous Pacific regions began entering the forests. They have, of course, no natural immunity to Leishmaniasis. From a mere handful, there are now thought to be 3-5,000 cases in the country – including a British journalist who had recently been travelling with the Contra.

The study of zoonotics in remote mountain/forest areas is difficult enough in time of peace; currently it is far from certain even which Leishmania parasite – *L.brasiliensis* or possibly *L.panamaniensis* – is involved. The most recent study in Nicaragua was undertaken by a French doctor, Pierre Grobsjean; in 1980 he was shot dead by the Contra at Rancho Grande. For a while, all research stopped but, on April 6th this year, MINSA and the Franco-Nicaraguan Scientific Committee announced a grand research programme: four years of investigation of animal reservoirs, establishment of laboratories, and training of local staff. It is, perhaps, no coincidence that this effort is being directed towards a particular affliction of the Army. In view of the desperate health situation of the country as a whole, it may be wondered whether a disease which is thoroughly unpleasant but only rarely fatal should justify the expenditure of $570,000 US.

But war has its own logic and its own particular health fears. In 1985, a ferocious epidemic of dengue fever reached Nicaragua, having previously attacked Cuba. There were tens of thousands of cases, some taking the fatal haemorrhagic form, and the government declared an emergency. Several million dollars from the country's very scarce reserves were spent on renewed efforts against mosquitoes and the labours of the *brigadistas* were redirected once again. Almost every house in Managua was visited, and Malathion was sprayed from aircraft over the capital. The epidemic was halted, but not the speculation as to its source; many Nicaraguans are convinced that the United States was implicated. Certainly, if one wished to perpetrate a biological assault on a poor nation's economy, the 'break-bone' dengue would be an excellent choice for incapacitating a workforce – the haemorrhagic deaths of children being merely regrettable collateral. Whether the US did it, or whether it would even be possible, are different questions which remain unanswered. But Nicaraguans are well aware of the existence of the biological/chemical warfare laboratories at Fort Detrick, Maryland.

On occasion, such fears become hysterical. On the 4th of April this year, the small northern town of Condega was hit by an attack of food poisoning. In the space of 24 hours, some 200 children and 40 adults had nasty symptoms. The local health centre was quickly overwhelmed, and buses transported scores of children, their parents and their IV infusions to the region's main hospitals. A few days later, the attack was shown to have been salmonellosis, focussed on the infant feeding centre. But the Contra have been very active in the area recently, and the people of Condega reached the obvious conclusion: 'Poison in the wells!' is a cry which students of European history meet in almost every century.

The strain to Nicaragua's 'Unified Health System' is increasingly apparent. The war is estimated to have cost MINSA some $70 million in direct damage from 1981-85. When MINSA does have money to buy drugs from abroad, it has almost no warehouses in which to store them, and when it can't store them it has too few vehicles to transport them about the country. If it had the vehicles, many roads to rural communities are frequently made impassable by the danger of Contra ambush. And even if the drugs get through, there might be no one to receive or administer them. There are reports from the Atlantic coast of junior doctors who have refused to go to their two-year 'social service' posts in the countryside, even though by refusing they fail to confirm their medical qualification.

The strain shows in all health facilities. In hospitals such as Managua's Lenin-Fonseca there are indeed beds in the corridors, and the trauma wards treat a steady stream of gunshot wounds – although it has to be said that many of these occur well away from the battlefields. Every *campesino* family given expropriated land is also issued with an automatic rifle to defend that land, and in Matagalpa recently I was shown a room of gunshot victims, all of whom had had accidents with their Kalashnikovs. Nicaragua is a society in arms, but not always very well trained. Meanwhile, on the streets of Managua, one meets the war wounded in wheelchairs which they have made themselves – that same ingenuity that helped the impoverished country to the gains that are now in danger of being lost.

What will become of the *brigadistas* under this onslaught?

Some writers [8] fear that their role has been badly eroded, that the decision-making responsibility they were supposed to take in conjunction with local health committees was perhaps always wishful thinking, their freedom to act more an ideal than a reality – that, as the pressure mounted, they would increasingly be used as the cheap foot soldiers of an overstrained system. There are some signs of resentment. In the Pacific port of Corinto, MINSA trained 90 *brigadistas* hoping that a minimum of 36 would become permanent unpaid local workers. In the event, only six remain in full-time work out of their own homes. These few are undoubtedly committed but they must wonder why they alone in the health structure should work for free, especially when their decision making is now so reduced.

By contrast, the Atlantic coast *brigadistas* and their community health committees are, of geographical necessity, so independent that their self-respect and determination has proved remarkably resilient; even with their health posts destroyed and their lives threatened, many Zelaya *brigadistas* have persisted with their work, such is their felt value. With the Contra war at last going the Sandinistas' way, the Zelaya programme is slowly being re-established. On the Pacific side, it remains to be seen whether the *brigadistas* will be trained up once more as the 'bottom line' in MINSA's strategy, or whether they can reassert themselves as health representatives of the local Defence Committees that spontaneously generated them after the 1979 Sandinista victory. They may emerge from the war battered but older, wiser, and more self-confident.

---

[8] E A Scholl. 'An Assessment of Community Health Work in Nicaragua', in *Social Science and Medicine*, 1985 vol.20 no.3.

MENTAL HEALTH IN NICARAGUA & EL SALVADOR [9]

Tropical disease units in Britain have several well-established categories of patients. Along with the nurses back from Sudanese famine relief, and the travellers returned from the East with worms, the world's refugees are our regular clients. One such that I nursed in London was Vietnamese. During the months that I knew him, all the care we gave his illness did little for his real problem: depression. With a string of language, work, family and social troubles added to his refugee status, he was often catatonic with misery, at times near suicide. Psychiatric opinions were sought. 'We must try to bring him out more,' we told ourselves vaguely, without really considering the terrible realities of his life story.

I had not expected mental health to be a research priority in Nicaragua, but I should have done. No one needs telling that war is a source of distress; many countries undergoing periods of repression and/or insurrection have had similar experiences – Namibia, for example. But the wars of liberation that have exploded in Central America have caught the professions completely unprepared for mental trauma on the scale that has resulted.

In pre-revolutionary Nicaragua, psychiatry was for the rich only. After the 1979 Sandinista Triumph, the whole aspect of the health service changed. In the first heady days of free care, there followed the spectacular vaccination drives, anti-malaria campaigns and radical attacks on infant mortality that earned Nicaragua its special World Health Organisation nomination in 1981.

---

[9] *Open Mind*, no.25, March 1987.

Mental health care, however, was slower to change. Many Nicaraguan professionals having taken their lucrative practices (clients included) to the United States, it was often left to foreigners to provide the core skills for the changes that the Sandinistas wanted. It will come as no surprise that a number of those involved were (and still are) Italians who, in their own country in the 1970s, had been making the running in returning psychiatry to the community. Under their influence, the one psychiatric hospital in Managua reduced its beds from 400 to 100 (for the whole country – pop. *c.*3 million), and a determined effort was made to put patients back in the hands of local clinics. Psychosocial day centres were established in the Managua suburbs and slowly – very slowly – the movement spread to the provinces.

But in the early 1980s, a new factor intervened, for now hundreds of refugees from the wars in Guatemala and El Salvador began crossing into neighbouring countries. In Nicaragua, their reception was generous in terms of land and legal status. What they could not be given, however, was peace of mind. It soon became clear that major problems existed.

I met a typical case in Managua. Isabel is a Guatemalan who had to leave her country in a hurry. The mother of three, she has had no contact with her children for two years. She does not know if or when she will see them again. On each occasion that we met, she had new aches and pains: a migraine, flue, stomach cramps, a recurrent bladder infection. Behind these, the roots of sadness and anxiety were clearly visible.

In the best Sandinista manner, a Refugee Mental Health Collective was set up. It produced a booklet entitled *Depression and the Refugee* which, in the comic-book form by now familiar from the Sandinistas' popular health campaigns, set out in some detail and with gentle humour the symptoms that the refugees were experiencing: depression, insomnia, physical illness, loss of libido, and many others. It explained their relation to the refugees' situation, and suggested remedies. The recommended treatment – for lack of any alternative but also out of choice – was indeed collective: occupational therapy, group recreation and, above all, group therapy sessions. 'That way,' says the booklet, 'you know you're not alone.'

By now, the Nicaraguans were not alone with the problem. El Salvador has no foreign refugees to speak of; what it has is tens of thousands of displaced Salvadoreans.[10] Today, perhaps one third of the country is a free-fire zone where the air force bombs anything that moves. In their drive to 'drain the human sea in which the guerrillas swim', the army has shifted large populations away from rebel areas, most notably the volcano Guazapa – which is so close to the capital San Salvador that the bomb flashes can be seen and heard there.

The state of psychiatry in Salvador today resembles pre-revolutionary Nicaragua. The top 15% of the population buys private treatment; for the remainder, the state provides almost nothing. There are some 300 psychiatrists for a population of four million, but 40% of these work solely in private practice, while 30% give most of their time to teaching. An elite profession, and very lucrative too. Meanwhile, in the one state psychiatric hospital, 250 patients are seen daily – up five times in five years. The increase has caught everyone by surprise, and the state has no

[10] When I visited El Salvador in 1986, the highly repressive government of President Napoleón Duarte was waging a ferocious war against scattered groups of insurgents who gradually gained the upper hand. A peace accord was reached in 1991.

plans for dealing with it.

But concerned voices may now be heard. In 1985, a Christian development agency provided funds to establish OCESAM, the Office for Training and Investigation in Mental Health. Their first report appeared not long ago.

OCESAM estimates that one in five Salvadoreans now fall into the high-risk categories of people displaced or otherwise directly affected by the war – one million people. The shattering of lives, families, church congregations and other social structures is taking a visible toll, as witnessed at the psychiatric hospital. Meanwhile, in their desperation to replace lost meaning and understanding in their lives, the people have fallen back on 'every type of magic practice, from witchcraft to religious sects which, far from helping them to confront their problems, only confuse them more.' (OCESAM)

In San Salvador, I was introduced to one such victim. Jorge was ten when the army attacked his village on Guazapa. His father had been killed some time before; Jorge now saw his grandmother, mother and two brothers shot in front of him; he alone survived under a pile of bodies. Too scared to move for days, Jorge finally made his way to a church refuge in the capital.

Since then he has been in and out of refuges, an orphanage (where he denounced the nuns to the army) and private homes. At one stage, he made his way back to the front and joined the guerrillas but even they couldn't handle him; after he had stolen money from the rebel commander, they sent him back, and he is currently living with a priest in the capital. Now 14, he is kleptomaniac and dangerous, by turns catatonic and viciously bullying. His condition is so grave that the day we met he'd had a brain scan to see if there might be some cerebral lesion. If so, funds may be found to send him to Cuba or Spain for treatment.

And if not? A small group of interested professionals – sociologists and teachers more than psychiatrists – are attempting to establish a programme of group therapy for use in the settlements of displaced people. Their methods are very basic. A sociologist told me: 'The peasants are naturally taciturn, but especially so if they have been tortured. Our first problem is to get them to talk at all. We use songs, stories, puppet shows, socio-drama, anything to draw out their experiences a little.

'We're not doctors; doctors are not interested, and also they are ill-equipped. What we have to face is not a multiplicity of individual illnesses, but a society which has undergone a profound collective trauma. Individual work is largely inappropriate.'

He did not mention the other feature of the work that discourages medical participation – the very considerable risk the helpers run from right-wing death squads.

As a basic text, the team has borrowed the Nicaraguan booklet, *Depression and the Refugee*, with Salvadorean modifications.

Meanwhile, in Nicaragua there are yet more problems. In 1983, when the Contra war escalated dramatically, general conscription was introduced. In December 1985, the first 1,000 conscripts were demobilised. Problems soon became apparent; there are reports of weed killer suicides, of young men threatening their own families with grenades. Britain is not unfamiliar with 'demob psychosis'. In Nicaragua there is a heady patriotic fervour to the war (as well as atrocious physical conditions), and an almost absurd courage in the face of a towering enemy – the United States and its proxies – that lends a particular emotional intensity to the experience.

But it is not only the troops who suffer. AMNLAE, the Nicaraguan women's association, has become increasingly concerned for the mothers, wives and widows of 'Sandino's pups' (as the conscripts are called). They have reports of women so anxious that they have set off for the front to find their men. And so 'The Mothers of Heroes and Martyrs' has been established, a network of mutual support groups to help the large numbers of women sunk in lethargic depression, isolated in their homes.

One psychologist remarked to me that, 'People don't know what is happening. They know, for instance, that the incidence of alcoholism is rising, but the connection with the war is only dimly made. We need to use our mass organisations, our health *brigadistas*, to bring these people out.'

Inevitably, the next victims are the children. A macabre feature of the past three months in Managua has been the spate of child burnings. Almost daily, it seems, children are being admitted to hospitals with all manner of burns, and several have died. The situation became so alarming that a campaign to prevent accidents was launched by press and television.

The war is undoubtedly responsible for the overcrowding of displaced families into shanty dwellings whose wood and cardboard walls catch fire and incinerate children. But perhaps there is more to it than this; last year, the director of the Child Mental Health Institute, Dr Jose Ayerdis Miranda, announced that he is convinced we are witnessing a syndrome of deliberate neglect behind the accidents. He puts the blame squarely on the war.

The state, with minimal resources, does what it can. An important source of assistance has been, indirectly, Argentina. Back in 1971, a furious quarrel broke out in the Argentinian professions – prompted by developments in community health in Salvador Allende's Chile – over the relation of psychology to politics, and the responsibilities of doctors. This led to a diaspora which took a number of Argentinians to Mexico.

In 1981, Marie Langer and Sylvia Bergman established a Mexican-Nicaraguan support group consisting of three Mexicans, a Chilean and eight Argentinians. The team instigated a survey of mental health problems amongst the 20,000 university students in the Nicaraguan city of Leon, and has since attempted to broaden psychiatric training by introducing sociological considerations that had barely been touched on previously, and by involving paramedics as well as ANDEN (the teachers union) and AMNLAE.

Resources are hopelessly inadequate. In the northern region of Las Segovias – frequently hit by the war – they have established a team of six workers in the town of Esteli. They have to cover a population of 335,000 spread over a large area, but have no vehicle.

European involvement remains (this time from Spain) and perhaps explains a feature of the programme which some might find disappointing: the core treatment is individual, with women's groups existing mainly because there are so many people to deal with. However, it seems likely that the common problems of isolation and depression are better faced in the local 'workshops of expression' than in discreet encounters with a medical professional. Could the Europeans perhaps learn as much as they can teach?

Nursing the Revolution [11]

'No firearms!' reads the sign at the door of Esteli hospital, but there's an AK47 in the pathology lab and another leaning on the fridge in the blood bank. Popular revolution, and the subsequent war to defend it, are a part of daily life in Nicaragua and, since the Sandinista victory, new values have profoundly challenged the health professions. Its self-confidence badly bruised, nursing in Nicaragua will never be quite the same.

During the Somoza dictatorship, the lives of the poor were sickly and short; for most Nicaraguans, a clinic was where you went to sell your blood for export to the United States. The rich 20% had private physicians and clinics and, if need be, regular flights to Miami.

Then came the revolution. The shock was profound: virtually overnight, with healthcare free to everyone, the hospitals and their staff had to cope with not 20% but 100% of the people, including 40,000 injured in the fighting. It was too much for some professionals; of the small corps of fully-trained nurses, several hundred left for the US, including many of the most senior and experienced. One entire hospital closed.

Nursing in Nicaragua, as elsewhere, began as the work of the religious orders. As the United States tightened its grip on the 'banana republics', so US influence was felt in nursing. During the late 19th and early 20th centuries, the Marines invaded Nicaragua four times and stayed as an occupying force for twenty years; military and civilian staff came in their wake and controlled nursing education, and the director of the school of nursing in Managua was an American until 1950.

---

[11] *Nursing Times*, June 1986

In many respects this influence was excellent. Previously, nursing had consisted of comforting the dying and little else. Only with the opening of a small nursing school attached to the remote mission hospital of Bilwaskarma in the 1930s did any idea of a more therapeutic role take hold, and the American doctor responsible, David Taylor, is revered by many as the father of modern Nicaraguan nursing.

The nuns were increasingly left to run the few charity hospitals while, for the new private clinics, nurses were recruited from middle-class families. With formal training, they came to see themselves as an elite, and had (it is now recalled) all the easy snobbery of the servants of the rich. It came as a shock when their wards filled with peasants with unwashed feet.

But the Sandinistas had promised, and were determined to provide, health for all. These first years of the popular health revolution in Nicaragua make heroic reading. Realising that the small number of professionals still in the country was hopelessly inadequate, the Sandinistas created the *brigadistas de salud* – large numbers of young health volunteers. The WHO marvelled that such a poor, war-torn country could achieve so much, noting that the key had been not only popular participation but popular initiation of schemes. Here, it seemed, was a community taking health into its own hands. Here were the neighbourhood committees with the poor thinking and acting for themselves. Here, in the slums, a popular awakening was being translated into popular preventive medicine.

But where did all this leave the remaining professional nurses? Back in the hospitals, out of the limelight and quite desperately overworked. In Nicaragua today there are two doctors for every nurse. Before the revolution, when the rich went abroad for treatment, there was little need for a large hospital labour force. The Sandinistas have increased the number of training schools from two to seven, but enrolment has been disappointing; the profession suddenly looked like very hard work for little pay and a severely eroded status. For a young Nicaraguan with academic qualifications, medicine was a more attractive career. So the Sandinistas put urgent emphasis on training auxiliaries (recently cut to a one-year course with reduced entry qualifications) and, as of 1983, introduced the *asistente de paciente* (patient assistant) with a brief grounding in basics. Some older nurses have come out of retirement, if only to assist in the mass vaccination campaigns.

There are still so few qualified staff that official policy provides for graduate cover in maternity and paediatrics only; elsewhere, auxiliaries are in charge. Where they exist, staff nurses are often obliged to be 'non-working' sisters – or, as the auxiliaries more scathingly put it, *enfermeras de escritorio* (writing desk nurses), shackled by the scores of reports to be written. They have so little patient contact that, in one hospital I visited, if there was an injection to be given the staff nurses preferred to ask a doctor to do it, having lost the knack themselves.

In the Matagalpa regional hospital, I met Jaime Fonseca. He is 28, and became an auxiliary immediately after the revolution.

'Before the Triumph I was a jeweller – but jewels don't matter now, do they? I've been nursing for six years, but many auxiliaries use the training as a first step to becoming, say, a lab technician.' I said I couldn't see the logic in that. He replied: 'It's a process. What we're learning is self-confidence and public responsibility.'

Jaime was in charge on the afternoon shift (3-10pm) in a mixed

33

ward of twenty-five beds, including urology, ophthalmology, orthopaedics and general male medical. Or rather, he was the afternoon shift. At the time, the ward was quiet.

'You can imagine what it's like when we're full. I can't do much for them.' What Jaime could and did do, as I watched, was a completely unsupervised drug round, including drawing up and administering IV antibiotics. I told him of British IV regulations, and he grinned: 'When we've got as many nurses as you, I'm sure we'll have as many rules.'

In another hospital, in Masaya, a young doctor had doubts about the auxiliaries:

'They've no vocation, they're only in it as a job. What we need are real nurses.' His hospital is better staffed, the staff nurses are in more frequent contact with patients and they are learning new skills as a result. 'We have no culture medium here, you know, because of the US economic blockade. So, in order to know what pathogens are in a wound, we have to use our noses. The nurses are good at that.'

Banis, the nurse-in-charge, wasn't too sure that she liked his idea of real nurses. She'd just come back from a year in Cuba. 'Nurses here need to learn from Cuba. They're more rebellious over there; they stand up to doctors. Our revolution's done a lot for women, but we can't do that yet. The doctors here can be very reactionary.'

Before the revolution, the health services were so limited that training abroad was the only way to specialise. Indeed, even for a basic qualification Nicaraguan student nurses had to go to Costa Rica for their psychiatric allocation. Today, there are scholarships to Bulgaria, Russia and Cuba – with language training, of course.

Lila Peña Pardilla, with four years graduate experience, is head of nursing at Granada hospital. A tough, humorous woman, she showed me her Sandinista military certificate. I asked her if she kept her AK rifle in the office. She smiled and shook her head, but said she wanted to go to Cuba soon. To study paediatrics?

'No, politics. You see, this revolution is about sharing responsibility, and we have to apply the lessons to nursing. What would happen here if I were called up or killed?'

Her fears are not idle. Even before the Sandinista victory in 1979, nurses were being killed; during strikes in 1976 and 1978, several were shot by Somoza's National Guard. During the insurrection, the Guard was liable to execute anyone found tending the wounded, for being rebel sympathisers, and today the Contra are no more sympathetic.

But now, one important extra resource is foreign support. There are several hundred foreign staff working in Nicaragua: Cubans, Italians, Mexicans, even (ironically) quite a few North Americans. Some have been killed. Many are extraordinarily selfless people. I met a Dutch nurse, Analöes, who had taken a year off to work, unpaid, in the country's only paediatric neurosurgery unit, to nurse children with shrapnel in their spines.

'Our hospital, the Lenin-Fonseca, was built privately with a casualty department designed to see 25 patients a day. Now we get 250. We have 45 children in a 30 bed ward, with only half-level staffing. This is when the strain shows. For example, the auxiliaries site all the IVs here – they're really good at it – but they have no time to check them so there's some horrific tissuing. And as for quarter-hourly neuro obs! We're lucky if we get to do a temperature round each shift. The children don't seem to die, but I don't know how the nurses keep going.'

Contradictions are apparent in the Ministry's attitude to foreign staff in hospitals. Both the work and the teaching of volunteers like Analöes are much appreciated by the unit of which – as the only nurse with specialised neurology training – she is frequently given sole charge. But the Ministry not only provides neither salary nor uniform: it has refused her any sort of contract or formal recognition of her presence.

Analöes and the Nicaraguan nurses do keep going, and the new schools are now producing their first post-revolution graduates. I recall one remark that will strike a chord in British colleagues: 'We'll manage; we have to. But we can cope best when we've learnt self-respect again. That's what we'd lost, that's what we're looking for now'.

BIRTH PAINS: NICARAGUAN OBSTETRICS [12]

The Nicaragua Health Fund was launched in London this spring to help counter the effects of the Contra war on health services. Even without the war, post-revolution Nicaragua has to cope with a system that is sorely strained.

But cultures cannot be recreated by government *fiat*, and still less medical traditions. Nowhere is the disparity between the new social structures and the old professional attitudes more pronounced than in obstetrics. And in the current crisis the professions have had no chance to adapt.

The Sandinistas' new Unified Health System has been heavily influenced by that of Cuba, with good cause; the Cubans have provided enormous assistance in both materials and personnel. Cuba's own achievements in reducing the incidence of

---

[12] *Hospital Doctor*, June 1986.

communicable disease and infant mortality are undeniable, and Nicaragua has replicated many of them. But the model does not transfer easily. In Cuba perhaps 90% of births take place in hospital, attended by doctors. Hospital birth for all is the stated policy of MINSA, the Nicaraguan Health Ministry. But MINSA is forced to recognise that 50-60% of births in fact take place at home.

There is the simple question of access to facilities. No country can expand its health services from covering 28% to 100% of the population overnight – and, as well as a war, Nicaragua has a US economic blockade to cope with. Much of the country is rural and remote; the few doctors (with fewer vehicles and bad roads) cannot reach the mothers; still less can *campesinas* going into labour reach the hospitals.

But would they want to? Against the relative safety of hospital must be set an experience of childbirth that in many centres is most discouraging. The overcrowding is acute. Managua's main women's hospital, the Bertha Calderon, was designed for 230 beds; the wards now hold 332 beds. No one has attempted to gauge the consequences in, for example, cross-infection. A comparable facility in Britain might see some 2000 births yearly. The Bertha Calderon sees 50 to 60 a day, 20,000 a year. The stay is brief; a few hours after the birth, the woman has to make way for others and go home – excellent were there any community back-up, but the hard-pressed state cannot provide it. And simply to get home is a struggle; the sight of a young mother with an infant a few hours old attempting to prise a foothold on a tight-packed Managua bus is truly alarming.

Privacy is non-existent. Wards and delivery rooms are open house; doctors, medical students, nurses and others come and go, modesty and dignity go by the board. The atmosphere can be strained, even downright brutal. The strain shows in the staff as much as on the women. The Managua press has recently carried articles complaining about sullen, secretive receptionists, stories of relatives denied information, of staff asleep on duty, of patients 'lost' by the system, of theft, of cleaning not done and rubbish abandoned in the corridors. The director of the hospital, Dr Jorge Orocena, doesn't deny the reports but points to other indices of low morale, a very high absenteeism above all – 965 absent days in the last eight months. Added to the already low staffing levels this means that the hospital runs on perhaps 50% of the required establishment. This stretching comes out in the behaviour of doctors and nurses towards the patients; Bertha Calderon staff are reputed to be aggressive, rude, dismissive and neglectful.

The problems are well recognised, but what can be done? In the face of the economic blockade and war, the steady deterioration of equipment (50% of Nicaragua's microscopes are out of action for lack of bulbs), the absence of any cash for improvements and the acute personnel shortfalls, it is only too easy to see how medical and nursing staff become depressed and demoralised, and how deviant behaviour begins.

They do what they can to counter it; lectures and discussion groups on doctor-patient relations have been started; there is a scheme for classes in 'humane nursing' and the Nicaragua Health Fund has been asked to support that. But there are limits to what pep talks can do when what is needed is material resources – hence the welcome for a private US fund's appeal for 'A Million Dollars for the Bertha Calderon.'

So far, a case for sympathy and aid; given time, more facilities and far more staff, things will improve. What arouses less immediate sympathy is the professional approach to women. Aggression may be ascribed to stress, but not the standard procedures. The woman gets no choice of place or position for the delivery. 'On the floor? Certainly not, there are microbes on the floor!' was the reaction of one nurse I spoke to. There is an understandable desire for the modernity and quality that under the Somoza dictatorship was so ruthlessly denied, but this has been translated into a formidable display of mechanical birthing chairs in aseptic rooms – a terrifying prospect for a *campesina* woman. As labour commences, the woman is forbidden to move about; she should lie down and keep quiet. Communication with staff is minimal. Episiotomies are done on primagravidas without exception. The doctor frequently removes the placenta manually without waiting for it to be delivered naturally. A Chilean midwife whose own child was born in Nicaragua described the process to me as 'Horrific – an assault on women.'

What is striking is the disparity between the very genuine advocacy of women's rights and of open consultation, and the reality in the maternity hospitals. But who's to blame? The Sandinistas? The Ministry? Recently a Canadian midwife working in the north of the country was reported by an outraged doctor to local MINSA headquarters for malpractice. When specific charges were discussed – no episiotomy, for instance – it was found that the official guidelines supported the midwife on every issue. It is the practice and teaching of doctors that does not agree with Ministry norms.

One can only suggest explanations. The medical schools of Managua and Leon are quite as conservative and quite as closed to 'lay interference' as schools in less harassed countries. But one also has to try and understand the reaction of the profession to the revolution. A small, elite group working out of luxury clinics was suddenly faced with an entire population in crisis, and quite new demands made by society. A defensive drawing together was perhaps the least that might have been expected.

A code of norms of practice has been drawn up under former Minister of Health Lea Guido, and was published in 1984. These were agreed by a national committee with the guidance of the distinguished Uruguayan obstetrician Roberto Caldeyro-Barcia. As official guidelines go, they are humane and intelligent. They warn, for instance, against rising Caesarean rates which are ascribed to a tendency for doctors to solve all problems at the highest level of intervention. But Caesarean rates (although not approaching North American levels) are still increasing, and with reports of some decidedly unsympathetic and scarring incisions.

In the face of such treatment, many Nicaraguan women have voted with their feet. The hospital at Jalapa has a new maternity wing – an East German donation – with a sophisticated delivery unit which is facing closure for lack of takers. Jalapa is in a northern border area made perilous by the Contra war; it would take very sympathetic attention to induce village women to make the journey. In such areas, only small hospitals with trusted local staff have any chance of rapport with women. What else can the Sandinistas do? They fought a revolution to bring health to the people. They can hardly now turn the people away.

There are other, more hopeful sides to the story. In the Bertha Calderon, classes in psycho-prophylaxis have been started and the first mother 'graduated' in March with a very successful, near-painless delivery. Elsewhere, the traditional birth attendant or *partera empirica* is strongly established – even though under Somoza the *parteras* were suppressed, even imprisoned, for

40

representing a threat to the private medicine establishment. Today there are some 15,000 *parteras* in the country and the Ministry has recognised that it needs their help. In Boaca region, the local director of MINSA announced in March this year a major new effort to upgrade *parteras*, and other regions are supporting schemes to raise hygiene and safety standards.

Courses and exchange groups flourish. Often it is found that the *parteras* have quite as much to teach as to learn. These are mature women, well-liked and trusted by their clients, often with many years experience. At the end of a five-day course they receive a certificate of registration and a UNICEF kit in a steel case. There are monthly workshops and, in theory, a six-monthly spot check on their work in the home village. In practice, the war and the chronic lack of vehicles make such visits a rarity.

The *parteras* have another name: *abuelitas del ombligo*, or 'umbilical grannies'. They have now achieved not only recognition but a certain cultural status. They've been filmed, there have been books and articles written about them. It remains to be seen whether in the long-term they will maintain their position or whether, with the backing of a government that would like to bring the entire population under its wing, the medical profession will assert full control. In the present circumstances that seems a remote possibility; for the moment, the Unified Health System is hard pressed to survive at all. Clearly there are limits to the pressures that socialised medicine can be expected to sustain. For the foreseeable future, the individual dignities of the Nicaraguan mother, and her joy in childbirth, must be regarded as in abeyance.

[Appendix: additional notes from a related article in *The Economist Development Report*, June 1986]

The Nicaragua Health Fund must ask itself whether it should send British doctors, nurses and technicians to Nicaragua, or whether the money would be better spent on drugs and equipment. There is a desperate shortage of medical personnel in Nicaragua, but the country does not lack for foreign health projects. At one extreme, a small American agency has a single midwife working there. At the other, the East Germans have constructed and staffed an entire hospital under canvas, the Carlos Marx, which sees 350 patients daily. Cubans and Mexicans, Scots and Canadians are all there. Some are remarkable figures, like the German brain surgeon who sold his home and gave up his career in Germany, came to Nicaragua during the insurrection, fought Somoza alongside the Sandinistas and now heads the leading neurosurgery unit in Managua.

But the revolution has brought with it challenges to conventional ideas of health care, and not all foreign expertise has proved sufficiently adaptable. Ironically, some of the difficulties stem from the arrival of foreigners who are more 'radical' than the revolutionary Nicaraguans. Rather than assessing the politics of primary health, the Nicaraguans' first concern is to provide any care at all in places where it does not exist. While the Nicaraguan system is famous for its emphasis on prevention and for its army of volunteers, the training and outlook of most Nicaraguan doctors is quite as orthodox as any in Europe.

The Catholic Institute for International Relations (CIIR) has sharply cut the number of doctors it sends to Nicaragua. Too often, the conflict of values and expectations leaves one side angry and the other disappointed. Part of the trouble may lie in the very ideals of the strongly motivated (and opinionated) foreigners who apply for posts in Nicaragua. A doctor feeling constrained by bureaucracy and conservatism in, say, the British NHS may look to Nicaragua for the chance to spread professional wings and develop radical ideas in community medicine. Once there, the doctor may find the system unattractively conservative.

For its part, the Ministry of Health finds that accommodating foreign personnel can be a headache. In Bluefields, on the Caribbean coast, locals have held three days of protests at the large numbers of Cubans. In 1983, the deaths of a German and a French doctor during Contra attacks led to the withdrawal of all foreign personnel from the war zones.

Outside intervention may undermine the achievements of the Sandinistas in the eyes of the rural population. A US/British funded health education group distributed the Spanish edition of the feminist health book *Our Bodies, Ourselves,*[13] but the book's emphasis on lesbian sexuality was too much for some peasant women to take. An attempt to distribute copies of *Where There Is No Doctor,*[14] David Werner's classic manual of rural health care, was halted in one region by doctors who felt it undermined their own position. Only the personal intervention of the then Minister of Health, Lea Guido, saved the programme.

---

[13] Produced by the Boston Women's Health Book Collective, 1970. It has been widely translated and distributed.

[14] Originally in Spanish, *Donde no hay doctor* was written for Mexican villages in 1970. It has been translated into close to 100 languages and often revised.

43

Rescuing Their Roots
The revival of natural medicines in Nicaragua [15]

On April 12th, 1979, Dr Alejandro Dávila Bolaños was at work on emergency operations in the hospital at Estelí, in north-west Nicaragua. His patients all had gunshot wounds; the Sandinista insurrection was in full flood and the fighting in Estelí was particularly savage. Late in the afternoon the National Guard arrived at the hospital. Bursting into the operating theatre, they accused Dávila Bolaños of aiding the rebels, and opened fire. Dávila Bolaños together with a junior doctor and a nurse all died, along with several patients.

Today, Dávila Bolaños is remembered as a hero and a martyr. But his death was a loss not only to surgery. A deeply cultivated man who had studied several indigenous languages, he had long been interested in traditional healing and the use of herbs. In 1974 he had published *Pre-Colombian Medicine in Nicaragua*, a survey of practices and potions learned from historical texts and from *curanderos*, local healers.

Under General Somoza, in spite of the fact that his regime was providing little or no healthcare for the population, *curanderos* had been persecuted, both for threatening the medical profession and then for aiding the Sandinistas. After the 'Triumph', the new Sandinista government opted for a modern hospital-oriented medicine. But in the six years since, it has become clear that traditional medicine has an important role to play. For a start, large areas of the country are so remote and inaccessible that it will be a long time before the national Unified Health System can

---

[15] *Eritrean Health News*, vol.1, no.3, spring 1987, 'Other countries' section, and a related version in *South*, February 1987.

effectively cover them. Secondly, resources are desperately scarce. Nicaragua's annual drugs bill is currently $40 million p.a. That almost exactly writes off the earnings of the country's gold mines. Traditional medicines are therefore not a crank's pastime, but are to be taken seriously.

The leading research centre is, appropriately, in Estelí. The project is called the *Rescate* [rescue] *Popular de Medicinas Naturales,* has Ministry of Health backing and is currently headed by a German sociologist, Juanita Brussel, with biologist Oriel Sotomayor, and Dr Jose Angel Lara. The skills of the sociologist are vital, since the project is attempting to rediscover popular knowledge and then propagate it once more.

The region of Las Segovias (around Estelí) was once particularly rich in Mayan and Nahualt culture; one may still come across stones with incised decorations of birds, plants and Nahualt symbols. The *Rescate* team feared that the medical knowledge might have been lost, but they undertook a large survey: 850 high school students went out into the villages asking *campesinos* what they knew of medicinal plants and how they used them; the students returned with 3500 completed questionnaires. A campaign was launched on local radio to gather further recipes – the *Rescate* staff point out that only the national literacy campaign of 1981 made it possible for *campesinos* to write in – and the end result was a list of 321 plants in current use of which 72 were regarded as of first importance.

A research garden was established at El Regadio (a village not far from Estelí) cared for by Ortelia Casco Cruz, a local woman who was first sent off to Mexico to a regional workshop on ethnobotany. The experience for her was mixed:

'Some Mexicans were unfriendly and suspicious; if I'd said I was studying herbal medicines I'm sure they'd have thought I was a witch. We met a very wise old man called Eugenio Martinez. He has problems in Mexico because his work in natural medicines threatens the big medical businesses. Such problems can't exist in Nicaragua.'

The plants are collected in Estelí where a report on the first 72 is in preparation. Each plant is carefully drawn, its various local names listed, its preparation and uses described.

There are some surprises. For example, cinchona is world famous as the 'fever bark' from which quinine is derived for the treatment of malaria. It has been known as such to Western medicine since the 17th century. But that is not its first use in Nicaragua where it is better known for inducing abortion up to two months into pregnancy. The logic to this is simple: chemical treatment for malaria, principally chloroquine, is widely and cheaply available in Nicaragua. But abortion is illegal, and clandestine abortions are either extremely dangerous, very expensive, or both. Cinchona bark, however, can be readily bought in the market.

The *Rescate* team are putting their discoveries to trial use and have opened a small clinic three days a week offering free herbal treatment. It is most important that the plants are tested carefully before over-optimistic clamour destroys their credibility. The uses claimed for each plant are limited and conservative. By contrast, in El Salvador – where the public health system is a disaster but the herbal market flourishes – herbs are sold in packets claiming the most fantastic cure-all properties. Only as uses are confirmed will the *Rescate* move on to the next stage of its work, producing simple wall charts and guides, training health workers and feeding information back to the *curanderos*.

Estelí does not have a monopoly. The Regional Committee for the Promotion of Community Health, representing agencies throughout Central America, set up the course in Mexico to which Ortelia Casco Cruz was sent. CEPA – the *Centro de Educación y Promoción Agraria* – has organised some forty workshops at community level throughout Nicaragua; for example, in the region of Granada, south of Managua, five continuing workshops investigate local knowledge of herbs and the results appear in the journal *Somos* published by AMNLAE, the Nicaraguan women's association, in a simple popular form encouraging families to use them. There is a further research group in the city of Leon, where a project working largely with *campesina* women teaches the use of herbal medicines and skin preparations.

Meanwhile, the *brigadistas de salud* – the volunteer health workers – have also realised that they have in local knowledge of herbs a resource that valuably supplements the over-strained supply system of the Ministry of Health, which – quite apart from a war, a US economic blockade, and a lack of foreign exchange – has few storage facilities. In such circumstances the use of a locally available, free and freshly grown botanic pharmacy makes obvious sense, and in some of the most inaccessible areas of the Atlantic coast, for example, the village *brigadistas* have been collecting and exchanging the knowledge of their communities.

There are many caveats and cautions to be heard. The director of the health eduction group CISAS, Mary Zuñiga, told me that they were introducing new herbs into their women's workshops only very gradually. There is, she believes, a danger of ill-informed confusion. A doctor on the Atlantic coast was thoroughly sceptical of the whole movement. Not only was much of it scientifically unsound, he felt, but:

'The revolution was fought on the promise of modern, professional care available to all. You can't then tell people they've got to go digging for roots!'

But there are other social questions. In Estelí, they told me:

'Our aim is not to persuade doctors but to restore to the people some measure of influence over their own health. We don't want to appropriate herbs for the medical profession, neither are we encouraging indiscriminate and excessive use; either course would be to simply exchange one dependency for another. That is not what the Sandinista Revolution is about. Finally, you must realise that we are not simply rescuing a few plants from disuse; we're engaged in rediscovering a whole culture which had been virtually obliterated.'

———————

LIMITS TO MEDICINE
by Ivan Illich [16]

The hospital in which I nurse has so few staff that a ward was closed last summer for 'redecoration'; it was in fact to allow us to be reshuffled round other wards where the situation was even more desperate.

Yet hours are spent vigorously debating the computerisation of the hospital's wards, and the Health Authority to which we belong is the proud possessor of a 'magnetic particle echo scanner',[17] a diagnostic plaything for which the magnets alone cost half a million dollars.

Most people say we are the victim of temporary financial stringencies. Ivan Illich would argue that our values are so distorted that we have reached our 'medical nemesis.'[18]

Illich, a perennial critic of establishments and orthodoxies, launches in *Limits to Medicine* a savage attack on the high priesthood of the medical profession. Doctors and their sidekicks, he says, have appropriated much of the private significance of our lives. From childhood to old age our rites of passage have been transformed into bizarre medical rituals. Parents are darkly warned that they 'risk' a home birth at their peril. Mothers must go into hospital to go into labour. They can no longer trust their own perceptions and won't even believe they feel a contraction unless it is confirmed on the read-out of the Hewlett-Packard

---

[16] *New Internationalist,* February 1985. 'Classic books.' Original published 1975.

[17] I was perhaps confusing this with what we would now know as an MRI scanner, a term not yet widely familiar in 1985.

[18] 'Medical Nemesis' was an alternative title (or subtitle) for the book.

monitoring system. Death likewise: a terminal experience of attachment to cardiac monitor.

Birth and death have become ceremonials for white-robed doctors. But what good has it done us? Our perinatal mortality rate is no better than China's, where they do very nicely without Hewlett-Packard.[19]

When the British National Health Service was established it was believed that costs would fall in the long run as greater diagnostic and curative ability reduced the morbidity of the population. This has been proved utterly wrong. Neither our skills nor our equipment have saved us from chronic illness or the appallingly unloved burden of geriatrics. And high-tech units have been almost totally defeated in their attempt to reduce coronary fatalities. Finally and ludicrously we are discovering previously undreamed-of diseases in formerly healthy sections of the population.

In preventive medicine, some screening (cervical smears, for instance) may, if better organised, be worthwhile. But the vogue for computerised general screening of workforces has been shown in no way to reduce sickness rates. Expensive medical techniques have a terrible cumulative power. If they are available, we must have them – although two-thirds of hospital construction costs are accounted for by equipment that becomes obsolete within ten years. Too bad if our local day centre for the elderly has had to close for lack of funds.

In the USA such is the warped logic of this technological imperative that hospitals have to buy all the latest gadgetry in order to exist at all; if they did not, doctors and their patients would soon move elsewhere. In consequence there are now often

---

[19] I doubt this is still the case, at least in Chinese cities.

a dozen vastly expensive scanners in an area of a few square miles. And yet, as Illich points out, in that same United States, home of unquestionably the most technically skilful medicine the world has ever seen, life expectancy has actually begun to fall. God forbid we should export such a medicine to countries where lives are short enough already – yet that is exactly what we are doing.

The World Health Organisation itself espouses the 'de-professionalisation' of primary health care as the most important step in raising national health levels. Yet year by year the grip of the profession tightens. The actual number of medical para-professions steadily grown as new specialities emerge, each demanding the taxpayer's support as of right.

Lest we imagine our situation new, Illich takes us back to origins: to Prometheus, primitive symbolism, the hubris of the priest who confront fate on society's behalf. He looks also to that fast-approaching future of psychological, environmental and genetic manipulation – 'engineering for a plastic womb'. He tells us to reclaim decisions about our own health, to resist categorisation, to 'die well' according to our own lights, and he does so with a breathtaking range of reference: historical, cultural, scientific and economic. For we are all health consumers, and *Limits to Medicine* is about us all.

DEFORMITIES OF LUST IN AMAZONIA [20]

A few months ago, at the village of Gorutire on the Rio Fresco (a tributary of the Brazilian Amazon), a Kayapo Indian woman gave birth to a monstrously deformed baby. It was promptly killed. Such a horror had never been seen there before. But the world around the Kayapo is changing fast and, in the last few years, the Maria Bonita district just upstream of Gorutire has been invaded by gold prospectors.

At Altamira earlier this year, while the TV lights were flooding the Kayapo-organised meeting of Indians protesting against hydroelectric dams, scientists from the Federal University of Pará (Belem) and a government mineralogist were presenting a side meeting with evidence of an impending health disaster.

Brazil is in the throes of the world's greatest-ever gold rush. Nobody knows how many *garimpeiros* – prospectors – have swarmed into Indian territory, but they must be numbered in hundreds of thousands. They are poor, desperate for gold, working in freebooting bands which come into murderous conflict with local Indian groups. Extraction is by simple washing of gold-bearing mud, but to speed the process, the prospectors use one of the most toxic of all metals: mercury. Thrown into the sluice water, mercury amalgamates with tiny gold particles, causing it to settle out quickly. The silt is panned, and the mercury is then burnt off with a short burst from a gas jet. Since 1980 the level of mining and the quantity of mercury used has increased

---

[20] *The Guardian,* June 1989. My sister-in-law Christine had been recruited as medical support for the Altamira protest meeting, and she recruited me (as a tropical diseases nurse) in turn. After the protest meeting we took a boat upriver and visited a prospectors' camp, witnessing the mercury process. The rather gothic title of this piece is a *Guardian* editor's, not mine.

dramatically.

At a very rough guess, 900 tons of gold were produced between 1980 and 1987. 1g of gold requires up to 2g of mercury to produce. Thus, perhaps 1,800 tons of mercury have been dumped into the Amazon ecosystem.

At Minamata, Japan (1962), the effects of mercury poisoning were demonstrated in a spate of deformed births and other illnesses in a poor fishing community. The Amazon catastrophe will be slower but nastier. Mercury from gold mining enters the ecosystem both directly (from the sluices, and as vapour from the burning process), and also indirectly as it reacts with bacteria and accumulates in the food chain.

The presence of mercury was detected in fish, plants and water in 1986. Pollution has been found hundreds of kilometres downstream from the mines, and the team from Belem now have results from tests on humans. Although the samples are as yet small, they show levels far above the 'safe' limit in blood, urine and hair, both in Indians and in the prospectors themselves.

'They must have been showing symptoms before,' says Professor Geraldo de Assis Guimarães, 'but local health authorities have been, for instance, describing toxic fits as caused by cerebral malaria – even in patients with no malarial fever. What we need, and at once, is a full-scale research programme.'

That is easily said. Neither the prospectors nor the local authorities are going to welcome such an exposé, besides which the resources required are enormous. Each sample analysis costs $50. Professor Guimarães estimates that he needs $100,000 for his proposed survey.

A further tricky question is the source of the mercury. Brazil imports all its needs – 1,336 tons from 1980-87 – but official figures can account for all of this in 'normal' industries such as electronics and alloy manufacture. In other words, large quantities are being smuggled. Meanwhile, Brazil has banned its use in mining, but clearly without effect.

'What we fear,' says Professor Guimarães, 'is a generation of Japanese monsters in the rainforest.'

THE POLITICS OF NURSING
by Jane Salvage [21]

This is not a kind book; nursing has been near killed with nurses' own kindness. The reality of NHS cuts, of acute stress (about 45% of nurses smoke), racism, hierarchy, the suppression of the individual (in the cause of professionalism) and the divisions between the Royal College and the unionised auxiliaries are not a pretty spectacle.

The Angels image does nurses little service either. Instead of skills given their just reward, there's the bamboozling of (mainly) women and the exploitation of their time and better natures. The entry of men into the profession, said to provide the management muscle that women couldn't find among themselves, hasn't helped; men simply reach senior positions at three times the speed. Fobbed off with public admiration, praised to the sky but politically abandoned by doctors (whom, to the delight of Mills and Boon, they persist in marrying[22]), nurses are often their own

---

[21] *New Statesman*, July 1985,

[22] I was wrong about this. I'm told the only preference they show is for firemen.

worst enemies. Currently they are obsessed by that professionalism, which means that nursing education is third-rate copy of the medical model and that nurses dare not strike; they forget that other professions don't strike only because they have no need. In Israel recently doctors had need, and did.

Jane Salvage, a founder of the Radical Nurses Group, writes as an angry feminist and a furious nurse, castigating many enemies. Still, she leaves a lot unsaid: about the way in which the professions appropriated healthcare in the first place, for instance, or the effects on developing countries of exporting our care models via 'expert' advisers, which we busily do. And it won't do to denounce the flattering of a spurious female image – all loving-kindness and domesticity – and then to claim that actually women really are better nurses because *etc etc.*

We undoubtedly needed provoking. But 'the book that every nurse has been waiting for', as the blurb claims? Another fond caricature, I fear.[23]

---

[23] An example of the perils of careless ambiguity. I meant that I wished my nursing colleagues really were waiting for such a book, and I was disappointed that they showed no signs of it.

This short notice came out more dismissive than I intended, and the author wrote to me to complain. I was sympathetic to much of her point of view; I and a few of my fellow nursing trainees tried to distance ourselves from the nursing establishment by (for instance) joining COHSE, a trade union, rather than the Royal College of Nursing. But I was antagonised by aspects of the book: firstly, the presentation was aimed low, with silly cartoons and a cover design meant to evoke the pink stripes of a staff nurse's uniform. The publisher's defence may have been that they wanted to appeal to a readership (nurses) not accustomed to reading books on the politics of health care, but to me it all seemed patronising, and betrayed the fact that, so far from waiting eagerly for an upending of the hierachy, many nurses seemingly liked their secure role. Worse was her rejection of men in nursing, on flimsy evidence as stereotyped as any *Carry On* film. I was struggling to survive as a male student nurse, an unusual thing in 1985, had faced considerable difficulty being accepted as a trainee at all, and was often the target of prejudice and preconceptions.

Rebels with a Cause
Training village health workers in Burma [24]

In the thickly forested mountains which stretch along the north/south border dividing Burma from Thailand lies a series of rebel states unrecognised by any government. At the end of the Second World War, as independence for Burma was being negotiated with the British, they expected regional autonomy at least, as the solution to centuries of hostility from the dominant Burmans. To their astonishment, the Karen and the many other minority peoples found themselves unwilling components of the Union of Burma. The sell-out did not fit their understanding of our relationship, and to this day they still occasionally send off letters to Buckingham Palace or Number 10, politely requesting explanation and support.

In Burma, in the late 40s, tension had mounted fast and several of these minority groups – notably the Karen and the Kachin – went into open rebellion in 1949, the former declaring the Free Karen State of Kawthoolei which today clings to a narrow strip of territory down the long eastern border of Burma and Thailand. They've been fighting for four decades years now, but I confess that until last year I had never heard of them. Nor, I suspect, had most people in Britain – another forgotten war.

Kawthoolei today[25] is home to perhaps 60,000 people who are scattered widely along 2000 km of river and forest in bamboo villages, which are vulnerable to Burmese army attacks. The

---

[24] This is a composite of two overlapping articles, from *Nursing Times* (June 1986) and *Hospital Doctor* (January 1987).

[25] Or so it was at the time of writing in 1986-7. There is little of it left within Burma today, in 2021.

forest is dense and most travel is done on the river. The machinery of government is run from wood and bamboo huts: schools, hospitals, tax officials, police and prisons, churches and welfare organisations. It suffers from all the problems of underdevelopment.

Protected and hampered by the forests, the Karen have little other than rapidly dwindling reserves of timber and a toll on Thai-Burma smuggling with which to finance their liberty.

In October 1986, I went with a colleague to Kawthoolei[26] on behalf of the London-based agency Health Unlimited, which has a specialised mandate to provide assistance to civilian populations for whom adequate modern healthcare is inaccessible because of war or political instability. We spent six months investigating public health in the rebel state, and the rest of our year in establishing a training course for community nurses – paramedics of the Kawthoolei government's Health and Welfare department. Health and Welfare faces formidable obstacles. It has to cover an area of hundreds of square miles of forested hills, with a population of about 7000 scattered throughout difficult terrain. Tracks through the forest can be awkward even in the dry season. During the monsoon, many become impassable. The main artery of the district is a river, broad and fast-flowing, liberally endowed with rocks and rapids, on which the Karen move rapidly in motorised dug-outs.

Further to the west there is an imprecisely defined front line, and a Burmese army poised at any time to launch a raid or full-

[26] This is the basis of my book *True Love & Bartholomew: Rebels on the Burmese Border* (Cambridge University Press, 1990). Health Unlimited, never a big organisation, was later absorbed into the larger agency War on Want.

scale offensive towards one or other Karen base.

Nationally, the Health Department is run by two Karen doctors trained in Rangoon hospitals. But they have to cover the whole rebel state; their visits to our district were few and irregular. They had time for a few crowded days of operations in the local hospital – mainly hernias, hydroceles and cysts – but could not give regular treatment. For the rest of the year, that is the responsibility of local Health staff, and of the army paramedics. They have some resources. At Riverside, the local administrative centre, there iss a wood-and-cement hospital of 24 beds run jointly by army and civilian staff. At some of the sub-district headquarters there are smaller dispensaries with a few beds, and a small laboratory donated by Médecins Sans Frontières (MSF), which gives them the capacity for simple diagnostic parasitology. There are a couple of Burmese-trained midwives, who work independently; the rebel state iss precariously reliant on these and other defectors deciding to 'come across'.

The handful of nurses already working there have an impossible task. Their responsibilities in the primitive hospital range from diagnosis to discharge. In theory, they also deal with environmental health, immunisation, midwifery, first aid, the war wounded, and drugs sales. Thai hospitals are out of reach for all but exceptional cases, so Karen nurses must be self-sufficient.

They cope as best they can, staffing the various hospitals and, when resources and the war permits, going on tour – with, of course, all the risks therein entailed. Casualties in this old, slow war are light compared to those suffered in, say, the Middle East. But people do get shot. Boats are not always safe from attack. One of our precious few nurses was captured in a Burmese raid, and those who go on tour in the frontline areas to the west run a constant risk of finding themselves in villages less friendly than they thought. I knew people who walked into what they believed was a safe Karen village, only to find it occupied by the Burmese army. One friend who made this mistake was beheaded for his error.

Under such pressures, it is hardly surprising that medical standards are low. My colleague witnessed an operation (removal of a neck cyst) by an army medical orderly. As a display of asepsis it was appalling: instruments casually rinsed in a little disinfectant, and others, if required halfway through, simply fished from a dusty drawer and pressed into service. Blood and pus-laden swaps went straight out of the window. It left my colleague pale, sick and angry – the latter because we knew that the hospital staff certainly had been taught the principles. The wearying realisation was that general education and many other concepts lie behind even such basic procedural teaching as asepsis.

Meanwhile, where drugs are available, even the hospital staff have little chance of understanding what the latest formulations from Thailand are – or are not – good for. The results are inevitable: wild and erratic over-prescribing.

The nephew of the district transport officer was admitted to the hospital with dysentery. I heard of his illness two weeks later, and visited. He had been given a dizzying cocktail: vitamin B complex, metronidazole, sulfaguanidine, diazepam and atropine. What he had not had, for two weeks, was anything to eat or drink. He died a few hours later. Such were the results not of stupidity but of an education irrelevant to difficult circumstances.

And the circumstances are getting progressively more difficult. A steady stream of refugees comes for shelter from the battle areas. They have nothing, but the state has very little to give them either. Recently an emergency 15-bed bamboo hospital was built at the main refugee reception centre – but there were virtually no drugs or staff for it. The financial problem gets worse by the day and, for what little cash there is, the priorities are rice and bullets, not antibiotics.

By far the most severe health problem the Karen face is malaria – and, by cruel irony, this is some of the most drug-resistant malaria anywhere; only quinine works well and quinine is exorbitantly expensive.

All of this has led to a particularly dramatic lesson in nursing education. Attempts at home-grown training have had very mixed results. The two doctors at GHQ are severely overworked surgeon-administrators, not educationists. Paramedic courses are held roughly once a year, but the urgency of the situation pushes the Karen into trying to train too many at once, with the result that they sat through a couple of months of lectures, take a written exam, and emerge with little grasp of either principles or practical skills. Practicality was what we worked on.

The district's Health and Welfare department was the responsibility of Bartholomew, a remarkable man with a palm-leaf bowler hat, extensive tattoos covering his thighs and hips, and an equally extensive knowledge of the forests, and their plant and animal life. Bartholomew had taken part in the Karen insurrection from the outset and was trained as an army first aid dresser.

Bartholomew had few staff – perhaps one dozen. Money was desperately tight, both for drugs and for infrastructure. In a place where river travel is the norm, the Department only now has a boat and outboard, because we bought one for the project.

Bartholomew had one or two other assets, not least his own expertise with regard to the geography, the patterns of disease, the natural pharmacopoeia of the forest and the wide range of equipment locally available. Bamboo, of course, is invaluable for everything from splints to measuring jugs. But what Bartholomew desperately needed was staff, and the means to train them.

Education in the Karen Free State of Kawthoolei differs from that of the Burmese, and often pupils are sent to Kawthoolei from outlying areas so that they receive 'proper Karen' teaching. After secondary education, boys normally go into the army whereas the girls often go into the health department. My colleague and I were in charge of eight pupils. Waterlily, one of them, came from an area outside Kawthoolei, but her parents were anxious for her to have a Karen education. The Health Department paid for her secondary schooling on the understanding that she would work for them afterwards for seven years. When Waterlily first arrived there was no village, no school, no hostel and no hospital, just a patch of forest that the Health Department had designated as their own.

Waterlily's nursing training began immediately and practically; she and her colleagues built the hostel they would live in, and she then helped build the hospital – a simple wooden building. From a dense forest, she and the other pupils created a working home.

Our job, as health advisers, was to teach our eight pupils – who had now completed their secondary school education – basic paramedical skills with which they could in turn train village health workers. Our attempt to teach even basic knowledge in twelve weeks was rather ambitious. We used as our textbook David Werner's classic manual *Where There Is No Doctor*,[27]

---

[27] See p.43 above.

originally written for the Mexican sierra but now used worldwide. However, we discovered pitfalls in attempting to transfer the lessons of primary health care from one country to another. As Werner and others have found, a village health worker system needs a referral structure behind it. In Mexico that was possible, but for the Karen rebels it is clearly out of the question to rely on Burmese hospitals, while there are severe constraints – financial, logistical and political – on how often they can send patients over the border to hospitals in Thailand. So, like it or not, Kawthoolei needs hospitals and staff to run them.

And the health problems differ too. Enormous efforts are made on an international scale in teaching oral rehydration therapy, which saves countless lives. But in Kawthoolei dysentery is not the biggest problem; rather, it is malaria. Everybody, including the students, suffers from it at one time or another. Mosquito control is impossible; it is not possible to fill in all the puddles in a rainforest, and the local strain of *P.falciparum* is resistant to almost anything except quinine, which is so expensive that we could not have conceived of Karen self-help fundraising that would have met even half the cost.

In Kawthoolei there are specific surgical issues also. The area we worked in used to be thought of as a backwater. But the Burmese are closing in. As yet there have been relatively few civilian deaths. There are, however, plenty of victims of landmines. Soldiers have long recognised that smaller mines create bigger problems. A dead enemy requires nothing more than burial. Maimed, they'll require carrying and nursing, hospitals, surgery and drugs and rehabilitation, and will be a long-term burden. We saw, distressingly often, the characteristic victim, minus a leg and one or both eyes.

Primary healthcare workers are often concerned with family planning, but here that is irrelevant; the Karen want all the babies they can get. Their nutritional status is fairly good, but hygiene and sanitation are atrocious. We did not see any cases of measles, only one case of leprosy (this is rampant in Burma), not much tuberculosis (widespread in Thailand), and little of the respiratory infections so problematic in the crowded, smoky slums of, for example, Calcutta. What the Karen do suffer from are the supposed complaints of affluence: diabetes, cancers, and gastric complaints. Almost the only thing they have which they should have is worms.

These are all real enough health problems, but what can you usefully teach a village nurse in the teak forests about cancer?

When our pupils had left secondary school, they had little experience of practical work, so our teaching was a process of discovery and invention for all concerned. We learned the hard way that you cannot, as many primary healthcare manuals advise, rely on simple antibiotics such as penicillin. Bamboo wounds, for example, often contain staphylococcal bacteria which do not respond readily to penicillins.

On the other hand, we could use the forests resources to practice suturing techniques – our pupils could sew up a 'wounded' banana in a trice. To treat skin infections we had only to speak to the nearest Karen hunter; he carries a home-made musket and sulphur for gunpowder, and when mixed with lard this makes an effective ointment.

Sometimes ideas went sour on us. I devised a colourful means of demonstrating blood pressure by using children's balloons, a length of clear tubing, and water tinted with potassium permanganate. No one warned me of the effects of potassium permanganate on rubber. The next morning, when I went over the lesson again, I paid a messy price.

We also played the card game which David Werner advocates as the perfect tool to teach pharmacology – all that a nurse of average intelligence needs in order to learn to prescribe as effectively as any doctor in a matter of weeks. Our aim was to interest the students in devising their own techniques for teaching; I was delighted one evening to hear Lotus Blossom, one of the students, sing a new song she'd composed about dehydration.

One day we went by boat to a cattle ranch in the forest above the rapids where three farmhands were lying sick in a bamboo hut. The students diagnosed the disease as shigellosis, fed and rehydrated the patients, and worked out the probable source and the route of infection which threatened the children next door. The students did this after only seven weeks training with only a book for guidance and using no drugs whatsoever. Their delight in their own success was moving.

After twelve weeks, the eight students were 'ready' for the village clinics, under our supervision. The hazards they face are enormous; the risk capture or death, and an infinite workload. Although the district is fairly quiet, the war is an ever present threat. The Burmese offensives mean that villages are full of sickly refugees, and the hospitals and clinics may be destroyed. Given all this, it is almost comical to point out that one of the problems the health and welfare department must tackle is precisely that which confronts our own NHS: the problem of recently trained nurses leaving the service early in order to start families. And given the urgent need for population, Kawthoolei certainly isn't going to deny them that.

INVESTING IN HEALTH THE WORLD BANK WAY [28]

The World Bank's annual *World Development Report* for 1993 examines the dire health of the developing world, and offers solutions fully in keeping with the Bank's predilection for the free market.

The *Report* pointed to four problem areas in health systems: misallocation of public funds (emphasising tertiary level provision), inequity, inefficiency, and cost explosion. These are all well-known. Citing 'innovative research', the *Report* proposed a three-fold approach for governments in the developing world and the 'formerly socialist countries':

1. Foster policies for an economic environment that will 'enable households to improve their own health... Income gains for the poor are essential. So, too, is expanded investment in schooling, particularly for girls.'

2. Redirect spending towards immunisation, micronutrients, and control and treatment of infection. This would reduce the burden of disease.

3. Encourage diversity and competition; decentralise services, promote competitive procurement, foster NGO and private involvement and regulate health insurance.

The *Report* elaborates on all of these. In July 1993, Save The Children (SCF) replied, point by point. As an organisation regularly at the sharp end of health crises, not just in the tropics but world-wide, SCF had recently completed their own three-year

---

[28] *The Health Exchange*, June/July 1994. This was a review of Save The Children's critical response to the World Bank's *Development Report*. I had worked for SCF in Darfur, Sudan, in 1991 and in Nepal in 1992.

study of sustainable health programmes. The SCF reply welcomes the *Report* for raising important issues. Thereafter, SCF's exasperation shows in every paragraph.

As regards the 'enabling environment', SCF retorts that 'the faith placed... in the power of policies seems excessive.' For example, good education policy is meaningless unless poor countries have the resources to implement it – which most do not. These countries are getting poorer, and the flow of aid is slowing.

Few would dispute that scarce resources are wrongly concentrated in urban tertiary care. The *Report's* first proposal would be to transfer much tertiary care to private control, thus releasing resources to essential primary services for the poor. SCF is unimpressed: 'In a country such as Malawi, total expenditure on health is so low that very little reallocation could take place even if tertiary care were privatised.'

Still, one should obviously target what little there is as best one can. How to decide priorities? The *Report* relies heavily on disability-adjusted life years (DALYs), measurements that allow comparisons between regions, risk factors, disease groups and sex. Thus, in sub-Saharan Africa, 80% of DALY loss due to diarrhoea results from infections in children under five. This is undisputed. But when DALYs are proposed as the basis for selecting cost-effective intervention, SCF loses patience:

'It is assumed that one intervention can be considered in isolation... This is an abstraction from reality. It fails to recognise the links...[e.g.] AIDS increases the incidence of TB, Vitamin A deficiency compounds the effects of measles, and so on... An integrated approach to the provision of healthcare is more likely to be cost-effective.'

Besides, insists SCF, you cannot re-allocate resources that

don't exist. For many countries, current spending would have to increase by a factor of 6 or 7 to create a minimally comprehensive system, 'an increase impossible to secure from domestic sources.' Meanwhile, whereas the need to investigate the quality of health investments is now well-recognised, the DALY method of resource allocation returns us to supposedly quantifiable outcomes from separate packages. It is, says SCF, 'of much more limited utility in determining decisions over health investments than the Report claims.'

Save The Children's greatest ire is reserved for the most characteristic World Bank recommendation: 'The challenge for most governments is to withdraw from areas of healthcare provision best left to the private sector.' But what exactly is the private sector? For whose benefit is it working? How should an already over-stretched (and under-trained) government begin to regulate cost, quality, safety and coverage? And what are the 'comparative advantages' that the *Report* claims private finance offers?

The *Report* suggests a system much like that in the USA. The *Report* says that, 'Beyond a well-defined package of essential services... the role of government should be limited to improving the capacity of insurance and healthcare markets to provide discretionary care.' In the US, millions of even fully-employed middle-class citizens can barely meet the costs of such insurance. How would it work in Chad? [29]

---

[29] The economic models recommended by the Bank are further aspects of the 'Washington consensus' lambasted by Joseph Stiglitz (see the review of his *Globalization and its Discontents*, p.77 below). The idea of the US health system being held up as a model in sub-Saharan Africa is quite weird. 'Discretionary care' means 'what you can get if you pay privately' which most Africans can't.

As Hillary Clinton throws the colossal machinery of US government into regulating health insurance, the *World Development Report* asks the bewildered leaders of the world's poorest to do the same. SCF's tone edges towards the withering: 'It must be plain to the World Bank that in many countries this [possibility] simply does not exist.'

As for the non-governmental organisation, that other 'private sector' advocated by the *Report*, Save The Children is quite candid: 'There is good reason to doubt the supposed efficiency of NGOs in large-scale service provision... SCF believes that it is vital for government to retain control of the health system and for NGOs to work with, rather than substitute for, the functions of the state.'

WORLD AFFAIRS

WORLD IN CRISIS
The Politics of Survival at the End of the 20th Century
edited by Julia Groenewold and Eve Porter [30]

Médecins Sans Frontières (MSF), founded in 1971 in the aftermath of the Biafran war of secession, is now one of the best known of the international aid and relief agencies, with offices in some twenty countries and, in 1996, operational missions in sixty-nine. At the tail end of a grim century, it must therefore be worth having this survey of a 'world in crisis' from the MSF point of view.

The book is a composite, with contributions on, for example, 'Frontline medicine: the role of international medical groups in emergency relief'; on 'The plight of the world's refugees'; on 'International law and reality', and others, followed by several country reports. It can be said straight off that this is a very useful volume, expounding pithily the outlook and dilemmas of that key player of our times, the aid worker. With caveats, however. The formidable list of contributors contains only two not directly involved with MSF, and it is not to be expected that the book will strike too hard at the fundamentals of the humanitarian movement. Nor does one necessarily want it to, but while there is a fair amount of self-scrutiny, there are certain issues that are side-stepped.

For starters, there is the question of the legitimate right of the

---

[30] *International Journal of Children's Rights*, vol. 6 (1), 1998.

non-governmental agencies to interfere in any of these dire situations in the first place. There are numerous instances – openly admitted by the contributors – of aid agencies and relief supplies becoming pawns in international *realpolitik*. There is an admission that the NGOs 'place themselves in one of the fundamental roles of a government: that of ensuring the collective safety of the populace.' Beyond that, there is a blurring of the 'fuzzy identity of the humanitarian action' to the extent that NGOs 'begin to look more and more like the UN.'

But one should remind oneself of the reality here: NGOs are just that: non-governmental, self-appointed, un-democratic, un-elected, often entirely un-mandated. They are private organisations, each with their own agenda, taking it upon themselves to engage with, and sometimes to arbitrate in, world events. Frequently one is grateful that they do – and yet we must never lose sight of the dangers of this surrogacy. Who is to control them, monitor them, regulate their follies and excesses? For excesses there are, and in situations such as the Kurdish 'safe haven' in Iraq, where dozens of NGOs squabbled over their respective patches of territory, the results were appalling.[31] The best this book can offer by way of control is well-informed news journalists. And when the agencies take sides in a conflict – as MSF openly admits to having done – what is the mandate or the political experience or expertise that justifies this? If (as the agencies claim) they can influence world events, there should surely be some accountability. But there is none. It is a remarkable situation.

If the NGOs have a mandate today (other than justified

_____

[31] The 'Millennium Tsunami' was perhaps an even worse case, especially in Sri Lanka.

indignation), it is in that very surrogacy role bestowed upon them by governments. It is dismally obvious that 'humanitarian aid' gives many a politician an excuse for doing nothing about a disaster. It is also true that governments nonetheless want a piece of the action, and they get this through more or less overt support of NGOs, whether through funding or other forms of patronage. For years it has been a source of grief to the British government that in so many crises it was the MSF cavalry (generally perceived as French) that came over the hill first. There have been repeated initiatives from the British Overseas Development Agency to establish a 'rapid response' rival.[32]

What, then, is the true nature of humanitarian agencies today? Are they 'non-governmental' at all? This and other issues are touched on in the MSF book, but the self-questioning is not followed through. Several contributors remark, for instance, that on a number of occasions the presence of aid workers or of UN soldiers has, far from protecting civilians, actually made their situation worse. Thus, the Blue Helmets of the UN gave the people of Srebrenica 'the deadly illusion that they would be protected when in fact they would not.' The NGOs in Ethiopia became the bait which drew people into camps from which the government could then conveniently and forcibly relocate them. These and other instances are cited in Rony Brauman's foreword – with the conclusion that the answer is to speak out, to go to the media and tell the world what is happening. What is not fully answered is the notion that in certain circumstances the agencies

---

[32] This began with various registers of UK aid experts, medical staff, engineers and the like, ready to drop everything and rush across the globe. I was interviewed in 1991 and placed on such a register which finally took the form of the British NGO 'Merlin', or Medical Emergency Relief International. This merged with Save The Children in 2013.

should not have been there at all.

That the question is unanswered is not surprising, perhaps – although there is now a small if vociferous body of opinion in the 'humanitarian movement' that repeatedly questions the advisability of direct intervention. It has been argued [33] that the colossal international effort to counteract famine in Darfur (Western Sudan) in 1985 was both a waste of money that saved almost no lives, and counterproductive in its distortions of the regional economy. It is noticeable that some of the NGOs – for example, Oxfam – are now distinctly more reluctant to be drawn into disaster relief operations than they were, say, two decades ago.

Furthermore, while there may be many situations that require speaking out, there are some in which there is no clear enemy or easy villain, or that are so complex that humanitarian organisations are frankly out of their depth – or, where it may not be entirely clear that there is a disaster occurring at all. Sudan, 1991, was one such,[34] and MSF was one of the agencies that quietly withdrew, even though some medical need was still apparent. Does this suggest that, even unconsciously, an ethos of speaking out leads to a greater readiness to be involved with humanitarian needs and relief programmes if, and where, there is also some speaking out to be done? That may be understandable, even brave, but it rather calls into question the disinterest that the

_____

[33] In particular by Alex de Waal in his 1989 book *Famine That Kills*. It was greatly to Save The Children's credit that they employed De Waal to research the book, attached to the SCF team in Darfur even as the famine relief programme proceeded.
[34] The 'donor countries' placed considerable pressure on the aid agencies and on the government of Sudan to instigate a full-blown food relief programme to Darfur, in order to avoid a repeat of earlier failures. But the evidence that a famine was occurring was in fact minimal.

NGOs, including MSF, lay claim to.

Brauman pins his (and his villains') colours to the mast. Much of MSF's task, he suggests, is at root 'Coping with Communism' (his subheading): 'We have been in most of the world's refugee camps, where fully 90% of their inhabitants were people fleeing communist rule'. This, bluntly, is rubbish. Of the book's five country reports – on Bosnia, Chechnya, Liberia, Rwanda and Sudan – not one concerns a situation that can sensibly be described as a flight from Communism.[35] It would be nice to think that the rapid demise of Communism would lead to a corresponding 90% diminution in refugee numbers worldwide, but I doubt it.

In many chapters of the book, one has a sense of writers doggedly attempting to identify the causes of ills, but unable to suggest answers that don't finally lead in circles. Thus, Iain Guest and François Bouchet-Saulnier trenchantly point out 'the Protection Gap between international law and [the] reality' of what it delivers – but have no answer other than more law and better enforcement. The Great Powers must 'rediscover their nerve and find a more efficient and legally acceptable method of intervention,' they conclude. But when the United States flexed its nerve and launched Operation Restore Hope in Somalia, the result was bloody chaos. The whole chapter, indeed, is a catalogue of floutings of international law – so why, we might sadly ask, do we bother? Guest and Bouchet-Saulnier admit as much with regard to the UN Convention on the Rights of the Child: 'The Convention has more ratifications than any other treaty... but the appalling cruelty meted out to children in Rwanda

---

[35] Not even Chechnya, which was a victim of Russian Tsarist imperialism from at least 1859, long before the Soviets weighed in.

and Bosnia suggests that describing their murder as a violation of the right to life will have no more effect on combatants than pleading for the Geneva Conventions to be respected.'

Similarly, the world's media are seen as both part of the problem and an important solution. This is a problem because it distorts and simplifies situations: the TV crews whip up political enthusiasm for dramatic interventions (Ethiopia, Somalia, Rwanda) but the crews are always pulled out just as things start getting better. What is the MSF answer? Ironically, the relief agencies (argues Mike Toole) need more media scrutiny, not only to highlight human rights but also to 'expose agencies, companies and governments that persist in malpractice'. In my experience, however, while desk officers in Europe and America are eager for television coverage that assists their profile and fundraising, field officers profoundly dislike it, since matters on the ground are generally horribly messy.

I raise these points not to undermine the MSF authors of these chapters, who nobly engage with some dreadful dilemmas, but simply to emphasise that these are problems of near-insuperable complexity – and to suggest, however cautiously, that more interference may not be the answer.

In such a world, it is perhaps not altogether surprising to find some authors grasping for certainties; thus, asserts Toole, in Mogadishu 'the provision of basic health services helped promote the restoration of a sense of dignity and justice in a highly traumatised community.' Sounds good – but how does he know? How can such a thing possibly be gauged? It is no more than a declaration of faith.[36] It is also understandable that, as Toole

---

[36] In retrospect, he was perhaps right; the existence of health services conveys a sense of some civil stability which could have a reassuring effect.

himself reports, efforts to broaden MSF's traditional role of emergency medical intervention into something more concerned with the fundamentals of ill-health – sanitation, nutrition, disease prevention, etc – have met with some resistance within the organisation. It is phrased in terms of, 'We are over-stretching ourselves'. One wonders if sometimes this might be rephrased: 'We don't want to exchange the rock of medical certainties for the questions of real life.'

In this respect, it is interesting to note some passing emphasis on the increasing personal dilemmas and psychological pressures faced by relief workers. 'The Relief worker: why do it?' asks Toole, noting that: 'While excellent guidelines on a range of technical issues have been developed and disseminated, no such guidelines exist to address the ethical challenges of relief work.'

A particular value of the book lies in logging the changes that are affecting the world's refugees and also the agencies that are attempting to respond to their plight. Few of these changes are for the better. Above all, 'asylum' becomes ever more elusive, as states and regions such as Europe that once accepted refugees with relatively good grace now do all they can to keep them out, to stop them moving beyond the 'first country of refuge' or, preferably, preventing them ever leaving the home country at all, such that they never even get to be refugees, only that lesser breed, 'displaced persons'.

For those who do make it into Europe or America, the safe haven is rapidly becoming hostile. An excellent chapter by Julia Groenewold and Stephen van Praet chronicles the increasing reluctance of state welfare systems to admit any responsibility for the stateless. Thus, for example, in the Netherlands 'the authorities can't enforce legal expulsion and therefore have turned to an indirect physical threat as a solution' – the threat being the withdrawal of any medical care. In France, MSF was involved in opposition to laws that withdrew health care and made even the provision of accommodation to a foreign national without a permit an illegal act – just as Moscow's *propiska* regulations and California's Proposition 187 threatened to do in their differing ways. Organisations such as Save The Children have known for decades that they have as much work to do at home as abroad; now MSF also is grappling with this uncomfortable realisation.

What does all this mean for children? There is little good news for them in the volume. In Zaire, huge numbers of unaccompanied children were found; either their parents were dead, or they had lost contact in the chaos of movement and forced repatriations, or sometimes they had been deliberately abandoned. In Liberia, a high proportion of the troops of the warring factions are teenagers, perpetually high on a diet of drugs and violence. In Sudan, the government flattens even the minimal housing available in refugee camps around Khartoum, 'forcing parents to dig holes in the hard ground so that their children can get some meagre shelter from the biting wind', while in one village massacre perpetrated by the Sudan People's Liberation Army, more than half of the victims were children – 127 of them.

The NGOs have, if nothing else, done a great deal to highlight the situation of children, and to alleviate it. There is a great deal to be said for the simple things, like clean water and vaccination. For that effort we must be grateful, whatever one might think of the NGOs' role in the ever-murky politics of survival.

GLOBALISATION & ITS DISCONTENTS
Joseph E. Stiglitz [37]

In the 1970s, I lived in the Indonesian city of Bandung, a cool and pleasant town high among the mountains of Java. The very name excites developmentalists; here, in 1955, leaders of the post-colonial poor, including Nehru, Zhou Enlai and Sukarno, declared themselves 'Non-Aligned' with either the Western powers or the USSR. The 'Third World' was born.

Thereafter, Bandung's reputation took an ironic twist: it became briefly the fastest growing industrial city in the world. Fortunes fluctuate, but friends tell me the pace is hot again. The lovely rice padi surrounding the city is vanishing under factories, many of them owned, directly or indirectly, by just those foreigners to whom Bandung once symbolised resistance.

In 1997, Bandung – along with most of Asia – was violently shaken, not by the local volcanoes but by economic collapse. The crisis, beginning with financial turmoil in Thailand, threatened to destroy the 'Asian Economic Miracle' and to rock the prosperity of the entire planet.

This crisis is central to Joseph Stiglitz's case: that the international financial systems have bungled globalization. Stiglitz, a Nobel-winning Stanford economist,[38] is a hero to the protestors who made Genoa and Seattle such uncomfortable places to be a trade negotiator – rather improbably, because he was President Clinton's economic adviser and, until January 2000, Chief Economist at the World Bank. There, his growing

---

[37] *Scotland on Sunday*, June 2002.

[38] I felt an odd and foolish sense of disloyalty about the criticisms in this piece, because Stiglitz and I once belonged to the same Cambridge college.

criticism of International Monetary Fund policies made his position impossible. He was eased out, but has responded eloquently in lectures and prose. This book encapsulates his attack.

His thesis – accessibly written, amply documented – is that the IMF has forced on poor countries policies that have beggared them, all in the name of aid and development. IMF standard terms – the 'Washington Consensus' – include financial liberalization, high interest rates, abolition of subsidies and the dropping of trade barriers. Governments desperate for loans have no choice but to accept the deal. These policies, supposed to create financial stability, have exactly the opposite effect. 'Hot money' washes in and out, speculators get rich, investors take fright. When food and fuel subsidies go, people riot and social tensions stoke the flames. Victims have included much of Asia, Africa, South America and Russia. The countries that have fared best are precisely those – Malaysia, Botswana, China – that declined IMF assistance.

Stiglitz asks bluntly: How can the IMF be so stupid? He describes a culture of arrogance and ignorance, of inflexible ideologies and hopelessly inadequate research in which an economic report on one country can be used as a template for another, with nothing changed but the names. He describes the vested interests behind the policies: the banks, the US Treasury. Indeed, was the catastrophic failure of free-market transition in Russia not just a dastardly ploy to keep the old enemy weak? No, concludes Stiglitz; there was no conspiracy, just grotesque incompetence coupled with a deeply immoral acceptance of corruption when it suits.

Stiglitz's case is trenchant, and based on vast experience ranging from aid projects in Kenya in the 1960s to meetings with

Islamic guerrillas in Mindanao. It is disappointing, then, that his vision here is so relentlessly narrow. His title, echoing Freud's *Civilisation & its Discontents*, hints at a broad canvas. His book, however, is not an examination of globalization at work: it is, entirely, an attack on the International Monetary Fund. While IMF ineptitude is lambasted on page after page, few of the 'turbocapitalists' – the pharmaceutical corporations, foods and electronics conglomerates – are named or their activities examined. Even the financiers remain shadowy. The World Trade Organisation, focus of the Genoa protests, is little considered. What globalization means on the ground is children sewing footballs in India, or women in the textile sweatshops of Bandung. You won't meet them here.

Globalization means more than the IMF, more than a nexus of finance ministers, failing banks and food riots. It is not simply an economic project, but draws in much of our lives, health, culture, even religion. Britons now travel to South Africa for heart surgery. Even symphony orchestras behave globally; some Russian cultural troupes, desperate for hard currency, are scarcely ever in Russia, always on tour. John Gray of the LSE has written: 'There are doubtless many reasons why Russia has not managed to achieve a modern market economy, but the anti-capitalist moral culture of Russian Orthodoxy must surely be among them'. Financial globalization is paralleled by the broad phenomenon known as 'global civil society', which includes the GATT protestors. Stiglitz mentions them as a symptom; there is little evidence here that he has spoken with them, or heard what their specific discontents are. Nor does he confront (as he doubtless could) writers such as John Mickelthwaite and Adrian Wooldridge for whom, drawing on J.S.Mill, globalization is a force for human as well as financial liberty.

As Stiglitz observes, although globalisation is essentially a post-Communist phenomenon, harsh austerity programmes and food riots are nothing new. Indeed, the whole debate feels oddly old-fashioned to anyone who has ever glanced at an issue of *New Internationalist*. What is new is the protest in the developed West. What has unleashed this? In large part, surely, the globalization of information and travel. The cheap technology and lowered barriers that allow money to flee Brazil also allow a tourist from Holland to witness exploitation in São Paolo, email friends in Toronto and nip on a plane to Genoa to speak her mind.

Meanwhile, globalization is coming home. I lately worked in an electronics factory in Fife.[39] I'd never heard of the company that ran the factory, but the VCRs went out in boxes labelled Panasonic and Toshiba. Stiglitz mentions small nations whose own soft drink manufacturers are being overwhelmed by the multinationals. Does he mean Scotland, where sales of Coke have now overtaken Irn Bru? Developmentalists have long cursed Western corporations that descend on impoverished countries, establish factories paying minimum wages and then, when the tax inducements end, up sticks and leave. What, though, of the former Hyundai semi-conductor plant outside Dunfermline, built with our public millions for a company that reneged on the deal when things got tough back in Korea? One empty factory in Scotland may not compare to mass unemployment in South Asia but now we too feel a 'discontent' that Stiglitz overlooks.

But make no mistake: Joseph Stiglitz is on the side of the angels. His prescription for change is clear: transparency; reform of voting rights in the IMF and WTO; fundamental changes in

---

[39] As an agency nurse in occupational health.

mind-set and governance procedures; an engagement in politics. He is realistic – the US will not surrender its IMF veto – but he reminds us importantly that the IMF is a public institution, funded by taxpayers. And, he insists, globalization has brought benefits: an end to isolation, the possibility of development. He writes, 'People in the West may regard low-paying jobs at Nike as exploitation, but for many people in the developing world, working in a factory is a better option than staying down on the farm and growing rice.' Well, perhaps. I think of the disappearing emerald green padi fields beyond Bandung, and have to hope he's right.

IN THE RAINFOREST
Report from a strange, beautiful, imperilled world
by Catherine Caufield [40]

Tropical rainforest once beautifully girdled the earth, but today that girdle is sadly frayed. An area the size of Britain is deforested or seriously damaged each year. Some countries, like India, have lost all their primary rainforest. Japan fiercely guards her own while macerating everyone else's. We have already destroyed half of what the globe once had.

In her travels to record this rape, Catherine Caufield met a mountain of circumvented conservation legislation and parades of official apologists speaking of a brave new monocultural world

---

[40] *New Statesman*, March 1985.

but confessing that 'not all factors have been allowed for'. Indeed not, and in surveying the problems worldwide, Caufield perhaps bites off more than she can chew – while for the reader a pithy detail in every sentence can become indigestible. Her aim is to describe the full gamut of threats to the trees. Torn aside for plantations and mines, pulped for paper (650lbs per American per annum), logged and sliced into 480 million disposable chopsticks yearly, the forests are exploited in the very worst sense, and Mother Nature's revenge can be ruthless; in Colombia the multi-million dollar Rio Anchicaya hydroelectric scheme silted up within 15 years.

With roads and power come the settlers. No one suggests that humankind should keep out of forests; the Lacandon people of Central America and the Lawa of Thailand have exploited the habitat in the better sense for centuries. But now inexperienced peasants are shipped in as settlers, disrupting the delicate eco-cultural balance, and attempting to supplant the knowledge of generations with a brief Departmental survey. That is not to dispute the courage of the settlers, many of whom are literally fighting for their lives.

But we are so deeply ignorant. 'It has been said that we know more about some areas of the moon than we do about tropical rainforests,' writes Caufield. While forest dwellers may distinguish several hundred species of useful tree, a mere handful of scientists, perhaps two dozen worldwide, are researching rainforest ecology in the field.[41] When the North does start prescribing for conservation, the people of the tropics look at our performance and quite reasonably take offence.

---

[41] It would be interesting to know how many are involved in such research in 2021.

Caufield, an American journalist best known for her pugnacious articles in *New Scientist*, catalogues our blunders and our selfishness. She throws herself energetically into the fray, her graphic writing largely making up for the lack of illustrations. There are dangers in attempting expertise on everything. I don't believe the Dutch colonial administration was up to no good on the island of Siberut in 1954 – Indonesia was at least six years independent by then.[42] She claims that naturally-derived reserpine alkaloids are 'widely used' to treat hypertension, but these drugs are inefficient and prone to very dangerous side-effects; a poor advertisement for a natural pharmacopoeia, reserpine is rarely seen in Britain at least. Caufield describes the bloody battle fought by Brazil's Txukarrama people against land seizures as a hopeless, misdirected retaliation. In 1984, however, the Txukarrama did win government recognition of their rights; the problem now is keeping officials to their own laws.

But nitpicking should not belittle the importance of the book. Pertinent and passionate, exploring not only the facts but the attitudes displayed by peasants, politicians and loggers, Caufield leaves us with tragically visible images. On the shores of Brazil's Tucurui reservoir they seeded grass to prevent the banks being washed away. But rains dislodged the seed, so now it is germinated under glass and the seedlings planted out over hundreds of acres, blade by blade.

---

[42] Depending on whether you date Indonesian independence to 1945 or 1949, the self-declared date or the final treaty date.

Weakness & Deceit
United States policy in Central America
by Raymond Bonner [43]
Out of the Ashes
The lives and hopes of refugees from El Salvador and Guatemala.
Edited for ESCHR / GCHR [44]

I was in Los Angeles last month,[45] and dutifully cut out anything the press reported on Central America. By the end of one week I had a large pile; some articles ran over three pages. If it used to be the case that Americans knew little and cared less, times are changing.

But what exactly do they know? Raymond Bonner, a *New York Times* correspondent, sets out with dreadful clarity how the US government has tried to dupe everyone, and principally themselves, as to what goes on down there. When their own embassy reported the truth of massacres in El Salvador, they got ticked off. When their own Human Rights Bureau sent in memoranda, they were not even stamped as having been officially received. When Bonner requests documents under the Freedom of Information Act, they 'cannot be traced'. Ronald Reagan conceals the truth from everyone, schoolchildren to Congress, while his staff briskly rewrite history.

---

[43] *New Statesman*, April 1985.

[44] The El Salvador and Guatemala Committees for Human Rights (UK), with War on Want (London).

[45] I was there because a play of mine, *Topokana Martyrs Day*, was in production at the Los Angeles Actors Theatre.

Contrast the finicky exactitude of the Salvadoran guerrillas' Radio Venceremos reporter: 'If we report that we took 20 rifles and the soldiers know it was only 15, they won't believe our other reports. Inaccurate reports are bad for morale.'

Throughout the US opposition there is terrible weariness, senators with their hearts in the right place asking the right embarrassing questions but never pressing the advantage home. And we can see why. A senior embassy official remarks, 'What would it matter if d'Aubuisson[46] had pulled the trigger on Archbishop Romero? Our policy wouldn't change.'

Bonner's thesis is that the policy might just as well change, since he sees the US as humiliated by its political impotence, its inability to obtain even the appearance of justice for murdered Americans, let alone peasants. 'Congress says one more massacre and no more aid. That was 10 massacres ago.'

The Vietnam echoes come thick and fast. 'The Gang that Blew Vietnam Goes Latin,' the *Washington Post* sniped at Reagan's team. Bonner is not the first Vietnam vet to report interference in El Salvador with disgust. But he documents brilliantly how wonky the lessons learnt have been. The star pupils are the Salvadoran military. Torture? 'Uh, well, the same thing you did in Vietnam. We learned from you the means, like blowtorches in the armpits, shots in the balls…'

The children of El Salvador, meanwhile, are in no doubt as to who is responsible for their suffering. In *Out of the Ashes*, published by a consortium of human rights campaigners, a refugee child writes that:

'The government of Ronnanrigan [*sic*] said to go and massacre

---

[46] Roberto d'Aubuisson (d.1992) was a military man and politician heavily involved with right-wing death squads in El Salvador, and widely believed to have ordered the assassination of Oscar Romero in 1980.

everyone and the military want to do for all the peasant people in the villages… But some people ran away to other countries and nothing's happened to them 'cos they're lucky.'

Lucky maybe, but if Reagan wants to reward doggedness in the face of adversity, here are his prizewinners. Briefly describing the slaughter that drove them over borders, the book concentrates on reconstruction, on what these Salvadorans and Guatemalans are doing to rebuild their lives and societies. Some have been luckier than others; in Nicaragua, refugees are quickly dispersed from the reception centres, settled on good land in cooperatives and given legal rights equal to Nicaraguans. In Honduras, Colomoncagua camp is neat and trim but overcrowded and sometimes bitterly cold. This is a community without adult men – they are either dead or back in El Salvador fighting. Other refugees have found their way as far as Washington, perhaps 80,000 of them, illegal and vulnerable, some of whom helped make Uncle Ronnie's birthday cake. It is these 'invisibles' that are the hardest to assist.

In the camps their problems are far from over. The Mexican and Costa Rican governments are grudging, the UNHCR erratic in its assistance. But the refugees farm, build and organise whatever they can. There are schools, workshops for embroidery, leatherwork, pottery and mechanics, committees overseeing sanitation and water supplies, libraries and news-sheets. There is even, in Nicaragua, a Refugee Mental Health Collective which produces booklets on how to cope with the depression that inevitably overwhelms them.

Their home lives cannot be recreated, but then they may not want that:

'In El Salvador agriculture was on an individual basis because we used to grow vegetables just for ourselves and not to share

86

with the community. Here in the camps, the agriculture belongs to the community, there is no intention of exploiting others. That is the progress we have made.'

So says the Colomoncagua camp bulletin. And when these communities do it for themselves they generally do it better. A large UNHCR farm was 'not a success. The refugees were expected to slot into an ambitious and complicated agricultural project rather than developing their own small-scale cooperatives.'

Absurdly, infuriatingly, even as this book is published there is an agreement afoot between the Salvadoran and Honduran governments for 'voluntary' repatriations of the refugees to model villages – complete with grid layouts and guard posts – financed by USAID.

Out of the Ashes is splendidly illustrated with photographs, drawings and songs by the refugees; the impression is of an inspiring resilience. And one picture is of a photography class for children. The Nicaragua Media Project, raising money to send photographic supplies, was something else I discovered in Los Angeles last month. Left in peace, the refugees might soon be producing books like this themselves; let's hope they find an audience as wide as that for Bonner and the *New York Times*.

AGAINST THE GRAIN
The dilemma of project food aid
by Tony Jackson [47]

Every day, 90,000 human beings die of malnutrition. Every year, £100 million-worth of food is sent to the Third World to relieve famine. Much more – three times as much – goes in project food aid: that is, food payments for work on irrigation schemes, or in school feeding programmes, or as inducements at health education centres and the like. The USA and the EEC lead the way. In 1979 the USA alone was feeding sixty million people through such projects. This colossal transfer is Tony Jackson's target.

Oxfam has, over the years, become increasingly vociferous in its opposition to food aid. *Against the Grain* catalogues in detail the evils food aid entails: grotesque wastage, dependency, the destruction of local market economies, corruption, a worsening of the condition of the landless (as the food merely pays for labour to benefit the landed) and – a particularly tragic irony – a frequent worsening of nutritional status as the food is misunderstood and misused. Jackson argues, from abundant examples of dismal failure, that only in a very few, very small and extremely well-planned schemes can food aid do anything to alleviate misery or to promote anything that could be called 'development'.

One might wish that he had given more consideration to the motives of the donors. The book bears witness to a vast mass of evidence against food aid, often gathered by the distributing agencies themselves. After the 1979 Guatemalan earthquake, field

---

[47] VSO *Orbit,* summer 1982.

workers begged their headquarters *not* to send food, yet the shipments kept coming. The US government is obliged by law to dispense 1.7 million tons this year whether anyone wants it or not.[48] Why? The reasons – dumping of surpluses, support for their own farmers, a political (or evangelical) desire to create dependency – are highly complex, and we should take Brandt's hint that we have to demonstrate the benefits to ourselves of more intelligent policies. Charity, we might say, begins at home. The power of Jackson's polemic – and his battery of evidence and quotation – is, however, beyond question. Will the agencies listen?

EMERGING INDONESIA
by Donald Wilhelm [49]

Emerging Indonesia presents a brief account of the country's history followed by a survey of current potential. The position of the author is unambiguous: the Evil is Communist (fundamentalist Islam being merely misguided) and Indonesia must be made safe for Western investors. The footpath to this conclusion is obstructed by smoke screenings, red herrings and half-truths. I can only sketch their extent.

For Prof. Wilhelm there is no question that the 1965 attempted coup was the work of anyone other than D.N.Aidit and the Partai Komunis Indonesia (PKI), an assertion that is, to put it mildly, unproven. Lt Col. Untung, the army officer who actually put the

---

[48] Under Title II of various 'Food for Peace' Acts.
[49] VSO *Orbit*, summer 1982.

coup into effect, is not even mentioned. The massacres of PKI sympathisers which followed were 'a national revolt against Communism' in righteous reaction to the PKI 'campaign of hate.'

There is a whole distracting chapter on human rights infringements in the USSR and China (what conceivable relevance to Indonesia has the discussion of Russian psychiatric hospitals?).

What else? The invasion of East Timor? Full marks. 'All three (US, Australian, Indonesian) governments feared the creation of an Asian Cuba which could have served as a base for outside Communist powers, and could have brought danger to the whole area.'

Corruption? Prof. Wilhelm prefers to call it administrative leakages.

Technology? Fine, so long as it's appropriate. And where should Indonesia go to purchase it? Why not that 'American [company] which engages in large-scale technology transfer... well adapted to the needs of emerging countries.'

And so on, by way of apologies for the Shah,[50] a cheer for the US Constitution, steam engines in Britain in 1835, the Warren Commission, and a clutch of colour photos. The villains of the piece, apart from Marx, are such 'ill-equipped' and less 'thoughtful' correspondents such as Brian May[51] whose doubts about the Five Year Plans were brought about by 'ideological naivety'.

---

[50] The Shah of Iran, who by 1982 was in exile in Paris. The Warren Commission was the official investigation into the shooting of President Kennedy. I forget the point of the steam trains, if there was a point.

[51] Brian May was the author of *The Indonesian Tragedy* (1978), a highly critical survey of corruption, incompetence and other abuses. The book was supposedly banned in Indonesia, but copies were passed around my VSO colleagues in Java.

The heroes? General Soeharto (a man of 'quiet dignity and strength'), the Indonesian Development Cabinets, the morally elevated directors of US banks, and all those 'thinking... responsible... reflective' men who shared their views with Prof. Wilhelm in 'off the record' discussions, above all the Western ambassadors. Perhaps they will enjoy the book's reassurances. It's of little value to the rest of us.

FREEDOM FROM FEAR
by Aung San Suu Kyi [52]
BURMA: INSURGENCY & THE POLITICS OF ETHNICITY
by Martin Smith [53]

Contemplating the life's work of a woman of the moral stature of Aung San Suu Kyi ('Suu') is a bewildering business. Few of us have a national liberator for a father, or feel destiny manifest within us. Absent from Burma for many years, Aung San's daughter was never in much doubt that she might one day have to return home to take up that burden and confront the armed swine who run her country. In 1972, she wrote to her Oxford academic fiancé, Michael Aris, to warn him: 'Would you mind very much

---

[52] Her phrase 'Freedom from Fear' is still used by the democratic opposition in Myanmar resisting the Army coup of earlier this year (2021).

[53] *New Statesman*, December 1991. The names Burma and Myanmar are both valid historically and etymologically. The Army imposed the latter in 1989.

should such a situation ever arise?'

There's no doubting the pride that all who meet Suu take in knowing her. They marvel at her faintly comical blend of ladylike probity ('There, among the sinks and the cubicles, in a setting deliberately chosen to mirror the distastefulness of the experience, she tried and rejected alcohol forever') with her astonishing courage, and delicate insight into the trials of her country, all of which are displayed in these essays and letters.

Intellectual subtlety is what you need for Burma. Suu insists that, in her country, Buddhism is the principle that underlies not just passive resistance (she's a dab hand at walking steadfastly towards levelled rifles), but also the Burmese perception of democracy itself. It was her own father who, imbued with Buddhist ideals of right leadership, founded the army that now imprisons her. Buddhist monks have, at many stages in Burma's history, played conspicuous roles in anything-but-passive uprisings. But she knows these things.

She insists, against a lot of evidence, that Burma has a 'quality of calmness and serenity that is precious' – not out of folly, but out of an understanding of the ways in which political misfortune distorts our true selves. There is an excellent essay contrasting the intellectual experience of colonialism in India and Burma. And a telling quote: the official Burmese term for 'Law & Order' translates literally as 'quiet-crouched-crushed-flattened.'

We see the bizarre harshness, the hard work, the young woman from Oxford addressing half a million adoring countrymen in Rangoon, who are soon to be shot at. She writes to Aris, 'Your Suu is getting weather-beaten, none of that pampered elegance left as she tramps the countryside spattered with mud, straggly haired, breathing in dust and pouring with sweat!' The book is a bit of a ragbag of miscellaneous writings and appreciations, but never mind. Suu is now held incommunicado under close house arrest. To hear her speak at all is a blessing.

Suu might be accused of some ingenuousness as regards ethnic reconciliation. Not so Martin Smith, whose dogged reporting and filming of the plight of the ethnic insurgents has kept them from being forgotten. Now his book becomes our standard reference. This is not light reading: 400-plus pages of dense type and minute detail, and another 50 of notes, all relentlessly chronicling the blunders, aspirations, mishaps and slaughter of several dozen insurgent groups.

It's a ghastly tale. The civil wars are estimated to have killed an average of 10,000 people annually for the past four decades. Smith has made frequent, difficult and dangerous forays into rebel territory and the book is based on innumerable interviews as well as a mass of documentation. He notes that, of the leaders who negotiated independence, more than half came to a violent end (Mountbatten included), eventually leaving the country subject to the brutal eccentricities of 'Number One', General Ne Win.

Burma today is a horrible mess, a rich and lovely place sunk to the depths of Least Developed Country status. Its troubles are not new; the ethnic conflicts are centuries old and have been stoked by successive rulers, Burman and colonial. Arguably, it was the British who, with stiff administrative notions of race, hardened the cultural edges and pushed the peoples into confrontation. Colonial policy has been nicely characterised as 'order without meaning'. Martin Smith lets us see some of the meaning behind the present bloody chaos.

A QUIET VIOLENCE

View from a Bangladesh Village
by Betsy Hartmann & James Boyce [54]

'A quiet violence stalks the villages of Bangladesh: the violence of needless hunger. It kills slowly, but as surely as any bullet, and it is just as surely the work of men.'

This is the inevitable conclusion of a pathetic catalogue of misery lightened only by the villagers' own humanity. Hartmann and Boyce spent most of 1974 observing and sharing the lives of the poor in rural Bangladesh. Their report only just avoids despair. The villagers of Katni – the pseudonym means 'hard labour' – are at the mercy of almost everyone: the landlords who lure them into hopeless debt and then take their fields; the merchants hoarding rice and salt so that, in a salt-producing country, 1974 saw scarcity and riots; the politicians – 'He told the shopkeepers, vote for me or you're a dead man!' – and the police who raided the village, ostensibly looking for criminals but actually bent on extortion; the moneylenders, the lawyers, the cartels, even the international aid organisations. Sarcasm is reserved for these, for each misguided scheme bolsters the position of the rich elite, whether it be the World Bank tubewells that somehow irrigate only the big landowner's fields, or the emergency relief blankets: the same landlord got those. All that reaches the villagers is ripples of farce. The authors witness the distribution of direct grant food-aid: one stale biscuit each from a US Defence Department tin dating from the Cuban missile crisis 10 years before. The villagers regard the cornucopia with dismay:

---

[54] *New Statesman*, March 1984 and in *Oxfam News*, summer 1984.

'I thought America was a rich country. Why do you eat these things?'

There is no sentimentality, no brotherhood of the oppressed, for the villagers are also at the mercy of each other, victims of Kamal, the miser whose 'greed verges on desperation', or wives of men brutalised by the struggle to survive. A farmer watches a starving woman stealing from his fields: 'But what can I do?'

Before anything else can be done, say the authors, land tenure must be reformed. Finally not all the half-baked advice and bungled projects in the world can compensate for landlessness.

NGOS AND BHUTANESE REFUGEES IN NEPAL
A reply to Rachel Hinton [55]

In early 1992, a large number of refugees left the Himalayan kingdom of Bhutan, fleeing repression and violence.[56] They made their way to the Jhapa district of Nepal in a rapid influx of (initially) some 50,000 who settled in five hastily improvised

---

[55] *Cambridge Anthropology*, 20.1-2, 1998. Rachel Hinton is a social anthropologist, now (2021) at the Blavatnik School of Government in Oxford. I had met her briefly in Edinburgh.

[56] Migrant workers from Nepal had been arriving and settling in southern Bhutan since *c*.1900, and their numbers had grown steadily. Buddhist Bhutan had become alarmed at the size of the Hindu Nepali population; by the 1980s discrimination was accelerating, with the immigrants forced to wear Bhutanese dress, and with the banning of their language in schools. When the immigrants began demanding citizenship and voting rights, it occurred to Bhutan's government that this sizeable constituency might even out-vote the 'natives' in some districts. Violent repression occurred, and the exodus began.

camps. A number of international agencies (NGOs) soon became involved with this crisis, including UNHCR and the World Food Programme, Oxfam, Lutheran World Service, and Save The Children (SCF). The latter was given responsibility for health care provision in the camps. I was, for a brief period at the outset, SCF stand-in team leader in Jhapa, and observed the first stages of the project at close quarters.

Rachel Hinton (*Cambridge Anthropology* 19:1) writes about the work of the NGOs with the refugees, arguing that there exists an ambivalence between the agencies' stated aim of 'empowering' such communities, and the reality on the ground. She suggests that the rhetoric of empowerment derives from the civil rights, women's and similar 'self-help' movements of the 1960s and 1970s. She remarks that the sort of 'guided participation' allowed by the NGOs often meant that the agencies retained most power in their own hands, excluding the refugee community from real decision-making regarding their own fate. Furthermore, that such empowerment as did take place was often imposed and damaging. I agree with much of her analysis, but not with all of her understanding of the reasons why.

I would like to change the emphasis a little. It is important to note that I was present at the beginning of the crisis, while Miss Hinton's research dates from a year or so later. Nothing wrong with that: but, in such situations, the picture can change dramatically as things settle down. Fundamental problems faced at the outset may not be apparent later, but may have set the agenda.

Aid is not an homogeneous activity. There is a world of practical difference between economic rehabilitation and the containment of a health or nutrition crisis, though they obviously

Bhutanese refugee camps in Nepal, 1992

overlap. While Oxfam was slowly and carefully establishing income-generating projects, SCF had colleagues from the Centres for Disease Control (Atlanta) advising that, in the squalid and desperately overcrowded camps with the monsoon threatening any day, cholera was imminent. Meanwhile, the neighbouring Nepali community was demanding protection, and the fragile local toleration of the camps was in peril; in such circumstances, one shoots first and asks questions later, setting up preventative measures and curative facilities as fast as possible. Tight discipline is crucial. The impression given by Hinton of an expatriate-ruled hierarchy in SCF is, however, plain wrong. The project manager and the senior medical officer were neither expatriate nor Bhutanese: they were Nepalis.

Which brings me to the central point. I have worked in aid interventions in several countries, including Burma, Sudan and Uganda, and in every case the issue of *national sovereignty* is paramount, the single most difficult and critical factor in deciding who is in control of whose fate. It affects how the NGOs see their role, and the risks they take, but above all it determines fundamentally the powers that they may either keep to themselves or transfer to the refugee or crisis group.

Indeed, how could it be otherwise? The situation is delicate in the extreme. A large number of foreign refugees arrive on a country's soil: what state in the world would readily cede any authority for control and management to that alien group? The more impoverished the host country, the more threatened they will feel, and the more hostile to any intervention that suggests that national authority is compromised. Nepal objected strongly: why should they allow refugees to politically organise or police themselves in any way outside the normal structures of the country? And yet, the impoverished Nepali authorities had to rely on international NGOs to provide food, water and other resources for the camps. For Nepal, this is a humiliating, unfamiliar and very confusing position. It is the assumed extraterritorial neutrality of the NGOs that makes them useful.

In return, the agencies rely on the refugees for labour, skilled or unskilled, paid for largely in kind (i.e. food) with minimal financial incentives. This is partly a matter of UN rules. Also it is pragmatic common sense: if there's cholera coming and there are Bhutanese nurses present, you use them. You cannot readily import a hundred British nurses, and Nepal has few to spare. But at once we have an example of how sovereignty raises its head: like anywhere else, Nepal sets legal minimum standards for health workers. If those standards are to be waived, on whose authority is it? Save The Children's? What if the newcomers prove to be dangerously incompetent? What becomes of legal redress?

The particular situation in Jhapa was more complex still, since the Bhutanese refugees were actually ethnic Nepalis – that is to say, of a large group who had been resident in Bhutan since the early 1900s. They could by some lights be regarded as 'coming home' to Nepal, and the Nepali government would be judged by its response to this emotion-charged demand. This led to great uncertainty. If the refugees were calling on their homeland for refuge, the homeland might well expect to regard them simply as ordinary citizens, with no special treatment: why the free food and healthcare, for starters? Were they to have tax-free self-rule as well? The ambivalence of the local Nepali community and the politicians' situation was profound. Hinton notes that the Government encouraged projects that kept the refugee men separate from the Nepali locals. This was not simply because of

Refugees constructing pit latrines in one of the camps.

the inevitable economic conflict, but because of the possible blurring of the boundaries between the two communities, and the political instability that was feared.

It must be remembered that in 1990 Nepal had teetered on the edge of civil war, with monarchists and Marxists in violent confrontation, and had just emerged with a very fragile democracy. In such a context, for an outside agency to encourage 50,000 desperate refugees to embark on grassroots organisation is not so far from sedition. Thus, any move to 'empower' such refugees is fraught indeed, and much of the NGO job consists of trying to smooth matters with local officials.

A concrete example: in the early days of establishing health services, we learned of the existence of a Nepali group who put on 'street theatre' shows encouraging people to take responsibility in health matters, and we engaged them to come to the camps. Two days beforehand, the group pulled out. They had been quietly informed that the local government would not approve, and that their own existence was in jeopardy.

Such delicate considerations abound in disaster work. It thus seems to me unsurprising that the rhetoric of empowerment is not matched on the ground, and I suggest that agency fieldworkers are rather more aware of this than Miss Hinton allows. I don't agree with her that NGOs see refugee communities as homogeneous. From Day 1, one is up against conflicts of interest within the camps. For example, SCF did its best to recruit refugees with any health training into the emergency programme, but immediately the several refugee doctors showed very divided loyalties. They wanted to be treated on a par with Nepali colleagues, with salaries and status to match. UNHCR rules would not allow SCF to provide that, and a very uneasy compromise was reached of raised incentives padded out with 'travel allowances', plus an appeal to their loyalty to the community. The doctors responded to that appeal – but no one was under any illusions about the strain of the situation.

So far from assuming unanimity in the camps, most agencies are painfully aware of the risks inherent in recognising self-appointed community leaders. Such leaders may have a genuine mandate from their people. Equally, they may have seized it; one only has to recall the hold of the murderous Rwandan militias upon refugee camps in Zaire and Tanzania. In the early days of the Nepal camps, the refugee self-help committees set up their own baton-wielding internal police force. On what mandate, under what law? There were rumours that the committees were (shall we say) less than democratic. Events in fact showed these fears to be unfounded – but one treads very warily in recognising the self-appointed, not least because the Nepali authorities are at one's shoulder, watching. A host government soon realises that the establishment of any internal organisation (brutal or benign) increases a camp's stability and durability, adding to the difficulty of dispersal or closure once the crisis has passed. Which is the last thing they want.

In such circumstances there is again, at least initially, something to be said for the remoteness of NGO control. We know very well that the structures and policies people decide, create and manage for themselves tend to be more durable. But one also notes that the situations are explosive and fraught, and that outside intervention can be calming and useful.

One day, in the first weeks of the crisis, we were debating the most effective way to operate healthcare. Some voices argued that a refugee health management committee was essential. At this stage, the negotiations over who had general authority were at a critical stage. The project head of UNHCR remarked to me that there was no way his handful of staff could run the camps.

'But don't you see what a remarkable situation this is?' he continued. 'It is most abnormal. Usually, UNHCR simply controls any refugee camp with a mandate from the UN and from the national government. We would just tell them what has to be done. The idea that the camps should run themselves, like a state within a state... It's bizarre!'

This, incidentally, from a thoughtful and effective man, well aware of what he was saying, who later held a dangerous post in Bosnia.

Thus, the issue of empowerment can seem in certain respects academic. The NGOs do not have great power with which to empower others. Still, the rhetoric persists. I suspect that there are sometimes other reasons, in addition to the intellectual fashion Miss Hinton cites, that account for this. One such reason is, to my mind, quite disreputable. Outsiders (from whatever country) may look at a certain society and decide that they dislike features of it: the position of women, maybe. When that society is in a state of upheaval, there follows the possibility for what in social work or psychiatry may be called 'crisis intervention': the notion that a stable society (or family, or person) resists change, but when they are in crisis, they are unstable and may be toppled in some more desirable direction. Some see this opportunity with disaster-smitten societies also.

More understandably, however, there is simple moral discomfort. Most NGOs can usually muster resources – money, food, vehicles, radios, drugs, et cetera – way beyond local capacity, and power follows willy-nilly. For example: in Darfur,

Sudan, in 1991, SCF had Land Rovers and the Ministry of Health had not; thus, SCF could visit, supply and influence remote health posts that local officials had not even seen in years. I daresay some of us are megalomaniacs, but many others are very uncomfortable with such situations. Talk of empowerment is comforting. But Miss Hinton is quite right to query its validity.

BIOGRAPHY

EMPIRES OF THE PLAIN
Henry Rawlinson & the lost languages of Babylon
by Lesley Adkins [57]

While I was an undergraduate, Cambridge University's chair of Sogdian fell vacant and was not filled. Teeth gnashed in senior common rooms: could this ancient university (Britain, indeed) not support one expert in Sogdian? It seemed not – a state of affairs that would have astonished and appalled the Victorians, in particular Henry Rawlinson, the subject of Lesley Adkins' fascinating book.

Sogdian? An ancient language, one of many that vanished until the formidable palaeographers of the 19th Century re-found them. Foremost among these was Rawlinson, a man who combined military daring, diplomacy among warring tribes, athleticism and endurance with a gift for language deciphering which would have excited Bletchley Park.

In 1827, aged 17, Rawlinson sailed to Bombay with the army of the East India Company. He would not see his family (few of whom ever wrote) for twenty-five years. In India he was homesick and bored. Time could be wiled away in horse racing and shooting (he was superb at both) and with study; he filled his days with Hindustani, Marathi and Persian, passing army exams. Here he found his destiny. A gifted schoolboy classicist, Rawlinson came from a family of scholars (though Adkins is

---

[57] *Scotland on Sunday,* July 2003.

wrong to credit a forebear of Henry's with a translation of Boethius; Christopher Rawlinson edited the Anglo-Saxon version by King Alfred [58]). Young Henry eclipsed them all.

In 1833, a military mission to Persia took Rawlinson as interpreter. These were dangerous times, early stages of the 'Great Game' as Russia and Britain vied for influence and power in Asia. Exploring the ruins of Persepolis, Rawlinson encountered the sculptures and inscriptions that were to obsess him, in particular cuneiform, the seemingly impenetrable script in which the languages of Antiquity were locked away.

Adkins neatly summarises the 'cuneiform conundrum', a complex story. Before its deciphering, the only records of the ancient Middle East were the Old Testament and second-hand reports by Greeks and Romans. Of Babylon, Babel, Nineveh and the empires of Mesopotamia (roughly equivalent to modern Iraq), no first-hand accounts existed. Or rather, inscriptions were known, but nothing was understood. There was a double block: they were written in languages nobody spoke and in a script that nobody could read.

Cuneiform means 'wedge shaped', though the script looks more like arrangements of little golf tees. It was the basic script used for some three thousand years. As Rawlinson rose through the ranks of military diplomacy, he spent every spare moment in seeking out cuneiform inscriptions, in particular the huge monument at Bisitun in western Iran. High on a rock face, a relief sculpture shows Darius the Great receiving homage. Around him are yards and yards of cuneiform text.

---

[58] Published by Christopher Rawlinson in 1698. This was a matter of luck, not learning on my part. My father had given me a 19th century edition of King Alfred's Boethius, and the introduction to that volume happens to mention Christopher Rawlinson's earlier edition.

Merely reaching the inscriptions meant hair-raising feats of rock climbing. One ladder collapsed, leaving Rawlinson dangling from a single spar over a precipice. One hundred feet up, the ledge under the inscriptions was too narrow for ladders to lean safely. Rawlinson had to saw off the ends, then stand on the top rung propping himself against the rock face, holding a notebook in his left hand while craning to copy the writing. He did this hour on hour, repeatedly, or employed Kurdish boys to swing on ropes and take papier-mâché casts. He then set about deciphering it.

Bisitun was trilingual, with inscriptions in Old Persian, Elamite and Babylonian. This was a key, just as Egyptian hieroglyphics could be deciphered only when the trilingual Rosetta stone was found. Proper names and grandiose formulas – 'Darius, King of Kings' – could be seen recurring and gave a toehold. Thereafter, the process was a fantastic labour of logic and grammatical prowess which was not complete at Rawlinson's death in 1895, half a century later. By then, Rawlinson and his many rivals had revealed not only the history of Old Testament cities but also the existence of the earliest writing and the oldest language known, Sumerian, dating back five millennia.

At the same time, excavations by A.H. Layard in Mesopotamia were uncovering those same cities. From beneath mounds of sand and debris, Babylon and Nineveh were exposed to view together with whole libraries of clay cuneiform tablets. The scholarly implications of all this were immeasurable. Myth became history; civilisations only known from passing mention in Scripture were shown to have existed in reality. But churchmen of the day were profoundly uneasy. If, for example, the first written record of the Flood was in the Epic of Gilgamesh, written in cuneiform on clay around 2,000 BC, where did that leave the 'revealed truth' of the rather later Bible version? And if Sumerian was clearly non-Semitic but much older than Hebrew, how could Hebrew have been the language of Eden? The public were agog; Prime Minister Gladstone himself attended the lectures.

This is the very heartland of classical archaeology and Adkins tells the tale with verve, apart from a few daft statements such as 'Cuneiform was last used in Babylon in AD 75' (how can anyone claim to know when a script was 'last used'?) If the reader is occasionally confused, that is forgiveable: we are dealing with Elamite, Median, Old Persian, Sumerian (also known as Scythian, depending on who you asked), Akkadian (which is Assyrian, but sometimes Babylonian), cuneiform and proto-cuneiform... Hardly surprisingly, some contemporaries refused to believe in the decipherments at all, and thought Rawlinson and friends were making it all up.

Rawlinson's career was beset by many difficulties. His study of Bisitun was interrupted for years by the military demands of the disastrous First Afghan War (with its infamous 1842 retreat from Kabul, in which an entire British army was annihilated). Years later he was still suffering from what we would now call post-traumatic stress. Though his diplomatic duties as Consul in Baghdad were not onerous, he (and Layard, and everyone else) were almost permanently ill, the result of heat, floods, war, malaria, typhoid, exhaustion, and alcohol.

Rawlinson at least was on the spot, able to view inscriptions at first hand. His greatest rival in the race to decipher was an Irish clergyman who seems to have rarely travelled further east than Dublin. Edward Hincks is the tragic counterpart to Rawlinson. While the latter received honour and promotion, was lionised by London society and fellow scholars, poor Hincks struggled with poverty and isolation in a rural parish, working with the few resources of his own library and genius. Hincks is almost forgotten now; his papers on cuneiform appeared in obscure Irish ecclesiastical journals that rest of European scholarship ignored. Yet, if there was one rival that seriously worried Rawlinson, it was Hincks.

Lesley Adkins' story is resonant now, as again the warring empires clash in Mesopotamia. In the aftermath of the US attack on Baghdad it was feared that the Iraq National Museum had been looted, its priceless antiquities dispersed. In the event, it transpired that little had been lost; just last month, the Museum put back on show the Jewels of Nimrud, found in a flooded basement. Of course, the looting had started rather earlier: Nimrud was one of the cities uncovered by Layard, its written history made legible by Rawlinson – and most of its treasure shipped with his help back to the British Museum.

WALTER & ALBERTINA SISULU: IN OUR LIFETIME
by Elinor Sisulu [59]

My grandfather served in the Boer War, training horses for Kitchener's cavalry. Afterwards, the government offered him land as an inducement to settle but his fiancée, a London girl, wasn't having it. But I could have been a South African. My uncle and aunt settled there, my cousin was born there; it's not so far.

But when, in the early 1980s, I became interested in apartheid politics and proposed a trip, my girlfriend of the time, a political martinette, was outraged. No, she told me: the ANC had asked us (an order was implied) not to put tourist cash in white South African pockets. I was not to visit my family, I was not to see for myself. We went to Nicaragua instead.

At much the same time, *New Internationalist* declared South Africa to be 'the moral front line'. I had to swat up. Attending rallies in London, I was shamed for not knowing the words of 'Nkosi sikelel' iAfrica' (never mind what they meant) and 'Free Nelson Mandela', and for not knowing that we were supposed to call the country not South Africa but Azania. In the 1980s, it was not for me to enquire or to hold independent opinions on South Africa. As a result, I felt less solidarity with the ANC than coolness, even a hint of resentment. I suspect that I was not alone.

But what is the image of South Africa now? One of the most violent countries on earth, where President Mbeki is in HIV denial, such that his people are denied essential drugs. Never mind truth: how altered are our gut responses.

This biography of Walter Sisulu and his wife Albertina comes,

---

[59] *Scotland on Sunday,* November 2003.

therefore, as a timely reminder of just how epic the South African story was. Walter Sisulu – who died in May this year aged 90 – was a guiding spirit of the ANC for six decades. He was Mandela's wise mentor, a man loved and admired in some respects more than Nelson himself.

He was made for the role. Walter's mother was a Xhosa-speaking country girl but his father was white, a lawyer who, if he showed no interest in his bastard offspring, at least never denied him. Little Walter became, by every account, one of the most endearing, selfless and courageous political leaders of the 20th Century. He was also very tough; I cannot imagine what it is like to be imprisoned for twenty-six years, but Walter Sisulu seemed never to grow sour or bitter, however angry he might be.

No great intellectual, he made the most of the school of hard knocks. There are striking vignettes here of Walter's early days as a political agitator, for instance his attempt to organise a strike at a biscuit factory where he worked. Confronting the mutinous workforce, the Afrikaner manager asked them one by one if they wanted at job. One by one, they abandoned Walter, leaving him standing alone in the yard.

There followed the decades of ANC activism and leadership, the desperate resort to military action, arrest in 1963 and the long years on Robben Island. The emphasis now shifts to Walter's wife Albertina who not only kept the family going in the face of dreadful police intimidation but, despite innumerable banning orders, managed to inspire and motivate the battered ANC. Again, there are remarkable scenes, some of which make one cringe. In 1989 Albertina toured world capitals, meeting Presidents Mitterand and Bush, Jimmy Carter and Shridath Ramphal.[60] But

---

[60] Sir 'Sonny' Ramphal, Commonwealth Secretary General.

only at the last moment did Margaret Thatcher deign to grant an audience at Downing Street. There, instead of listening to Albertina, Maggie gave her a lecture.

This book is an exhaustive history of the Sisulus' career, with some surprising lessons. One is the courage of a significant section of the South African judiciary; time after time, trumped-up charges were thrown out of court, or ANC defendants acquitted. Meanwhile, the ANC and MK – its military wing – are shown to have been, in the face of ruthless Security oppression, fairly ineffective, their greatest achievement being to keep going (no mean thing). Neither general strikes nor guerrilla strikes achieved much. The apartheid regime was brought to its knees more by the rioting schoolchildren of Soweto and by Chase Manhattan withdrawing its investments than by anything the ANC actually did. What the Sisulus and Mandela achieved was, rather, a degree of unassailable moral authority. Their magnificent personalities counted for everything. By the mid-80s, even white SA motorists who would never have supported the ANC as a party were sporting *Free Mandela* stickers on their cars.

Elinor Sisulu is Walter and Albertina's daughter-in-law and, as a result, her writing is well informed. She makes, however, slightly hard work of this grand tale. She is loyal to the point of hagiography. Not a breath of meaningful criticism stains her pages. Walter's slightest failings are hastily explained away. Why did he leave school in Standard Five? 'It could be that he had a learning disability like dyslexia.' (Maybe he was just academically poor.) Why did his estate agency business go bust? 'This was because the kind-hearted Walter behaved more like a social worker than a hard-headed businessman.' (Maybe he just wasn't very good at it).

112

Nor is she entirely reliable, for example citing a British Prime Minister called McMillan, referring to a meeting in Botswana that seemingly took place four years before that country existed, and confusing Christian Aid with Christian Action. It would have been nice, incidentally, if she had acknowledged that one reason the ANC's legal defence performed so stalwartly is that Christian Action raised money running into millions to pay the fees.

Her sense of irony is AWOL. In 1976, Walter wrote from Robben Island to Minister of Justice Kruger, denouncing the ill-treatment of his family. Such a magnificent letter, trumpets the biographer, must have 'impressed' and 'unnerved' the Government. But a page later she notes without comment that Kruger never received it. The prison authorities simply stuffed it into Walter's file.

There are other absences; for example, any serious analysis. Walter was an almost life-long communist who visited Moscow in 1953. What did he think of Stalin? And why communism? We are only told that he was attracted by its 'intellectual appeal' and its 'coherent theory of society.' That is hardly adequate in a major political biography.

The result is a study that seems sometimes naive and dated, a work for those unquestioning 1980s but a little disappointing as a retrospective now. That, however, should not take away one shred of the honour due to Walter and Albertina Sisulu.

THE PERFECTIONIST
Life & Death in Haute Cuisine
by Rudolph Chelminski [61]

Not long ago, staying with friends in France, my wife and I offered to cook a pudding for dinner. Something simple: apple crumble. We were watched with deep suspicion throughout our work; at the meal, we found that our hostess had prepared something else, 'just in case'.

The same hosts met us for lunch in a local restaurant, 'the best in the neighbourhood.' Though the meal was pleasant, I've eaten better in Fife. But we were learning again the unshakeable belief that the French have in their own culinary culture, and its supremacy.

The principle guardian of that culture is the Michelin Guide. Since 1933, Michelin has been awarding stars for culinary excellence and those stars represent the supreme accolade. For a chef to gain three stars means public fame and enormous professional esteem. At any one time, less than thirty restaurants in the whole of France have three star status. People drive all day to dine there; the chefs enjoy a prestige beyond the dreams of any British TV cook. To earn that prestige, top French chefs subject themselves to terrible pressure, working fantastic hours to achieve perfection not once-off, but again and again. Do it for lunch for the most discerning clients, then do it all over again for dinner. Only the Michelin inspectors match this regime; poorly paid, they must eat and report on two meals every day. Briefly, that may be fun, but year in, year out...

---

[61] *Scotland on Sunday*, February 2005.

114

In 2004, a former Michelin inspector claimed that the company had just five travelling staff, that visits took place at most every three years, and that top establishments are considered sacrosanct. There have been hints of corruption also. The furious ensuing row has gone to the courts which, just three weeks ago, refused to award Michelin a substantial sum for 'denigration'. Reputations have paled; foundations have trembled.

In February 2003, the business claimed another victim: Bernard Loiseau, patron of a three-star establishment, shot himself for fear of losing his third Michelin star. He was not the first such suicide, but was by far the most celebrated, a household name in France. This book charts his rise and fall.

It is a genuine three-act tragedy: a man of great gifts and greater ambition, destroyed by that ambition and by a fatal flaw – personal doubt – while at the peak of his success. Loiseau fought his way up the steep ladder of his profession, undergoing a most arduous apprenticeship and punishing work schedule to forge a distinctive style of cuisine: only the finest ingredients, lightly cooked at the last moment and combined with subtlety. He matched his hard labour with charm and personal generosity, and with an assiduous courting of publicity; he could smell a journalist – or, more importantly, a Michelin inspector – at one hundred paces. Throughout his career, his ambition never wavered. 'I want three stars', he declared, even as a scullion.

Rudolph Chelminski, a Paris-based American journalist, has a long track-record writing about French culture generally and food in particular. He knew Bernard Loiseau personally, has met many of the great chefs and has put a good few of their meals under his belt. He tells the sorry tale of Loiseau with panache and understanding. He understands the issues, the high stakes, the burn-out and the food, much of which receives careful description. We learn of the master-strokes of the light Loiseau style: snails in nettle soup, fillets of pike in wine sauce, frogs' legs with parsley and garlic purée.

Chelminski backs up the story with a brisk survey of the development of modern haute cuisine, focussing in particular on the profound change that 20th century motorcar culture brought about – for now it was not only grand metropolitan establishments that could command a distinguished clientele. The phenomenon of the provincial inn grew rapidly. A gifted restaurateur could open house in a small town almost anywhere in France. As long as they were within striking distance of a main road, they could achieve national celebrity.

Motorised gourmets might not always drive on Michelin tyres, but they would carry a Michelin guide. For years, Michelin itself equipped its inspectors with humble Citroen 2CV cars. Arriving unannounced and supposedly anonymous at a top restaurant, its car park packed with luxury limousines, the solitary Michelin man would be spotted before he sat down. Michelin was a byword for parsimony, paying inspectors the equivalent of a primary school teacher's salary, and requiring office staff to turn envelopes inside out to reuse them.

Bernard Loiseau was the antithesis of parsimony, generous to the point of absurdity, always kind, always grand in manner and gesture. His third Michelin star was finally won in 1991. President Mitterrand came to dinner. The restaurant grew and grew, becoming an auberge with fabulous bedrooms. The old bywords were revived: '*Calme, luxe et volupté*' (and serious prices).

And yet he killed himself. Prone to depression, colossally in debt (rich Americans being too craven to fly after 9/11), his tables empty on dreary winter days, fearfully overworked and sleeping badly, feeding on Prozac, Loiseau became terrified that his reputation, his grip would fail. Like Ibsen's Master Builder, he felt the pitiless pressure of a new generation of young chefs coming after him. Meanwhile, the certainties of French culture were wobbling: McDonalds and Disney had arrived; rival chefs were incorporating Japanese ingredients. Then, in 2003, Loiseau began to hear rumour that his third Michelin star was in jeopardy. The mere possibility was too much for him to bear.

So: a tragic tale. How well does it read? Sad to tell, very irritatingly. Why, in a book edited and published in London, must we submit not only to US spellings but American terms, such as 'rutabaga' for swede?[62] Chelminski's prose tends to cheap and wearisome journalese, replete with fatuous asides and chauvinisms. The Michelin Guide is compared to *The Thoughts of Chairman Mao* on the grounds that both books are red and have long print runs. Loiseau's second wife is 'slim, attractive and intelligent' in that order. Wooing his first wife, Loiseau employs food; Chelminski writes: 'Oh yeah, great, more foie gras, more fattening deserts. Just the thing for winning a woman who watched her ligne like a junkyard dog watches his favourite 1983 Pontiac.' This is trash; it might do for a magazine article, but in a 400 page book it curdles. It confirms a suspicion that those who boast of their taste buds often have very little taste at all.

But, it may be said, there was always something vulgar about haute cuisine, that culture of thrush paté and reductions of

---

[62] The answer, of course, is that books are prepared for simultaneous publication in Europe and the US, and the latter is by far the larger market and won't tolerate our spellings and terms. I knew that, but felt like striking a feeble blow.

sacrificial veal. Bernard Loiseau, for all his talent, could be exceedingly vulgar. For a look at the Loiseau manner, run him up on Google. The Relais Bernard Loiseau website reveals the '*calme, luxe et volupté*' apparently unchanged.[63] The business, the name continues; death was never a problem for legends.

AT THE EDGE OF EMPIRE
The Life of Thomas Blake Glover
by Michael Gardiner [64]

Thomas Glover seems the quintessential Imperial Scot. The son of an Aberdeenshire coastguard, he engaged with that quintessentially Imperial Scottish firm Jardine Matheson in 1857 and, aged 18, was soon hustling in the China trade, dealing in the 'big three': silk, tea and opium. The times were heady, the profits huge, the scruples few. Soon after the US Navy forced Japan to open to trade (1853), Glover was there for Jardine Matheson. He spent most of the rest of his life in Japan, and his career was remarkable. He was a 'player' in politics, helping to unite the samurai clans whose rebellion led to the Meiji Restoration; he supplied the Aberdeen-built ships which founded the modern

---

[63] The website today (2021) shows that the empire run by his family has grown substantially since his death in 2003, now with five dining locations around France including Paris. Prices remain high. The website does not mention BL's suicide, or the stresses of his career, but notes that the *Relais* maintained its three stars for 25 years. Today it has just two stars, and its sister restaurants one apiece.

[64] *Scottish Review of Books*, May 2008.

Japanese Navy; he ran coal mines and founded a brewery, then spent many years as an adviser to the fledgling Mitsubishi company. He died rich and successful; his house in Nagasaki remains a tourist attraction, and he was reputedly the model for Pinkerton in *Madame Butterfly*.

Glover's story, however, contains many ironies that Michael Gardiner highlights in this intriguing if wayward biography. The *Butterfly* connection is no more than romantic myth. Glover's contribution to Japanese shipping was not only immense in itself; he also brought in (from Aberdeen) a modern pre-fabricated slipway which allowed Japan's own shipbuilding industry to develop – and thus to help kill off Scotland's shipyards. As a mine-owner, Glover was a failure; his Takashima coal mine bankrupted him. Although, at his death in 1911, he was wealthy and honoured, Glover was a disappointed man, no longer his own boss but a hireling of Mitsubishi. Although intimate with leading politicians, and an ardent advocate of Japanese military expansionism, he was eventually placed under the surveillance of the *kenpeitai* (secret police). Finally, for all his devotion to Japan, he was never fully trusted. Nor was his family. The tragic figure in the tale is Glover's son Tomasiburo. Not much of a success in business or scholarship, the boy became an ardent patriot, but his half-British parentage made him deeply suspect. The louder he shouted for the Emperor, the closer he was watched. Tomasiburo committed suicide in 1945, shortly after a single bomb devastated his father's adopted city of Nagasaki.

It is a fascinating tale. Gardiner's telling is, however, decidedly erratic. Was Glover Scottish at all? His father was not. Does it matter? Gardiner worries away at this and Scottish national identity in general, starting with the observation that 'the word

'Scotland' does not appear on any passport'. Nor do the words 'England' or 'Wales', come to that. There is little evidence that the point bothered Glover who was, as Gardiner admits, 'mostly too busy making money for any such reflection'.

The book needed a competent editor, and didn't get one. It gets off to a bad start with: 'The wisterias are a lilac deep enough to cling to the clothes.' Lovely stuff, but what does it mean? Then: 'The dragonflies are aircraft circling the ponds.' (I think Gardiner has been to Ian Hamilton Finlay's garden at Stonypath, where the bird tables are in the form of Japanese aircraft carriers.) What does he mean by 'Newtonian laws of supply and demand'? Is he confusing the great physicist with Adam Smith and David Ricardo? He describes Glover as 'dissatisfied with the routine of working, drinking and prostitution' – so the poor man was selling his body as well as opium. He states that, by 1905, 'the Japanese Imperial Navy had by now overrun Russia,'[65] which suggests sailors eating sushi in the Kremlin.

His account of the Anglo-French naval bombardment of Kagoshima (1863) is so muddled that I resorted to Wikipedia to sort out who sank what. Gardiner down-grades the incident: 'There was nothing much battle-like about the Battle of Kagoshima, in which the British Navy fired on the wooden town with large cannon, only receiving the occasional hit in exchange.' But on the facing page he writes: 'The Satsuma counter-attack caused the destruction of eight allied ships… It was nevertheless a punitive strike rather than a battle.' Confused? Me too.

Such solecisms litter the writing. This is a great shame, since Gardiner is good on the ruthless trading world of Asia in the

---

[65] To this day I puzzle over this strange statement, and wonder what the biographer meant by it.

1860s, and perceptive and candid about his 'hero'. The fact is, Thomas Glover was in many ways a most unattractive character. He was a womaniser; Tomasiburo was his son by a prostitute. He beat up his servants. He lied to his business associates. He was ruthless and unscrupulous, making a fortune out of flooding the Japanese market with guns. He treated his mine workers appallingly. He was, writes Gardiner, 'amoral, fickle and lacking in finesse.' Nevertheless, Glover was a formidable man, and undoubtedly cuts a figure in the histories both of Japan and Scotland – whatever it said on his passport.

HISTORY

INFIDELS

The conflict between Christendom and Islam 638-2002
by Andrew Wheatcroft [66]

I have a small painting by Mortimer Mempes, a friend of Whistler. It shows an 'eastern scene', three figures in a Turkish souk. I'd always assumed that Mempes made a sketching trip to, say, Constantinople. But in Andrew Wheatcroft's fine new book there is reproduced a German print of *circa* 1886 characterising 'Old [Turkish] Bosnia' with a very similar composition. Mempes's picture is, in fact, an entirely stock image.

Much of *Infidels* is concerned with such stock, and with tracing the growth of mutual fear and hostility that has bedevilled Christendom's relations with Islam. Wheatcroft declares that his interest is with how this happened, not with why. He manages, however, to combine martial history with analysis of hatred and misunderstanding, right down to difficulties for Westerners in telling the time in Ottoman states. He begins at the beginning, with Arab armies bursting out of the desert to brush aside garrisons of Byzantine troops, then continues through the Moorish conquest of Spain, the Crusades and the interminable bloodbaths of Greece and the Balkans, right up to the events of 9/11.

His keenest interest is in southern Spain, and Wheatcroft retells with verve the arrival of the Moors in 710 and their demolition of

---

[66] *Scotland on Sunday,* May 2003.

the Visigothic kingdom, followed by the nearly 800-year Christian reconquest. It is a tale that has been told before, but he makes astute points It is fashionable, for example, to favourably contrast Islamic tolerance of other religions in their Spanish domains with the Christian intolerance that followed. Wheatcroft shows in detail the limits of this. Harmonious *convivencia* was shortlived and 'while Christians and Jews might be tolerated in Muslim lands, they were nonetheless to be shunned'. A Muslim, for instance, 'must not massage a Jew or Christian nor throw away his refuse'. Among these communities, economic interdependence was inescapable but the boundaries of defilement remained. What developed was not exactly tolerance, more pragmatic compromise.

Wheatcroft highlights linguistic changes, for example the varying names given to the Moors in Spain at the time of the Reconquest: *mudejar, maranno, morisco*. Each contained subtly different levels of insult, governed by changes in relative power. When the victorious Catholics forcibly converted the remaining Moors, and attempted to alter every aspect of their lives, the reluctant converts received instruction from Islamic leaders in North Africa on how to remain good Muslims in secret: 'Remember, God is not concerned with externals, but with the inward intention of your hearts. Pray silently, or by signs. Make the ritual ablution before prayer if only by rubbing your hands on the wall.' When the Catholic authorities tried to discover who was performing illegal circumcisions, they were met by silence or misinformation.

Throughout, the book scores by balancing points of view. For every European picture of the vile Turk, there's a counterpart from the Arab experience. Shifting his focus to Palestine,

Wheatcroft shows both Crusaders and 'Saracens' believing the other had defiled their holy places, and how the Arabs were nonplussed by the sheer vulgarity of the Frankish knights, while acknowledging their military prowess. He reminds us that the Islamic world was no more homogenous than Christendom; in Jerusalem, the Ottomans oppressed local Muslims as much as they did Christians. As the centuries passed, mutual fear meant the image each side held of the other became progressively less rounded, more of a 2-D caricature. Branding the menacing Turk as Antichrist was a comfort, for the Bible made it clear that Antichrist would be defeated eventually.

Conversely, Wheatcroft notes there was little Islamic study of the Crusades until the mid-19th century, when popular histories first appeared in Arabic. Muslims were now recalling the despoliation of 'their' holy land, at a time when the Imperial powers of Europe were conquering and exploiting them all over again. The term for Crusader – *al-salibiyyun* (the crosses) – came to signify the new colonialist enemies of Islam.

And so to the Balkans; and here the book tends to become a disheartening parade of one massacre or mass-impaling hard on the heels of another. All too frequently, a 'final solution' was suggested. Back in 16th-century Spain, one proposal for getting rid of the troublesome *moriscos* was to tow them out to sea in ships which would then be scuttled; in the Greek Peloponnese in the 1820s one song went, 'not one Turk shall be left'.

This is an imaginative, thought-provoking book, and I have just a few reservations. It is difficult to agree that Europe's fear of Islam was artificial. Arab armies really did erupt out of the desert; a good deal of slaughter of Christians immediately ensued, even if Europe repaid it in good measure. Meanwhile, in his search for

124

developing images and attitudes, Wheatcroft might have spent less time on familiar battles and given more space to, for example, contemporary Spanish literature, such as the *fronterizos,* 15th-century Christian propaganda songs often of great beauty and power. One of these, Luys de Narváez's *Paseavase,* was probably a reworked Moorish melody. It tells of the Moors' despair at the capture of Alhama and includes the famous grieving refrain, '*Ay, mi Alhama!*' It was banned in Granada because it so upset the Moors that they threatened riot, and it was translated by, among others, Lord Byron. And there's no mention of the great *Chanson de Roland,* a fight between Charlemagne's rearguard and the local Basques transmogrified into an epic struggle with the Moors.[67]

Wheatcroft focuses on areas where Christians, Jews and Moors lived in proximity, though Jews play little part in his tale. He thus limits his study to the Mediterranean basin. But what of Indonesia, the world's largest Muslim community, where the pattern of Islam's arrival was quite different (and, being based on trade, far less violent) but where there is now serious conflict with local Christians?[68] What of Nigeria, Africa's most populous country, where (unlike anywhere Mediterranean) Islam was established centuries before Christianity, and where interfaith murders are sparked by Miss World competitions? Such countries may not bulk large in the Nato range-finder (though both have oil) but, without them, generalised conclusions about Christian-Muslim conflict are suspect.

As regards Iraq, something has changed, surely. When

---

[67] These songs and lyrics were my own agenda at the time, as I was working on recording performances of them. See p.200 below.

[68] Disputes inextricably bound up with separatism, as in the Molucca islands.

President Bush mentioned a 'crusade' he was lambasted for his crassness. Western leaders, whose countries have ever-growing Muslim populations, scrambled to stress that this was not an attack on Islam.

In Spain this Easter there was a remarkable conjunction of processions. There were the famous Semana Santa parades, in which colossal tableaux of the Passion in wood and silver are borne on the shoulders of Christian fraternities around Malaga, Seville and Granada, the cities recaptured from the infidel Moors up to 1492. This year, in the same week, there were also large demonstrations against the war in Iraq. The Spanish were energetically decrying the massacre of Muslim innocents. Which is a scruple that, as Wheatcroft shows, would not have troubled previous European generations.

FIVE PAST MIDNIGHT IN BHOPAL
by Dominique Lapierre and Javier Moro [69]

Remember Bhopal? The Indian city that, in 1984, was smothered in a cloud of toxic gas from an American pesticide plant, killing more than fifteen thousand people? In Britain the memory has perhaps faded somewhat, but not in India. It was the worst industrial disaster in history. Quite apart from the dead, possibly half a million people were permanently injured, their eyes, lungs and brains ruined – while the Union Carbide Corporation got off

---

[69] *Scotland on Sunday,* March 2002.

with paying compensation of roughly $350 per victim.

Lapierre and Moro's exposé of Union Carbide's activities tells a dismal tale. The Bhopal plant produced methyl isocyanate (MIC), precursor of an effective and valuable pesticide but, in itself, as nasty a substance as chemist ever concocted. Placing such a facility on the edge of a swarming slum-city was a bizarre decision. Even before the plant was built, many within Union Carbide saw a disaster waiting to happen. It poisoned the water supply, it leaked. The American engineers went home. Because the plant was losing money, the safety systems were turned off to save cash while it was run down. The corroded, ill-maintained valves and gauges failed, and it blew up on a night when the shanty towns were full of wedding guests. Union Carbide blamed sabotage and went into overdrive to protect its share price.

Dominique Lapierre has been successfully telling 'the human story' behind great events for decades now; I recall, thirty years ago, reading his book on bullfighting, and another on the liberation of wartime Paris. More recently, he has returned repeatedly to India with, for instance, *City of Joy* successfully filmed. He has done well out of this and, to his great credit, has spent huge sums on charitable works for the Indian poor, establishing health care, housing and schools in the slums. Half of the new book tells the story from the point of view of the victims, the impoverished labouring classes (principally children) of India.

It seems churlish, therefore, to have reservations about this undeniably passionate and painstaking investigation, but I do. The presentation is Hollywood (co-author Moro is a scriptwriter), the prose style is *National Geographic*, every page heavy with portent and 'humanity' and ludicrous dialogue. The facts are well marshalled, but the audience is patronised to the point of comedy.

Can there be anyone in Britain who doesn't know what sort of food a samosa is? It merits an explanatory footnote here. Glib, homespun generalisations are legion, such as, 'In India, like anywhere else, it was the womenfolk who were most perspicacious.' The effect is of passion pre-digested, a McDonald's Outrage. Even with a case so flagrant as this, I prefer to reach a few judgements for myself.

Bhopal's story is not over. In 1991, summoned to an Indian court on a charge of manslaughter, Union Carbide's CEO disappeared from his Florida home and has never been seen since, but the writs are still out.[70] Even now, the law suits drag on, the key issue being where the cases should be heard: in India, or in the US, where damages paid would be far higher? In November 2001, after this book was completed, a US Appeal court upheld Bhopali claims for environmental damage and there is now some hope that the victims' lawyers will at last gain access to Carbide files. Union Carbide, meanwhile, has set up a website, where you can admire the 'anguish' they feel, and their unstinting generosity to the injured who today still die at a rate of a dozen each month.

---

[70] The US refused to extradite Warren Anderson, who died in 2012. Some 16,000 citizens of Bhopal died quickly from the accident, with a further c.40,000 maimed and a total of possibly 150,000 injured, with high long term risks of e.g. cancers. To this day, the site has not been demolished or decontaminated, and continues to rust.

THE BROKEN STRING
by Neil Bennum [71]

The Bushmen (or San) of the Kalahari, the oldest known culture
in Africa, may be the ancestors of all of us. There is even a theory
that the entire human race may be traceable to one Bushman or
woman of some 60,000 years ago. When, in 2001, the Botswana
government forcibly removed them from their last protected
hunting grounds, the action was likened to "kicking grandfather
out onto the street". The reasons for the expulsion are unclear; it
may have been diamonds.

The Bushmen's cause has made unlikely bedfellows, including
Roger Scruton (arch-conservative philosopher) and Hugh Brodie
(indigenous peoples activist). There is a fierce tradition here; for
150 years, people have been persecuting and espousing the
Bushman with equal passion.

Neil Bennum focuses on the Bushman languages, possibly the
most ancient on earth. In the mid-19th century, a remarkable
scholar began to study these. Wilhelm Bleek was a Prussian
linguist who had made himself an expert on the languages of
southern Africa even before setting foot on the continent, then
held an official post in Cape Town Library that allowed him to
compile some 12,000 pages of stories, songs and other texts,
largely from Bushmen serving prison sentences for murder and
cattle rustling. Bleek – and his brilliant collaborator Lucy Lloyd –
compiled a record of a dying culture that still survives, in 118
notebooks.

As Bennum emphasises, this is a cultural archive of great

---

[71] *Scotland on Sunday*, June 2004.

power and beauty, the story conveying a view of the world based on thousands of years of intimacy with animals and landscape. Bennum's book is filled with tales and anecdotes that confirm this.

Unfortunately, it is a perplexing book to read. The typography slips in and out of italics apparently *ad lib*, while the historical record of Bleek and Lloyd's project is interleaved with Bushman material in a perverse manner.

Thus, one subsection concludes: '[Bleek's] first four years in Cape Town he could consider a success – but we used to be springbok and the man who shot us is above morals and has not owed us a thing since he made us stand up.'

I don't know what this means, or who is speaking: Bleek? Bennum? Bushmen?

It is difficult to trust such an assemblage; is this book history, poetry or polemic? As history it is inadequate. It implies that the slaughter and dispossession of the Bushmen was entirely the work of the Boers. But in fact there are eyewitness accounts from the early 19th century of incoming Bantu peoples butchering and enslaving Bushmen also.

Bennum's heart is in the right place. But it should be axiomatic that the more remote the culture that you are trying to evoke and describe, the more you should assist the reader, guiding considerately rather than putting wilful obstacles in the way.

THE CONQUEST OF NEW SPAIN
by Bernal Diaz [72]

I first read Bernal Diaz's eyewitness account of the *conquistadores* at an age when I wasn't sure where Mexico was; it seemed an horrific tale of fabulous courage in a fantasy world. I read him again as a student just before visiting the Third World (India, in fact) for the first time, and some faint notion of parallels came to me: of decadent, luxuriant, gifted but sadistic empires shattered by tiny bands of ruthless European adventurers, with their respective governments' blessing.

In my recoil from the abjectness that subsequently overtook both India and Mexico, I put Bernal Diaz away for years. Rereading now, it seems once again a tale of unreal heroism in a mythical landscape – because that is how, as an old and impoverished man writing of the great adventure of his youth, it seemed to him.

Between 1519 and 1521 Hernan Cortés overthrew Montezuma and his successor Cuatemoc, each able to command tens of thousands of disciplined and ferocious Aztec troops, with a force of just 400 Spaniards including Diaz. There were innumerable factors in this bizarre triumph. The Mexicans had been so unpleasant to their neighbouring subject states that Cortés very quickly found he had armies of dedicated Tlascalans fighting for him, hungry to avenge rape and pillage, slavery and tax extortion. His unfamiliar cannon and horses terrified the Mexicans – though Diaz insists that it was their skilled swordplay that counted most.

---

[72] *New Internationalist*, April 1988. 'Classic books.' The *Historia Verdadera de la conquista de la Nueva España* was written in 1568-71, and published in full in 1632.

131

Montezuma's indecision and faction-ridden court prevented the Spaniards from simply being pushed straight back into the Caribbean. But Diaz has no doubt who won the fight for them: the more absurd the peril they find themselves in, the more they put their faith in Christ.

The Spaniards lust for wealth (or even just enough gold to pay off military surgeons' bills) went constantly hand-in-hand with an intense religious zeal; this is too easily forgotten. Indeed, the money and the metaphysics can hardly be separated. In one town Cortés gives the citizens 'an image of Our Lady and a cross which would always aid them, bring them good harvests and save their souls.' Remembering the norms for dealing with 16th century heretics in Europe, the Spaniards can seem paragons of moderation. They do except gifts of virgins, but nicely insist that they be baptised first. Human sacrifice disgusts them, especially when they have to watch 80 of their own captured comrades being cut open and eaten, but the expedition chaplain cautions Cortés not to force conversion too fast: 'It was too much to expect the Chiefs to destroy their idols until they had a better understanding of our faith.'

In every town they cleared a pyramid and erected a cross. 'What's the point?' muttered the common soldiers. 'They'll only sacrifice again as soon as we leave.' There was a point, though, when during the final battle Cuatemoc presented to a warrior the arms of the Sun-War god Huitzilopochtli with which to annihilate the Spaniards. This ultimate weapon failed; Cortés and his allies tumbled the image of Huitzilopochtli down the pyramid and the War of the Gods was lost.

Below this cosmic struggle snarl harsher realities. Every time the Spaniards climb a temple pyramid, the open sores on their legs throb with pain. They live in their armour day and night throughout the final three month siege. They suffer malaria and cold, fight amongst themselves, fart in front of Montezuma to goad him into giving them jewels and have Cortés snap at them to 'behave like a gentleman.' They burn their boats (literally) to push themselves on against the ridiculous odds while the Pope gives them dispensation for any wickedness committed during the struggle.

And, of course, they hunt out gold everywhere. But you cannot read the account and still believe that economic gain was the only driving force behind the conquests. The subtlety of motivation the old man describes is extraordinary. My student 'politico-economic' reading of Diaz – of conquerors on whatever continent as mere instruments of long-term plunder – left me with a glib, inadequate understanding. I now revert rather to the sense of wonder.

Which was the reaction of the Spaniards to Mexico. 'And when we saw so many cities built in the water... we were amazed and said it was like the enchantments they tell us of... And some of our soldiers even asked whether the things we saw were not a dream... Everything was shining with lime and decorated with different kinds of stonework and paintings which were a marvel to gaze on. But today all that I then saw is overthrown and destroyed; nothing is left standing.'

MEMOIRS

A Tale of Love & Darkness
by Amos Oz [73]

Amos Oz polarises people. *Newsweek* called the Israeli novelist 'a sort of Zionist Orwell.' The Arab Media Network was less flattering, labelling Oz 'a cheap political propagandist.' When, in 2001, the English branch of PEN invited him to speak in London, it was inundated with protests. William Dalrymple threatened to resign (but didn't) and rival meetings were organised.

Oz arouses such passions because of his unabashed loyalty to the state of Israel, his refusal to condemn West Bank settlements, and his advocacy of partition. In a *Guardian* article in 2001 he blamed Yasser Arafat for the election of President Sharon and the consequent hardline approach that dashed his predecessor Erhud Barak's moderate peace efforts. For this, Oz has not been forgiven in some quarters.

But friendly voices are equally forceful. Earlier this year he won the Prix France Culture, and last month was awarded the Premio Catalunya. The Catalans made their praise unambiguous by lauding Oz both for his literary work and for his efforts for peace, and by making the award jointly to Palestinian writer Sari Nusseibeh.

Oz presents himself as an advocate of reconciliation; for many years he has headed an organisation called Peace Now. He also,

---

[73] *Scotland on Sunday*, August 2004. This book hovers between fiction, autobiography and history. It is reputedly the biggest selling work of Israeli literature worldwide.

134

however, advocates the partition of the disputed lands; the Palestinians and Jews cannot live together, he argues, and must therefore live separately. His new book – part autobiography, part history of his family, part memoir of the creation of modern Israel – goes some way to explain what brought him to this position.

His father was from Lithuania, his mother's family from Poland and Russia. The two family stories, traced back several generations, encapsulate the European Jewish experience. In the Polish town of Rovno, the Germans killed 23,000 Jews in two days in November 1941.[74] In Vilnius, Lithuania, his father's family were scholars and rabbis with huge private libraries. They were passionately European: 'These over-enthusiastic Europhiles who could speak so many of Europe's languages, recite its poetry, who believed in its moral superiority, cultivated its heritage, dreamed of its post-national unity and adored its manners... had done everything possible to please it, to break through its cool hostility with frantic courtship to be accepted, to belong, to be loved.'

Only the terrible experience of the 1930s and 1940s could send such people to 'some drought stricken Levantine province where a few desperate Jews tried their hand at creating a segregationist armed nationhood.'

But they went. Jerusalem in the 1930s was an extraordinary place, packed with refugee intellectuals. The University reputedly had more professors than students; there was a rabbinical scholar in every cupboard. And in the evenings, because no one had a radio, they sat around writing, agonising over the country they had come to and the culture they were creating.

It was not a happy society. David Ben Gurion, the political

---

[74] Not exactly what happened, but the correct details are just as bad.

pragmatist from Tel Aviv, described the Jewish population of Jerusalem as '20% normal, 20% privileged, 60% weird.' Amos's uncle Joseph would lecture the family from his own *History of the Second Temple,* noting its suitability as a model of heroism for modern Israeli youth. It was, says Oz, a place in which everyone could speak of nature and Freud for hours on end, but could not discuss emotions. And they certainly had emotions to discuss. The heart of the book is a tragic story: the slide into depression and finally suicide, when Oz was still a boy, of Fania, the author's mother. Afterwards, he and his father never mentioned her death. When Oz was a teenager, he left his father's home, changed his name and went to a kibbutz, vainly trying to acquire a suntan and to be a young pioneer, and to put the sadness of Jerusalem behind him.

The birth of Israel was a violent one; for a British audience, much of this account makes uncomfortable reading. Especially shameful was the British collaboration in the 1948 Arab assault. In one incident during the siege of Jerusalem, Arabs ambushed a convoy carrying staff to the University.[75] Nearly 80 people were shot or burned alive in the buses. British troops saw what was happening and could have intervened – but did nothing. Unsurprisingly, there was a long-lasting bitterness. Even as a child, Oz and his chums constructed pretend rockets for launching against London.

Oz does not shrink from accusation and account reckoning. The Arabs, he writes, were more set on ethnic cleansing than ever the

---

[75] I wish I had known, at the time of writing this review, that the convoy massacre was in retaliation for the Zionist slaughter of 107 Palestinian villagers at Deir Yassin in April 1948, and the subsequent razing of the village. Amos Oz gives no more than a passing mention of this atrocity, without naming the village.

Jews were. But his view of the siege of Jerusalem is that of a boy trapped in a stifling, sandbagged flat with a dozen unwashed and terrified neighbours. They survive on rissoles of wild mallow. His pet tortoise is sliced in half by shrapnel. He manages, however, to keep a grip on humour; there is a glorious description of his bookish father being issued a 'home guard' rifle, being unable to load it, and trying to charm the bullets into the magazine by reciting poems. The rich detail with which this self-revelatory book is crammed may not win over Oz's detractors but the overall impression is of honesty, compassion and strength.

Whatever you think of his politics, you cannot be left cold by his story. But the text is sometimes repetitive; a number of statements and tropes are repeated, for example the notion that, 'If I could grow up as a book, a copy of me might survive somewhere,' and the irony that in Europe the graffiti said 'Jews go back to Palestine' while in Jerusalem they read 'Jews get out of Palestine.' These are telling points; they don't need making twice.

WONDERFUL ADVENTURES OF MRS SEACOLE
IN MANY LANDS
by Mary Seacole [76]

The stereotype of the black woman in the British Health Service is appalling: a nurse or auxiliary, perhaps on permanent night duty in geriatrics. I have heard my colleagues in the 'caring

---

[76] *New Internationalist,* January 1986. 'Classic books.' Original published in 1857.

professions'[77] express bigoted distaste, and have seen nurse managers practice outright discrimination against coloured staff. In case you wondered, it was ever so – as the career of Mary Seacole (1805 – 1881) illustrates.

She was a West Indian creole – not exactly black, and certainly no slave. She refers to herself as an 'old yellow woman' and her family ran a boardinghouse in Kingston, Jamaica.[78] From her mother, and from British Army surgeons, she learnt to treat all manner of ills. When cholera savaged Kingston in 1850 she learnt skills in fighting epidemics which she was to use repeatedly.

She left Jamaica following her brother and a 'disposition to roam' to Panama where she opened a hotel. There, in the squalid and lawless town of Cruces, crowded with migrants chasing Californian gold, the cholera caught up with her. The yellow woman alone had an idea of how to cope and she bustled around the town treating the victims and cajoling the population into some basic hygiene. Not content with curing, she felt a little science was in order – and carried the corpse of a child off into the undergrowth for a furtive autopsy.

In Panama she saw the races in collision, and anatomised them too. Apart from acknowledging their courage, she generally disliked Americans, 'dangerous neighbours' who then, as now, regarded Central America as private property and 'would fain whop all creation abroad as they do their own slaves at home.' But in Panama the escaped slaves stood up for themselves and

---

[77] At the time of writing this piece (1986), I was a qualified nurse in specialist tropical disease training in London. The ward sister took against an Iraqi auxiliary, a pleasant woman whom she accused of sloppy and lazy work. I and my trainee colleagues disagreed, and I stood up for the woman, writing to the hospital authorities and speaking to the ward sister. I don't know the final outcome but it didn't make me very popular.

[78] I was born in Jamaica myself.

occasionally the local government would stand by its own constitution and defend them. A woman found viciously beating her black slave girl was taken before a judge who, the slave owner snorted, 'must be a drunk or a fool to interfere between an American and her property' – only to fall into a rage when the judge freed the girl.

Seacole was the victim of similar bigotry. Having taken passage on a ship back to Jamaica she was confronted by irate Americans: 'Guess a nigger woman don't go along with us in this saloon. I never travelled with a nigger yet, and I expect I shan't begin now. If the British is so took up with coloured people, that's their business, but it won't do here.'

But then the Crimean War broke out. The black Jamaican regiments volunteered to go; the War Office couldn't stomach that. Their white officers – Seacole's Kingston clients – sailed off to the diseased misery of Balaclava. She decided she would nurse them, and took ship for London and volunteered her services to Miss Nightingale:

'I made long and unwearied application at the War Office, in blissful ignorance of the labour and time I was throwing away…'

She tried Department after Department, and charities also:

'Was it possible that American prejudices against colour had some root here? Did these ladies shrink from accepting my aid because my blood flowed beneath a somewhat duskier skin than theirs? Tears flowed down my foolish cheeks…'

And so she went under her own steam. Setting up in business as a caterer to the convalescent, she built her British Hotel on the high road from Balaclava to Sebastopol. Not content however with merely nourishing the ill-managed army, she went out into the lines whenever there was a battle, a skilled and (at last) widely appreciated paramedic carrying dressings, medicine, water and food to British, French and Russian wounded alike.

And she was showered with accolades and thanks, even a eulogistic poem in *Punch* entitled 'A Stir for Seacole'. It did her little good; the end of the war found her back in London, bankrupt, with her army admirers making another stir to collect funds for her. And here she wrote down her *Wonderful Adventures* to rescue her finances.

What are we to make of her career now? It foreshadows uncomfortable trends. While Florence Nightingale was establishing the future pattern of British nursing – concerned above all with domestic management, hierarchy and the crisp execution of medical orders – Seacole was the quintessential independent practitioner, curing and nurturing equally, forming her own judgements. But Seacole was forgotten and the Nightingale style swept the world.

Recently, a certain British regional health authority was visited by an enquiry into racism. 'No black ambulance crews at all?' the commissioners wondered. 'None,' came the reply, 'and there won't be while I'm Director.'

I told that story at a polite dinner; my audience was unmoved. 'After all,' said a lady, 'at the crunch, in those first moments, one wants to be picked up by one's own people.'

OUT OF AFRICA
by Karen Blixen [79]

There's a suburb of Nairobi named 'Karen' in honour of a Danish baroness – all that is left of one woman's remarkable and distinctive experience with another culture.

Karen Blixen had married her aristocratic cousin, and they went to Kenya to plant coffee. But the venture was not a success. The land was too high, the coffee never did well, and the Baron's rakish career ended in his squandering their capital. After their divorce in 1921 she was left to cope alone in a strange country. She remained an aristocrat ('The Prince of Wales did me the great honour...') and was nothing if not colonial. But being both Danish and free-spirited she identified only hesitantly with the ruling powers, and indeed often acted as an intermediary between the mutually incomprehending British and Kikuyu.

Following the financial failure, she wanted to take the almost unprecedented step of step of granting some of the land to the local people, who were classified as 'squatters'. She spent long hours in government offices coaxing the officials. And she succeeded. It was a move of rare sensitivity – too rare, as Mau Mau was to prove.[80]

'The squatters are Natives who with their families hold a few acres on a white man's farm and in return have to work a certain number of days in the year. My squatters, I think, saw the

---

[79] *New Internationalist*, April 1985. 'Classic books.' Original published 1937.

[80] The Mau Mau (or 'Kenya Land & Freedom Army') revolt of 1952-60 pitted Kikuyu and Meru rebels against white settlers, their black workers, and the British Army in which my father-in-law was serving as a young officer with the King's African Rifles. It has been described as a howl of despair by the disenfranchised and dispossessed who had lost their land to the settlers.

relationship in a different light, for many of them were born on the farm and their fathers before them, and they saw me as a sort of superior squatter on their estates.'

The interface between the lives of Baroness and Native grew acutely tender: 'The discovery of the dark races was to me a magnificent enlargement of all my world.' But without glib claims to understand:

'When I came to our station, one of my people would be there with a mule to ride home on. When I asked how they had known I was coming they looked away or seemed uneasy, as if frightened or bored, such as we should be if a deaf person insisted on getting an explanation of a symphony from us.'

She presents Africa and its interlocked cultures without pleading; its value must be self-evident if its nature is to be revealed. Whatever impinged upon her had her attention. She had a passionate eye for difference without prejudice, and extraordinary people came by: a High Priest from India, an old Danish sailor who tried to save her fortune with charcoal burning, Somali virgins and Maasai warriors, an unkempt renegade Swedish barman fleeing on foot from Tanganyika.

Always she let people speak for themselves. She persuaded an English doctor to save the life of a Kikuyu woman in labour: 'Afterwards he wrote that although he had, for once, treated a Native, I must understand that he could not let that sort of thing happen again. He had, before now, practised to the elite of Bournemouth.'

She revelled in the entangling of her life with the Kikuyus and spoke her mind to them, especially of their justice.

' "You old men," I said, "are fining the young men in order that it shall be impossible for them to collect any money for themselves. The young men cannot move for you, and then you buy up all the girls yourselves." The old men listened attentively, the small black eyes in their dry and wrinkled faces glittered, their thin lips moved gently as if they were repeating my words; they were pleased to hear, for once, an excellent principle put into speech.'

A Kikuyu named Kitosch enraged the whites by exercising his 'firm will to die' after a mere beating from his English master, thus throwing the law off-balance and leaving the Europeans perplexed to evaluate motives and guilt.

'By this strong sense of what is right and decorous, the figure of Kitosch stands out with a beauty of its own,' Blixen wrote. 'The country is his native land and, whatever you do to him, when he goes he goes of his free will because he does not want to stay.'

She laughed at herself often. A Danish missionary taught her Swahili but could not bring himself to pronounce their number 'nine' because 'it has a dubious ring in Danish' – so she was persuaded that Swahili does without the number nine altogether. She wrote of Kikuyu pride, ideas of history, God, poetry, cooking and death, and then of locusts, giraffes, iguanas and bush fire with a poised intensity, a heady sense of the felt presence of Africa.

'The little spring hares were out on the roads, moving in their own way, sitting down suddenly and jumping along to a rhythm like miniature kangaroos. The cicadas sing an endless song in the long grass, smells run along the earth and falling stars run over the sky, like tears over a cheek.'

A settler mentality; but interminable developmentalists have seldom, with all their doctrines, matched her openness to Africa.

THE GATE

by François Bizot [81]

The gate now lies wrecked in the compound of the French embassy in Phnom Penh, Cambodia. In 1975 it was firmly closed in the faces of Cambodians desperate to escape their Communist 'brothers', the Khmer Rouge (KR) who had just taken over the capital. The sentinel at the gate was François Bizot, a French ethnologist and intermediary between the thousand or more people – Cambodian and foreign – trapped in the embassy compound.

It was Bizot who had the appalling duty of turning away anyone without a foreign passport; Bizot who went foraging through the deserted city gathering food for the besieged, pillaging abandoned shops and houses; Bizot who rounded up expatriates stranded in distant corners, bringing them to safety; and Bizot who conducted much of the delicate negotiation to arrange the massive convoy that finally took the hundreds of foreigners over the border to Thailand.

These tasks fell to Bizot by virtue of his fluent Khmer and because of his empathy with the people (he had a Cambodian wife and a child), in particular the strange understanding he had reached with the Khmer Rouge four years earlier. Bizot was working for a conservation agency frantically seeking out venerable Buddhist texts, artefacts and indeed teachers before war engulfed them. In 1971 the war in Vietnam was in full swing while Henry Kissinger's 'sideshow' in Cambodia was gathering

---

[81] *Scotland on Sunday,* January 2003. Bizot's memoir carried an adulatory foreword by John le Carré. I now find that some online Amazon reviewers find the prose 'poetic'.

pace, the North Vietnamese backing the Khmer Rouge in sweeping away another hopelessly corrupt US-backed republic. Doggedly pursuing his researches into Buddhist trance rituals, Bizot set out to visit an elderly monk – and was captured by the Khmer Rouge.

He spent the next three months in a forest prison camp, frequently shackled to a tree and surrounded by other men who were being led away to be beaten or to have their skulls smashed. Bizot was treated relatively well; he was not beaten, and was allowed to wash. But the KR were convinced that he was a CIA agent and interrogated him again and again, until he formed a powerful, creepy relationship with the commandant of the camp, Comrade Douch.

This relationship is the emotional heart of his book. A strange affection develops, as so often noted between hostages and their captors. Bizot and Douch argue for hours on end on the justice of bloody revolt ('Did you French not have a revolution and execute hundreds?') until at last Douch obtains permission to release Bizot, on condition that he carries the KR manifesto back to the French embassy and translates it. Bizot decides that, for all Douch's ideological dogmatism, 'This terrible man was not duplicitous; all he had was principles and convictions.'

But terrible is indeed the word for Douch; he later ran Tuol Sleng, the infamous former school where thousands of the KR's perceived enemies were tortured and slaughtered.

Bizot's story is extraordinary, and this is a riveting book. It raises many questions. Why, for instance, has it only appeared just now, nearly thirty years after the events? Seemingly because previously Bizot could not bring himself to write it, and this is only partly because of the traumas of the time. There is, also, his rage at the *trahison des clercs*, the manner in which intellectuals of the day (especially French) refused to recognise the truth – even when put under their noses – and loudly acclaimed the supposed peasants' struggle for liberation, even as the evidence mounted that the KR were barbarians intent on extermination. When French fellow-travellers in Phnom Penh declare that the liberation is going to be 'fun', Bizot cannot contain his contempt.

His fury at his compatriots is only equalled by his contempt for the Americans. He refuses to speak English because 'I could not bear to be taken for an American... It was the Americans' uncouth methods, their crass ignorance of the people, their demagogy, their misplaced clear conscience and that easygoing childlike sincerity that bordered on stupidity.'

Bizot's attitude towards French colonial policy is, however, a tad disingenuous. He claims, for example, that in the countryside 'the French had seen fit to preserve traditional methods' – which is one way of describing the colonial norm of milking a country with minimal investment.

As a keen traditionalist researching Buddhism, he is suitably shocked to be asked to pack precious books to be spirited away to France. I wonder how he would answer Edward Said's charge: that Orientalist scholarship, from Napoleon's Egyptologists onward, was essentially a weapon of imperial control? As an anthropologist himself, Bizot must know – but does not mention – that in 1970, one year before his capture, the American Anthropological Association had torn itself asunder over accusations that US scholars in Thailand, Laos and Cambodia were in fact stooges for the CIA, gathering information on the 'loyalty' or otherwise of villages and ethnic groups who might need to be bombed to save them from Communism. It is surely little wonder that the KR were suspicious of a foreigner scurrying about the countryside asking questions in the middle of a war.

There is one other serious flaw in this book. Commenting on the difficulties of debating with Douch, Bizot remarks that it is not only words but ways of thinking that differ between cultures. He claims that, 'I have learned that simple words convey more intense truths.' If only he and his English language translator had learned these things sooner.

Bizot's prose veers between the earthy and the high-falutin'. While the former can be vivid, the latter is often embarrassing. A bank with nobody present must be called 'an immense theatre of death.' Sexual attraction to a Vietnamese girl quite undoes him: 'Beneath unfathomable layers, I had felt her body against mine, capable of extracting from the very depths of the universe that mysterious energy that has always linked man to the brilliance of the stars.' When he slips into high intellectual mode, he completely loses his translator, who will give a strict rendition of a sentence without apparently knowing what Bizot is talking about. Even apparently simple statements are problematic, for example: 'One seldom laughed in the camp because one's lungs had contracted in the rib cage.' Meaning what, exactly?

But never mind. There is ample compensation in the plethora of unforgettable scenes: the wealthy Khmer lady who steps from a Mercedes and, when Bizot cannot let her into the embassy, tries to hurl her baby over the fence to safety; the terror of a night attack when the Communists call to the petrified local soldiers by their individual names; Bizot and friends streaking nude in the rain during the liberation; the untouched meal, several days old, on an expat's table, the wine glasses full and the chicken rotting. The details are vivid and disturbing; did you know that, if a man who has eaten nothing but rice for weeks manages to catch and devour a large spider, it will alter the colour of his shit?

Perhaps you saw Roland Joffe's remarkable film of *The Killing Fields* some twenty years ago. Doubtless you recall Pol Pot. If by chance the memory is now fading a little, *The Gate* will bring it all flooding back.

THE MALAY ARCHIPELAGO
by Alfred Russell Wallace [82]

I worked for a publisher in Java once, and edited a small educational edition of Alfred Russell Wallace's Indonesian travels between 1854 and 1862. Few people in Indonesia had heard of Wallace, although no country can ever have had such a glorious portrait painted of it. Indonesia is a vast country, comprising some 13,000 islands in an area the size of Europe. To explore even a fraction of these cost me considerable effort.

Effort, however, was never a problem for Wallace. In that age of the meticulous and industrious, he was unsurpassed. Sometimes, wondering perhaps if I had the energy to make an overnight bus trip across Java to visit friends, I'd blush to read a chapter of Wallace:

'I was just eight years away from England, but as I travelled about 14,000 miles and made 60 or 70 separate journeys, I do not think that more than six years were really occupied in collecting. I

---

[82] *New Internationalist,* May 1988. 'Classic Books.' Original published 1869.

find that my Eastern collections amounted to 125,660 specimens of natural history.'

But what journeys! No night buses then. Wallace went by horse, canoe, or simply on foot. In many areas he was the first European visitor, and the difficulties involved were staggering. Once, sailing in a small boat to the island of Miscol, he missed the island by just 50 yards, helpless against the currents and the primitive design of his boat, which led to his being swept back out to sea again. He never visited Miscol. He ran the gamut of risks from pirates to tigers, by way of sickness and serpents – once he shared his bedroom with a 12 foot snake without realising it. He almost drowned. He often starved. On the remote island of Waigiou, prostrated by fever, he reports that, 'My life was saved by a couple of tins of soup which I had long reserved for some such extremity.'

But nothing stopped him from collecting. From the moment he touched shore anywhere, he was in hot pursuit of Nature. One day he found thirty species of butterfly. On another, ninety-five species of beetle in six hours. Many were new species, but preserving and transporting the treasure was not easy. Ants ate many of his specimens. His jars of preserving alcohol, although full of toads and lizards, were surreptitiously drunk by his Dayak hosts.

Nor was he a mere collector. He observed and explained the divide between Asian and Australasian flora and fauna (today still called the Wallace Line). And while lying sick in a shack somewhere, he wrote down some interesting thoughts about natural selection which he sent to Charles Darwin in England, prompting the latter hurriedly to publish his *Origin of Species*. Yet Wallace never resented this. In fact *The Malay Archipelago* is dedicated to Darwin.

I flatter myself that I have wide-ranging interests, but comparison with Wallace is humiliating. He wrote (in delightful witty prose) of trade and tiger hunts, of Dutch missions and the manufacture of native flint-locks, of head-hunters and Birds of Paradise, of the customs and laws of the Malay princes. Some of these he applauded. Others – such as tying naked adulterers together back to back and throwing them to the crocodiles – repelled him.

The book is the product of a different intellectual age. For Wallace the natural world was a cornucopia of infinite and unadulterated riches. He had no need of the modern naturalist's preoccupation with pollution or extinction. He was a High Victorian, much concerned not only with the classification of birds, but also of peoples. Having sorted out the human types of the Archipelago, he concluded that 'the intellect of the Malay seems rather deficient'. He makes similarly sweeping judgements about Papuans and others. Unable to resist moralising, he ascribes the rapid ageing of Malays to 'bad habits and irregular living.'

While generally impressed by the efficiency and wisdom of the Dutch colonial administration, he nonetheless looks everywhere for evidence of more natural laws of social behaviour. After some weeks in the remote seasonal trading station of Dobbo, with no official or police presence whatsoever, Wallace decided it was the safest and best-regulated place he'd ever been: 'Trade is the magic that keeps all at peace,' he commented.

The Malay Archipelago is as trenchant a statement of the 19th-century social conscience as one could wish. At every stop Wallace compares British industrial civilisation with 'savage' society – and finds the latter superior, almost ideal: 'I have lived

150

with communities of savages where each man [*sic*][83] scrupulously respects the rights of his [*sic*] fellows. Our vast manufacturing system, our gigantic commerce, our crowded towns and cities, support and continually renew a mass of human misery absolutely greater than has ever existed before.'

I used to try hard to imagine what Wallace would have made of the Indonesia that I knew. There is quite as much human misery there now as in Victorian cities. And the cornucopia has been thoroughly plundered and befouled.

MOVING MOUNTAINS
by Claire Bertschinger [84]

Some years ago, a play called *A Map of the Heart* ran in London's West End. The plot concerned a man who volunteers for work in an African famine and is kidnapped. Before that, he has an affair with the medical director of the relief operation, a woman known internationally as 'the Angel of the Camps'. The playwright (William Nicholson) was using shorthand that post-Live Aid

---

[83] The *sic* was added by a *New Internationalist* editor. I was dismayed by what I thought both a patronising intervention and a lack of historical intelligence. This was the last piece I wrote for that magazine.

[84] *Scotland on Sunday*, July 2005. This coincided with the G8 Gleneagles Conference and the launch of the first report of Tony Blair's Commission for Africa. I was also asked to give a lecture about aid at Edinburgh's Traverse Theatre in a City Council series, 'The Edinburgh Conversations', running alongside Gleneagles. The *SoS* editors asked me to tone my review down a little, for instance diluting the claim that the foreign agencies "knew what was happening" to a more cautious "must have known", to avoid libel writs.

audiences everywhere would recognise and respond to. If ever there was an irresistible call to our deepest wells of generosity, it is mass famine – and if ever there was a prototype for this Angel, it is Claire Bertschinger.

In 1984 Bertschinger worked for the International Committee of the Red Cross (ICRC) at Mekele in Ethiopia. She was in the ghastly position of attempting to provide medical care for thousands of starving people displaced by drought, crop failure and, above all, war. She was forced to choose between hundreds of famished, emaciated children, deciding which should be fed and which were beyond saving. She was obliged to wait, hoping against hope, for aircraft bringing supplies of food and drugs, aircraft which often failed to materialise. Her chapter describing this is suitably headed: 'A Living Hell'.

And then, in a chapter headed 'Saved', she describes the arrival of the BBC, of Michael Buerk and his 'Biblical' reports, and then just ten days later of an RAF plane packed with food. An astonishing bandwagon – Band Aid, in fact – was rolling. As we have seen in the last week or two, it is rolling still.

Bertschinger's new book describes her career in international disasters and crises: Lebanon, Afghanistan, South Sudan and elsewhere, in addition to Ethiopia. It is a book in the great tradition of personal memoirs of nursing heroism, a tradition that always includes telling doctors what's what. In South Sudan, Bertschinger informs a bossy Finnish surgeon that he may think he's the most important person around but he's not; more important are the cleaners who keep the infection rate under control. Nurses worldwide will applaud, not least those struggling just now with MRSA in British hospitals.

It is decently and clearly written, although bearing all the hallmarks of extensive ghost writing: for example, the arresting image at the outset of each chapter:

> Nine hundred pairs of eyes looked up as the furious buzzing grew louder.

Or again:

> July 1984: the smells of death, sweat and shit mixed with the fragile scent of eucalyptus hit me immediately as I stepped off the Ethiopian Airlines DC3 Dakota at Mekele.

The ghost writing is fair enough; not the least of the challenges Ms Bertschinger has overcome in life is dyslexia. But certain aspects soon become worrying: the emotional language; the lack of analysis (and of an index), the appeal to spiritual values and heroic neutrality in place of serious reflection. Granted, this is a memoir, not a study. But it is soon apparent that her story contributes to a view of international aid that is uncritical, based on gut response and a belief that the human will can triumph over adversity, and can 'move mountains'.

Bertschinger – like many who gravitate towards aid work – had a taste for adventure and crisis long before she reached Ethiopia. Indeed, she writes: 'I wanted to be the first on the spot whenever there was a disaster in the world, as a disaster relief coordinator.' This impulse – which drives recruitment for all the major international agencies – is dangerous. Perhaps we must have a rapid response capability for disaster. The problems begin when the aid industry (which is what it is) becomes self-perpetuating. Intervention is the *raison d'être*; they are not capable of thinking otherwise.

Some will think this an unpleasantly grudging point of view. But it is important to be clear-sighted, to separate admiration for personal courage from necessarily approving the cause. In the view of a stubborn minority (by no means only me), the international aid effort in Ethiopia was disastrously misconceived from the outset.

The facts won't go away. The famine in Ethiopia was largely man-made. The regime of Colonel Mengistu was fighting three wars at the time, in Eritrea, Tigray and the Ogaden, attempting to rebuild and indeed expand the old Ethiopian empire. Depopulation – by means of starvation, roadblocks and scorched earth tactics – was a strategic weapon. By 'draining the sea in which the rebel fish swim', Mengistu attempted to asphyxiate the insurgents. When food aid became available, he took full advantage. He refused to allow food to be delivered to rebel areas (only Oxfam ever managed to circumvent this). When starving people were inexorably drawn to the emergency feeding centres, they were rounded up by troops, forced into trucks and shipped off to remote areas of the country, journeys of anything up to six days on which many were given no food or water.

Nobody knows how many people died in the forced migration, but there are good estimates that it may have been upwards of 100,000. Besides this, Mengistu extorted huge sums of money from aid agencies (by means of fantastic currency exchange rates), using the money to pay for arms that devastated more rebel areas. And for good measure he purloined food and vehicles for his forces. The conclusion is inescapable: many people in Ethiopia died not in spite of the aid effort, but *because* of it.

You will find little recognition of this in Bertschinger's memoir, nor is Bob Geldof of Band Aid given to admitting anything, preferring to argue that 'it was worth it' if just one life was saved.[85] Bertschinger writes (of Tigray), 'These displaced

---

[85] In 2010 Geldof threatened to sue the BBC if they repeated the accusations

people had been driven out of the interior of Ethiopia by the civil unrest and the desperate need for food.' She, and many aid agencies, refuse to face the corollary: that the people moved because the aid workers were there to feed them.

Just one major organisation – Médecins Sans Frontières – stood up and publicly objected to Mengistu's behaviour. MSF was forced out of Ethiopia as a result. All the others, including Oxfam, Save The Children and Bertschinger's ICRC, took the line that, if they had to remain quiet in order to remain in-country to save lives, then so be it. I find this position indefensible. The agencies played straight into Mengistu's hands, allowing him to use food aid as a weapon of war, and conniving in a policy that possibly saved many lives but which was also responsible for the deaths of tens of thousands of others. The agencies must have known that this was happening.

Furthermore, the long term consequences are dire. As long as the 'international community' willingly springs into action at the first mention of a hungry refugee, then unscrupulous governments will use that reaction cynically to rid themselves of inconvenient populations. Mengistu couldn't believe his luck when 'aid' financed the depopulation of rebel territory, and the lesson has been learned: today, the government of Sudan is playing the same card. In order to rid itself of opposition in Darfur, it gleefully encourages (at gunpoint) the Fur people to flee to Chad, where angels much like Claire Bertschinger are waiting to feed them.

Careful analysis of aid operations suggests that they are often, in reality, neither effective nor even helpful. In the 1985 famine in

---

about the consequences of the aid, in particular Band Aid's complicity in money transfers to Mengistu. The BBC World Service had reported claims that 95% of the cash raised had gone to arms purchases. The BBC later apologised to Geldof for statements for which it had insufficient evidence.

155

Darfur, millions of dollars were spent by aid agencies on ships, warehouses, trains and airlifts, Land Rovers and of course expatriate staff [86] – let alone the agricultural surpluses dumped on the country by the 'donor nations'. And yet, few people in Darfur received more than a few kilos of food. All that effort and expense saved almost no one. Where people survived, it was because they had resources (hidden food and wild food) of which the agencies knew little. In the current Darfur crisis, the people ask not for food but security. In an interview published in *The Independent* last year, Fur villagers said clearly, 'We do not need food; we can find that. We need protection.' But what they got was food.

Some insist that there is often no choice, that in order to 'move mountains' we must have the courage to take painful decisions. But there is another, rather different courage: the courage to refuse, to insist on thinking rationally not emotionally, to risk popular condemnation, to resist the 'we must do something' clamour. And, from time to time, to just say no.

---

[86] The events of 1985 were examined in painful detail by Alex de Waal, employed as a researcher by SCF, who published *Famine That Kills* in 1989. I was medical programme coordinator for Save The Children in Darfur in 1991.

THE COUNTRY BENEATH MY SKIN
by Gioconda Belli [87]

The Sandinista revolution in Nicaragua of 1979 seems to belong
to another age. Ronald Reagan and the Soviet 'Evil Empire' still
held sway. There is also something uncomfortable about
Nicaragua that suggests that we – left and right – would almost
rather forget it. On the one hand, our US allies (with our own Mrs
Thatcher's eager approval) were implacably opposed to what was,
after all, the just overthrow of a tyrant. On the other hand, like
many revolutionaries, the Sandinistas finally betrayed themselves
from within.

Gioconda Belli – author of this 'memoir of love and war' –
begins as a rich girl in Managua high society. Early photos show
a beautiful debutante packaged up for breeding the next
generation of the elite. As her marriage sours, she falls among
intellectuals, starts sleeping with poets and is soon drawn into the
furtive networks of the Sandinistas. There were always several
'tendencies' among the rebels. Belli sees little of the dismal
poverty that drove peasants to take up arms; she moves, rather,
among urbanites concerned more with President Somoza's
corruption and political oppression. Her work in advertising gives
her access to corporate information which documents the grand
larceny of the Somoza-controlled state. Soon Belli is being
watched, her friends caught and shot. She flees into exile in
Mexico and Costa Rica, labouring on with the Sandinista

---

[87] *Scotland on Sunday*, December 2002. The *SoS* books editor, Andréw
Crumey, wanted a rather longer review of this, but I suggested the book just
wasn't worthy of such attention, although other reviewers have taken it more
seriously. I still use Belli's memoir for teaching students how to identify
grotesque over-writing.

leadership to organise insurrection from over the Costa Rican border. Finally, in the immediate aftermath of the 'Triumph' of July 1979, she flies into Managua with 40,000 copies of a newspaper proclaiming Somoza's overthrow.

Thus far, it's an interesting insider's view of events. What happens next is a great pity, both for her and for us. She falls in love with Modesto, a top *comandante*, then gives up her post running revolutionary television and follows Modesto about the country as his PA. She spends a lot of time agonizing over this, and the fact that she has thrown away a chance to contribute significantly. She ends up marrying an American journalist and moving to California.

The book is thus frustrating. Exchanging one social elite for another (the Sandinista leadership), her account can seem like an episode of *Dallas*: 'We grew angry with each other but we ended up on the carpet, making love tangled in chair legs underneath Somoza's conference table.' Real evocation is sparse. A prizewinning poet and novelist, Belli nonetheless writes flat, superficial prose both about people – 'Ricardo radiated the rare energy of an absolutely centered person' – and about events – 'I felt I was living in an extraordinary time filled with historic resonance.'

Her most perceptive remarks concern the failings that finally undid the Sandinistas: the vanity, naivety and megalomania of men like Humberto and Daniel Ortega who found, in the US blockade and Contra war[88] that followed, too much reason not to relinquish power, not to free the press, nor to allow for dissent.[89] Daniel

---

[88] See pp.14-48, above.

[89] The Sandinista leader Daniel Ortega has held power off and on since the revolution, and in 2021 won another 'landslide' election confirming him as president, but only after he had imprisoned most opposition candidates and arrested critical journalists. Many Nicaraguans now regard him as just another

Ortega was later accused of sexually abusing his stepdaughter, while the Sandinistas generally were prone to chauvinism and homophobia. Belli herself is not free of self-importance: 'Given the considerable international relations experience I had accumulated...' she writes, heading off to Cuba to meet Castro.

When I visited Nicaragua in 1986, idealism was still evident, but more in the villages where hard-pressed teachers and health workers struggled to sustain the remarkable achievements of the vaccination campaigns and literacy brigades. Belli surely moved among such people also, but tells us little about them. That's where the heart of the Revolution lay, not in Somoza's bunker into which the Sandinistas moved the day after the Triumph, slipping all too neatly into the corridors of power.

CONTACT WOUNDS
A war surgeon's education
by Jonathan Kaplan [90]

'Observe; don't just look,' was a key lesson that Jonathan Kaplan's surgeon father passed to his son. This memoir is part autobiography, and part observation of a succession of conflicts – Iraq, Angola, Israel and others – in which Kaplan father or son offered their medical services.

Jonathan Kaplan grew up a South African, observing but

---

dictator.

[90] *Scotland on Sunday,* February 2006.

bemused by apartheid and other notions of supremacy. As a teenager, he was sent with other young Jews to work on a kibbutz in Israel shortly after the 1968 war. His habits of observation made a good start here. Dismayed by the bigotry of his companions and his hosts, he ended his stay thoroughly disillusioned by Israel.

As South Africa became involved in conflicts (such as Mozambique's civil war) which his parents could not support, the family departed, and Jonathan began a rootless existence, any idea of a steady medical career (or relationship) disrupted by the call of some new trouble. He also launched into environmental campaigning as a film maker. His book moves between periods of intense experience, his life in between remaining shadowy.

The result is a portrait of a disaster junky: 'Every day I scan the war news like job-vacancy ads, searching for peace.' But we never learn much of his motivation, or why he gets into film making, or why he drifts from one horrific scenario to the next, beyond a desire to be 'lost in this incomprehensible communion' of fellowship under fire. We learn about the grim education, but not so much about the person it produces.

Nonetheless, this is a powerful book. Kaplan observes with a keen and un-illusioned eye. He stumbles into a role as the only surgeon at a hospital in Kuito, Angola, with desperately scant resources and faced with an endless stream of war wounded, many of them women and children. He is ready for Iraq long before the war starts, and his description of Baghdad after the US invasion is appallingly funny; before the fighting reached the city, there were eighty humanitarian agencies waiting in Amman, Jordan, most of them American and all regarded by Bush and friends as a legitimate branch of their war effort. Many have laughable names – Human Appeal International, Oasis of Love, the Good People – which don't stop them offending Muslim sensibilities at every step. The daily official briefings by the Coalition Provisional Authority are an exercise in smoke and mirrors. The whole ghastly mess is strongly reminiscent of Vietnam [91] – an analogy Kaplan draws.

It is satisfying that he also turns his contemptuous gaze on the pig's dinner that political meddling has made of the NHS, an institution he clearly loves while despairing of the 'initiatives', 'improvement plans' and 'empathy audits to identify those requiring training in caring, communication and warmth-building.'

Kaplan is, like a few medics, a tad prone to self-importance, given to statements such as: 'The possession of a surgical training is a responsibility that cannot be sidestepped',[92] or the description of his learning-journey as sharing 'the nature of all mythical quests'. One may balk, also, at a view of the world that seems to see almost nothing but conflict. But, with these caveats, he writes very well, sharply and clearly. This is a sad, painful book, but engrossing.

---

[91] The daily military press briefings in Saigon were known as 'the Five o'clock Follies'.

[92] This may be true, but it surely applies to any profession, including pilots, bus drivers, refuse collectors, or janitors, *viz* Claire Bertschinger on the role of cleaners in refugee camps, p.152, above. There are, however, many points in common between Kaplan and Bertschinger, both self-confessed disaster junkies.

HEARTLAND

by Neil Cross [93]

The father-and-son memoir is a remarkably durable literary form, its lineage stretching back through the likes of John Mortimer[94] and David Daiches[95] *via* many a thin fiction to Samuel Butler and Edmund Gosse[96] and beyond – back, if you like, to God and Adam. It has proved far more persistent and potent than its female equivalent and it is easy enough to see why. We witness epic battles of will between two generations of testosterone, the elder determined to mould the younger in its image and the latter kicking and defiant. Think of Lord Chesterfield, whose letters to his illegitimate son,[97] begun when the lad was only seven, exhort him to avoid laughing aloud (*so* vulgar) and to shun low types like violinists. Not surprisingly, the boy was a failure – which is to say, he did his own thing.

Religious dogma is often in the mix: Christian fundamentalist for Gosse; Jewish for Daiches. Take a little English boy adrift in Edinburgh playgrounds, and we can add chauvinist violence too. Neil Cross's childhood had all these, and strange love.

Abandoning a dead marriage in Bristol, his depressive mother brought him to Dalry and a new 'father', one Derek. This man enthralled hapless mother and son equally. An unsuccessful shop manager, Derek's career and personality were compounded of lying, adultery, vicious hatred of blacks, theft and daydreaming.

---

[93] *Scotland on Sunday,* May 2005.

[94] J.Mortimer: *A Voyage Round my Father* (play), 1963-82.

[95] D.Daiches: *Two Worlds: an Edinburgh Jewish childhood* (1956)

[96] S.Butler, *The Way of All Flesh* (1903). E.Gosse: *Father & Son: a study of two temperaments* (1907).

[97] Published in 1774.

Yet he was in some respects an excellent father; he explained to young Neil many clear hard truths about the world; he introduced him to books, sitting by his bed to read him *Tom Sawyer* but not disdaining to give him cash to buy science fiction; he took him out walking and sang silly songs to a ukulele; he paid him serious attention. In return, the child adored him.

But there was a much darker side. Derek's frustrations filled him with barely suppressed violence. Being a coward, he took this out on the family dog which he beat so hard that he broke the umbrella. And at last he broke the family's heart, abandoning them for a series of other women, though not before a final act of deceit and betrayal so callous that this reader wanted to find out where he lives and to go and punch him one. Meanwhile, throughout little Neil's childhood other boys are punching, kicking and spitting on him for being weird and English.

Then, one day, the Mormon missionaries come to call. Instead of shutting the door sensibly, Derek invites them in, and before you know it the whole family are Mormons, with Derek ending up a Bishop *via* wacky rituals with Derek and mother wearing nothing but white ponchos, having their privates blessed by the celebrant. Does elevation to the clergy stop Derek's mendacious career? Not one bit – but I won't spoil the grisly story, which is written in good, clean, dispassionate prose.

Neil Cross looks out of the jacket photo with a wry grin; one can hardly imagine how he survived. His publishers should have talked him out of his dreadful cliché title (*Heartland* is also the title of a saga series of equine novelettes: 'Healing horses, healing hearts.') Cross's book deserves better. In all other respects, this is a distressingly fine piece of writing.

When Heaven & Earth Changed Places

A woman's journey from war to peace

by Le Ly Hayslip

Romancing Vietnam

Inside the boat country

by Justin Wintle [98]

'Vietnam was what we had instead of happy childhoods,' said Michael Herr. Here are two journeys to Vietnam, attempting to put that past to rest. For Justin Wintle, it's the Vietnam of movies, *Green Berets* to *Platoon*, that 'assault course for the American psyche'. For Le Ly Hayslip, the ghosts are those of a childhood blown apart by enemies – French, Americans, Koreans – and her own people, Republican and Communist.

Can this *be* childhood: murder, torture, prostitution, one's village a battlefield, one's neighbours the cannon fodder. 'My duty is to avenge my family, to protect my farm by killing my enemies,' the young girl tells her father, who replies, 'No, little peach blossom, your job is to stay alive.' She just succeeds. The compensations come from family and friends and, bizarrely, a string of American lovers and protectors, one of whom, 30 years her senior, she finally marries, thus escaping to the safety of the US.

In 1986, Le Ly went back to see what had become of her people. In 1989, Justin Wintle went to look for 'Vietnam now', spending three months touring with a succession of official

---

[98] *New Statesman,* March 1991. Wintle met the photographer Don McCullin in Vietnam and managed to get himself portrayed in black & white, posing like a brooding Ernest Hemingway with a curl of cigarette smoke.

164

though sympathetic guides. For both, the major issue is that of the present regime and its ideology. Wintle is led to meeting after meeting with spokesmen and People's Committees, occasionally breaking through to 'reality'. Le Ly spends much of her return trip frightened that, even now she's a US tourist, she may be rearrested as a traitor. As a child she was brought up to idealise Uncle Ho, but creeping doubts had set in (not helped by being raped by VC cadres) about what sort of better life the communists offered. Finally, there came the unsettling notion that she was happier and safer under the wing of those 'barbarian saints' the Americans, from whose country she now runs a reconciliation organisation.

Wintle, meanwhile, constantly chafes at the Party's plans for his tour and education, and can never develop much sympathy for *Doi moi*, the current state philosophy of renovation. He doesn't take time to wonder why emergent states need such philosophies, however seemingly trite and obstructive, to establish their new identities: *Ujamaa* in Tanzania, *Pancasilla* in Indonesia, and many others. He tries hard to see 'Vietnam now' free of the taint of the wars of the past – but could such an image ever be possible? As a cadre says to Le Ly, this country is run by people who have been fighting for freedom since the 1940s; how can that fact not possess the present? With none of Le Ly's grounding of birth, tradition and time, Wintle should not have expected to do more than scratch the surface in three months.

Nor does he display much sympathetic delicacy of mind. Tourists in exotic lands can be revealing – *viz* Colin Thubron in China – but not, I think, when they write such excruciating prose as this, full of cheap modern idiom, ending a passage of ironic analysis with 'Cute, huh?' When a man is shot in the belly and defiantly hurls his own intestines at his executioners, Wintle credits him with 'guts in the face of the enemy'. Is that offered as wit? And a last cavil: there is (*pace* the style) interesting and useful information in Wintle's book. But with neither chapter headings nor an index, it is un-retrievable. Could neither he nor his publisher be bothered? Or don't they care?

FICTION

YOUTH
by J.M.Coetzee [99]

A short novel by a 'colonial' writer, entitled *Youth* – echoes of Conrad's eponymous story are inevitable. But Coetzee's bleak new tale is Conrad reversed. Conrad's young seafarer, after misadventures on a burning ship, awakes from exhausted sleep in a small boat to find the faces of the Orient staring down at him from a jetty, mysterious and thrilling. By contrast, Coetzee's journey is of a young South African would-be poet coming to London to make his literary career *c.*1960, and finding it anything but tantalising. Indeed, it comes close to destroying him entirely.

The arrival of tropical innocents with ambition has been variously described by, for example, the Trinidadian V.S. Naipaul and the Sudanese Tayeb Salih. Like Naipaul, Coetzee's work is semi-autobiographical. The protagonist, John (Coetzee's own name), follows the path that the author himself did, journeying to London with superficial qualifications in literature and mathematics, obliged to make a living in the new-fangled business of computer programming even as he searches for kindred spirits, inspiration and love, the which he sees as inextricably linked. John finds none, only IBM, frozen pipes, dreariness and soulless sex.

Youth is a book about failure. He is 'in the vale of testing and not doing very well'. There are days when he speaks not a word;

---

[99] *Scotland on Sunday*, May 2002.

he marks these in his diary with an *S*, for 'silence'.[100] He persuades himself that he is going through that essential time of experience that any great writer needs. He thinks of T.S. Eliot drudging for a bank. Frequently exhausted by his work at IBM, he tries to believe that tiredness is the first cross that, as a suffering artist, he must bear. He asks himself: can he perhaps get the same inspiration from exhaustion and misery as poets once did from opium and alcohol? It hardly rings true.

Meanwhile, he awaits his destiny and the love that will set him afire. He succeeds only in deflowering an even younger South African virgin in a shameful, callous manner.

It is not only John who fails. The Britain he finds is not a glamorous or successful place, but the land of the TSR2 bomber, of ICL and CND, of doomed challenges to US superiority, of small-minded poets writing on humdrum themes. But when he contemplates a return to South Africa – to the Sharpeville massacre and Dr Verwoerd's apartheid – he is filled with horror. Like Naipaul, Coetzee is not kind to his homeland.[101]

Youth is hardly a cheery read,[102] but it is a fascinating one. As ever, Coetzee dissects alienation and its settings with a prose that is never flowery, never less than evocative, precise and un-illusioned. Many of his sentences are questions: If enlightened British writers exist, where will he find them? What will cure him of babyhood? Where will he find what he needs to know? On and

---

[100] Coetzee is not known for conversation even today. I read an account by someone who had invited him to a dinner party and who, at evening's end, realised that he had said nothing at all.

[101] I was referring to Naipaul's ferocious books on India, his ancestral homeland, not Trinidad his place of birth.

[102] I am a firm admirer of Coetzee, but I found this book hard going as did other reviewers, who described it as 'a strange, bleak performance' (*TLS*).

on, he questions his own writing and himself, mercilessly, destructively, driving himself into silence and sterility. Other scribblers have the guts to put their lousy poems in the post.

It makes a curious difference knowing what actually did happen next. In *Youth*, John witnesses the death of his own spirit. Coetzee himself, thank goodness, fled Britain for Texas, at last returning to South Africa to become one of the great novelists of our age.

THE GRANDMOTHERS
by Doris Lessing [103]

New Nobel laureate J.M. Coetzee, in his latest novel *Elizabeth Costello*, created a character that rang bells everywhere. Miss Costello is an elderly Australian novelist revered for one early work, now noted for her frequent appearances at seminars and conferences, and for her reserve and intellectual hauteur – a public figure and an icon. Coetzee has dropped broad hints that one model for Costello is Doris Lessing, now in her 80s and mostly honoured for novels such as *The Grass is Singing*, published half a century ago. There is, however, one big difference: unlike Costello, the redoubtable and publicly frosty Lessing has by no means stopped writing. With two dozen novels, operas, plays, stories, poetry, essays and an autobiography to her name, Lessing is going strong, even if her reputation is now a

---

[103] *Scotland on Sunday,* November 2003. Doris Lessing made frequent appearances at the Edinburgh Book Festival, including 2003.

troubled mixture. This collection of novellas continues the mixture.

The great triumvirate of white South African novelists – Lessing, Coetzee, and his fellow Nobel Laureate, Nadine Gordimer – share obvious preoccupations in the new South Africa. The post-apartheid world is only in the background in Lessing's four new stories, but familiar themes re-emerge.

The Reason For It revisits the fantasy-science fiction that Lessing explored in her *Canopus* novels, and is an unoriginal tale of a sort that every sci-fi writer produces eventually. It describes a foundering civilisation, soon to be overrun, with the obligatory postscript from a future archaeologist noting that the ruins sit upon evidence of yet another culture. So far, so hackneyed: Arthur C. Clarke and J.G.Ballard were there decades ago. Reading with South African glasses adds interest, however. The fictional people were themselves invaders once, who swept in over simple rural folk. They bring about their own destruction through arrogance and stupidity, turning from their academies of learning to place their faith in walls and an army to put down the barbarians outside. Like white South Africa, yes, but also like Rome, Byzantium and Russia and even the US. In Lessing's tale, the chief agent of decline is a monarch who turns out to be nothing but a fool.

Here is a theme Lessing shares with her compatriots. In Nadine Gordimer's recent novel *The Pickup*, white South African culture seems secure and smug, while the 'barbarians' are pathetic illegal immigrants. But, for the rich white heroine, only a journey to the land of the barbarians gives her own life any meaning. J.M.Coetzee's 1980 masterpiece, *Waiting for the Barbarians*, portrayed an empire skulking behind its walls, its decaying civilisation sustained by the menace of the barbarians beyond. Coetzee's starting point was the eponymous poem by the Alexandrian poet C.P.Cavafy in which, again, an expiring empire needs the threat of barbarians in order to cope with internal decay.

Once a doughty Communist, Lessing now offers no obvious solutions to decadence. Coetzee, reviewing Lessing's autobiography, observed that, in considering her own career as a young activist, Lessing 'must be admired for broaching... unfashionable questions... She knew she was behaving badly [but] cannot get to the bottom of why she did what she did.' But at least she acted. In this new story, there is no action left that can stem the rot.

The other three new stories are more personal, the best being *The Grandmothers* itself. Two white women in the Tropics, inseparable childhood friends, become glamorous young mothers and both produce dashing sons. As their marriages fade, both begin passionate affairs with each other's teenage boy, affairs which endure for years. The story has a cool restraint, a calm clarity in its prose: 'He lay face down on the rock and sniffed at it, the faint metallic tang, the hot dust, and vegetable aromas from little plants in the cracks.'

Lessing's prose has been criticised as flat and grey. To me, such precise, evocative and unpretentious sentences are the work of a long-practised expert. There is also a lack of moralising. Lessing's work has sometimes been marred by the author telling us what to think, but there is none of that here. If there is a morally limited character, it is the young 'outsider' wife that one of the boys eventually marries, a girl who cannot cope with what she discovers about the past.

Victoria and the Staveneys tells of a black girl in grim, rainy

London, entangled with a family of wealthy white liberals. She has a child by one of the sons, watching sadly as her daughter drifts away from her, seduced by a world in which the comforts and the opportunities are infinitely greater than anything she can offer. The tale is muddled in its telling, with a clatter of secondary characters. There is a poignancy, though, in Victoria's realisation that, while the arty liberal Staveneys are enchanted by the half-breed child – 'my little crème caramel' crows the grandfather – they want nothing to do with Victoria's other baby, Dixon, who is black and wild and who 'sweated easily. Sometimes sweat flew off him as freely as off an over-hot dog's tongue.' Lessing's grasp of black Britain is not so sure as it is of South Africa. She describes 'the wave of immigrants invited... after the Second World War... to take on the dirty work.' But they weren't: the 'wave' of Jamaicans came in the 1950s, and they came to run London Transport: not especially dirty, just ill-paid. Of contemporary mores, however, she is a wryly funny observer, noting how people dying in hospital are now 'suspected of knowing everything that was going on around them, even if in a coma or half dead. Or even dead.'

Lastly, *A Love Child* describes a modest English lad called up in 1939. He is a poetical soul, and on the sea voyage to India he falls for a broody girl in Cape Town looking to get pregnant. He is there just four days, but the intoxication he experiences is all that gets him through years of tedium as an army administrator in India. He becomes an emotional mollusc, shut down to war, suffering, and end-of-Empire politics. Nothing touches him except the belief that the Cape Town girl has borne his child, for whom he later searches without success.

This is Lessing in her bleak, grey mode. Critics have

complained that her emotional range is narrow and hard, that she describes human circumstances without empathy. In this strange tale, though, we have the reverse: a man charged with emotion who cannot find the one point of contact that might allow his deep springs of love to flow. It is a chilling portrait, for which we may be rather frigidly grateful.

THAT OLD ACE IN THE HOLE
by Annie Proulx [104]

A curious fashion has developed in recent years of, I believe, US origin. It is the trend for novelists to make elaborate, effusive acknowledgement of their sources. Barbara Kingsolver, for example, prefaces *Prodigal Summer* with practical thanks to 'Chris Cokinos for his wonderful book, *Hope is the Thing With Feathers*', and with toe-curling thanks to 'my sister Ann [who] has expanded her soul for my support in ways that sometimes resemble wings'.

Annie Proulx keeps things calmer, but *That Old Ace in the Hole* begins nonetheless with three pages of thanks. Proulx being Proulx, a strangeness enters even here. What in other authors would be pedantry now has its own odd interest: she thanks 'District Manager C.E.Williams of Panhandle Ground Water Conservation District No 3 [who] made useful comments on the agricultural use of the Ogallala aquifer.' She even thanks people

---

[104] *Scotland on Sunday*, January 2003.

173

whose information she did not use: 'Retired Park Service Ranger Ed Day gave a fine exhibition of flint knapping (deleted in the final version).'

What is going on? I have no objection to proper gratitude, but I do not think previous authors were being ungracious in keeping their research private. The trend for extended acknowledgements has been noted in non-fiction also; suggested reasons include an attempt by anxious authors to shore up their case by mustering all the authorities they drew on (Chaucer and Dante did the same) presenting, as it were, a group photo of their backers. This, in its modern incarnation, has the unhappy effect of dissipating the fiction, undermining the willing suspension of disbelief. It lends to a story a fake air of documentation, even of 'truth'.

There was no question that Annie Proulx's previous novels, *Accordion Crimes* or *The Shipping News* – which produced a memorable film performance from Kevin Spacey – were anything other than works of a full-blooded imagination. *That Old Ace in the Hole* is somewhat different. It sets out to collate and portray.

There is a story, certainly; a man called Bob comes to the Texas town of Woolybucket as a 'site scout', to find land suitable for purchase by a pig-farming corporation. Knowing that hogs are unpopular for their stink, he tries to keep a low profile as he investigates the locals, hoping to discover who might be willing to sell up. This narrative thread is not particularly strong; the novel is, at heart, an anthology of stories. This is, perhaps, a development of a trait that was always present in Proulx. There was no great narrative drive in *The Shipping News* either, while *Accordion Crimes* was a set of novellas linked by little more than ownership of a musical instrument. Indeed, I believe that Proulx is more naturally a writer of novellas and short stories whose finest work is to be found in the superb *Close Range* collection: tales such as 'The Half-Skinned Steer' are masterpieces of concision and evocation, sharply focused and clear in their narrative direction.

In the new novel, Proulx places her 'scout' in a succession of settings in which others can tell him stories. Bob Dollar himself (notwithstanding the publisher's tag of 'unforgettable') is a rather colourless figure. He is simply the ear, listening to LaVon Fronk, her colleagues in the ladies embroidery circle, and others evoking the curious folk of the 'panhandle', that squarish chunk of territory that juts up from the north-west corner of Texas. Everyone Bob meets has stories to tell; LaVon Fronk is the self-appointed archivist of panhandle life, compiling a huge compendium of personal histories from friends and neighbours, which she knows she will never finish.

In Proulx's hands, these stories are generally worth listening to, though some are slight and sentimental: there's the tale of a cowboy who is sacked for absence from work when it transpires that he is holding the hand of a little girl who is dying. There is the tale of the barbed-wire salesman and the angry rancher who make a wager as to whether the wire will hold back a herd of thirst-maddened steers. These stories usually have a point: in the case of the sacked farm hand, there is argument over whether such a tear-jerking legend can actually be true. In the case of the wager, the point is the familiar one that the modern age arrived in the form of wire, which spelled the end of the open range.

These are not narrative points. They are part of an exercise in evocation, documentation and plentiful nostalgia: '[Of] the great ranches all but the battered remnants of a few had fallen away, cotton growing up against the foundations of the houses, verandas buried in the dirt, the costly imported stained glass windows slivered by bullets.' The storytellers are the eccentrics of the panhandle, people of sometimes limited education but shrewd as hell. As the sheriff warns Bob the scout: 'These illiterate old coots can figure you right out o'your socks.' Eccentricities are valued and cultivated: 'Crusty old ranchers who worked an embroidery hoop, or the man building a full-size locomotive in his garage... But dark skin colour, strange accent or... homosexuality and blatant liberalism were unbearable.' This adds up to a portrait of a place and a way of life, as one might have expected after all those acknowledgements. There are splendid scenes of windmill building and cockfighting – 'a combat with sexual overtones rooted in the deepest trench of the panhandle psyche' – and people with names like Coolbroth, Freda Beautyrooms and Ribeye Cluke. Then there's Brother Mesquite from the monastery that ranches bison, and a nice joke about a cowboy who wears clothes all made of brown paper, and gets hanged for rustling.

The prose often has a wonky syntax that puts a queer kick into the descriptions. She has a lovely line in images: 'The legs of the running horses twinkled like spinning coins.' Her throwaway observations are delightful, describing, for instance, a gormless woman carefully picking the heating elements out of a new electric blanket. '[You recall] when her gas stove blowed up? Just melted the nylons right onto her poor legs.' The villains of the piece are Bob's employers, Global Pork Rind, who, to emphasise their status as alien invaders, are based in Tokyo. They and the shameless hustlers they employ get their comeuppance, and the book ends in a homey sort of victory for the forces of resistance. *That Old Ace in the Hole* does not stand up with the best of

Proulx's work. It is, however, thoroughly enjoyable as an affectionate picture of a battered corner of the US.

WHITE LIGHTNING
by Justin Cartwright [105]

In the seventh novel by South African Londoner Justin Cartwright, a South African Londoner goes home in comically humiliating circumstances. He is a film director who has nursed ambitions to be an auteur. Attempting to bolster his faltering career, he has shot a soft-porn horror called *Suzi Crispin: Night Nurse*, with the result that his career dies. Thereafter, the only work he is offered is a propaganda film for a neo-Fascist millionaire founding a new British political party. His son dies of asthma, his wife throws him out. So he returns to the Cape to be with his impecunious mother, who is dying too. If this sounds cheerful, never fear, it gets worse.

Cartwright is a skilful storyteller, and the tale is an engaging one. In South Africa, our cineaste – whose name we don't hear – is drawn into a succession of doomed relationships: with a white divorcee, with a squatter family afflicted with Aids, and with a caged baboon on a run-down farm which he buys, thinking it to be a misanthropist's heaven. But though he views people objectively, he is powerless to prevent himself being manipulated and taken for a ride.

---

[105] *Scotland on Sunday,* August 2002.

Along the way, Cartwright has a lot of fun, notably with the night nurse, more *Carry On* than carnal. The narrator's style is perfectly judged, having a fleshy glibness that reeks of sham. He speaks the language of post-modernism, larded with (mis)quotations of Voltaire and Marvell. The one author that matters is Virgil writing on bees, because our narrator's father wrote best-sellers of popular science on bees, and the son now hankers for that dream of reflective solitude, the life of the beekeeper.

Like many a paunchy, golf-playing advertising man, he cannot see the ludicrous pomposity of his own opinions, which tend to start with the words, 'In my experience, women...' Or they are would-be shocking in a clunky way: 'I too shall die, and I don't give a f***.' Or feeble clichés: 'This city has a kind of heartlessness.' He can recognise affectation in others, and has little time for whites who say boastfully, 'I am an African'. But he cannot see his own folly as he attempts to outsmart the landscape of scrub plants: 'I will learn the botanical names.' Thus far, thus mildly distasteful. Quite how far below this entertainingly unpleasant surface Cartwright takes us is perhaps another question. At times he seems to view South Africa with a bleakly honest gaze. At such moments, the present tense prose focuses on the strictly immediate: smells, voices, the poorness of things described without judgement. That is how we are now meant to write about Africa, after all. But he can't keep it up; when the temperature is rising and the modern condition is becoming unbearable, we nip back to London for another episode of farce. So we have Coetzee-with-laughs.

The jokes are funny enough, but the epiphanal moments are perhaps too slick – for example, the mother's death: 'She had slipped across the border without her papers.' If we have sympathy for the narrator, it is because, after everything he's learnt, he'll still be stuck for all eternity with his own trite formulations.

LETTERS FROM THE GREAT WALL
by Jenni Daiches [106]

Just as many young Germans are reputed to know nothing of Hitler, so many Chinese under the age of thirty are said to be unaware of the significance of Tiananmen Square in their country's recent history. While the spectacular protests and their crushing have come to symbolise a vast People yearning for democracy, the truth was as usual far more complex. The death toll, for example, is given at anything from 23 (by the Chinese Communist Party) to 2300 (by the Chinese Red Cross). Even the motivation for the protests was confused; in one corner were students who considered the regime corrupt and the current wave of reforms inadequate, while in the other corner were many labourers who had been enjoying relatively good times and saw the reforms as a threat. What few would dispute, however, is that the demonstrations/protests/rebellions or whatever were directed predominantly by youth clamouring for self-determination against oppressive old men.

Into this frame steps a (fictional) Scottish lecturer in literature,

---

[106] *Scottish Review of Books*, vol.3 no.1 (2007)

a young woman bent on escape from another regime of men who, if not all old, still represent the manifold varieties of male deceit and oppression.

Jenni Daiches (a.k.a. Calder) has for many years held a succession of well-respected positions with the Museum of Scotland, editing and writing books on Scottish history and literature. *Letters from the Great Wall* is something different: a novel of self-discovery and liberation. Her heroine is Eleanor, a first-class honours graduate now lecturing in English at Edinburgh University. Eleanor is the product of a stultifying male-ruled home in Linlithgow who has allowed herself to be cornered by Roy, a University anthropologist hungry for academic success, a pliant wife, and babies. Eleanor is gradually suffocating. As Roy and her parents pile the pressure on her to wed and procreate, she suddenly decamps to China, giving a few lectures for cash but then touring the major sites, while subjecting her nearest and dearest back home to cold scrutiny. In the meanwhile, disaffection is brewing, and when she returns to Beijing she is just in time for the tragedy of Tiananmen Square.

As she moves around China, Eleanor sends (in her mind, or to some unspecified recipient) a series of letters describing China and pondering her reasons for fleeing Edinburgh. Thus, much of the novel is a description of her life in Scotland, and very depressing it sounds too. Eleanor herself seems lifeless at times, and is not wholly convincing; supposedly 33, she feels middle-aged throughout, able for instance to refer to 'youngsters necking' in the park. Her putative husband Roy is so tedious that one can't imagine why she shacked up with him in the first place, or why she has the slightest compunction about cutting loose. Western men as a breed come off badly. Her father is a tyrant of the quiet sort, a dead hand of conformity. Her brother is a careerist going the same way. In China she is assaulted by a Pole, used by a cool Canadian, and robbed by an Englishman. Back home, the only man she ever loved is heavily differentiated: not a real Scot but a semi-man, an effete bisexual Jewish restaurateur – and he deceives her too. By contrast, the one woman she gets to know in China is Dutch, big-boned and determined, making her own forceful way through life. Most of these are two-dimensional figures, and Eleanor's attitude to them just a string of resentments. Only the Chinese men – a returned democracy activist, and a doctor-poet – are sympathetic. Men, says Eleanor, are basically irrelevant to her self-knowledge.

Nonetheless, Daiches' debut novel has considerable virtues. Her evocation of travelling around China is sharp and effective: the vast and drab 'Friendship Hotels' in every city, the silent men spitting in trains, the extraordinary sense of eternal struggle (oxen ploughing just as they did in the Bronze Age). The prose is efficient. Perhaps a little too efficient. The style is clipped. Very clipped. Rather like this.

The final pages are the best, and are very well done. Daiches resists the temptation to draw back and take a grand overview of events. She barely mentions the politics behind the Tiananmen protests. The villains Li Peng and Deng Xiaoping, the epic hunger strike, the great statue of the 'Goddess of Democracy' that was erected in the square, none of these things gets a look in. Instead, Eleanor is simply there with her friends, confused, frightened but determined, hearing gunshots in the distance, or creeping terrified through the dark streets. And there she leaves it, inconclusive just as the Tiananmen protests were, but with the world and Eleanor herself unmistakably changed nonetheless.

THE SUCCESSOR
Ismail Kadare [107]

Accepting his Man Booker International prize earlier this year, the Albanian novelist Ismail Kadare said modestly, 'Everything I did was quite normal; I just did it in an abnormal country.' This is a little disingenuous; much about Kadare's situation is very odd.

For decades, Kadare was one of a tiny handful of Albanian writers who managed both to achieve international recognition and to survive the bizarre brutalities of Albania under Enver Hoxha. He survived by walking a very fine line between storytelling and criticism of the regime – so fine a line, indeed, that not everyone agrees that he deserves the name of dissident; recently a debate about his record raged in the *Times Literary Supplement*. Kadare finally left Albania and applied for political asylum in France just weeks before the Communist regime collapsed.

Kadare speaks little English, and there are, apparently, no decent translators for Albanian into English. So the versions of his books that we have are at two removes, put into French by Tedi Papavrami, an Albanian violinist resident in Geneva, and from French into English by David Bellos. All very odd.

Odd, too, is this very entertaining novel, closely based on historical events. The Successor in reality was Mehmet Shehu, who had been named as the official next-in-line to rule Albania after Hoxha. Not long before he was due to take power, he was

---

[107] *Scotland on Sunday*, January 2006. At about the time of writing this review, I and several other authors were invited by Fife Council to help out with a 'reading day' in Glenrothes. I was able to nominate a book for my sub-group, and chose *The Successor* – which some in my group roundly said they hated. I much enjoyed both this and other novels by him, such as *The Seige*.

found dead, shot in his home. Was it murder? Suicide? To this day, no one knows (or is saying).

The novel – like Kurosawa's *Rashomon* – examines the mystery from several points of view, mostly people who blame themselves for the death. There is the daughter, whose attempt to marry a member of the old pre-communist elite brought disgrace on the Shehu family. There is the architect who believes that, by building the Successor such a fine home, he caused murderous envy in others. Finally (and just as in *Rashomon*) the dead man is contacted by a spirit medium, and spills the surprising beans.

It is all told with wonderfully sly wit. When the failing Hoxha visits the fine new house, Shehu's mother boasts of the dimmer switches – the first in Albania – only to have the blind dictator pathetically groping the wall to find them, to try them out. When the Successor's daughter dreams of meeting her slaughtered father's ghost, she tries not to get his blood on her clothes while he's trying to avoid her lipstick. No need to be scared of ghosts in Albania, someone says: we're all the living dead here.

There was nothing normal about Hoxha's Albania, a country reputed to have had one concrete bunker for every adult male of the population. Kadare's achievement (and his double-translators' also) is to maintain a deadpan tone that makes the bizarre credible and thereby more bizarre. There are, for example, wonderful scenes of the entire Party membership being summonsed to the Fourteen Halls of Tirana to hear taped recordings of Hoxha speaking, all the audience frantically trying to unravel the runes (Who's in, who's out? as Lear would say) suggested by subtle changes in the seating plan. In such a land, to be powerful is also to be very vulnerable.

With this short novel, Kadare evokes a place of smoke, mirrors and arbitrary execution, and does it with elegance and compassion.

No More Angels
Stories *by* Ron Butlin [108]

Ron Butlin's new collection carries an 'appreciation' by Ian Rankin. This is fitting, since the stories inhabit a landscape Rankin knows well. Most are set in or near to Edinburgh, most involve copious alcohol, and two thirds are about death.

Only a few murders, admittedly. Most are deaths remembered, usually of family: the wife killed in a car, the brother drowned, the mother collapsing with a coronary, another mother falling downstairs, plus one victim of Lockerbie. A husband is killed by remorseless disease, and his wife waits for her own death. Another family's exotic birds are on the way out, literally, with the cage door left ajar: 'They'll die out there; they need looked after.' Butlin's characters are not good at looking after each other. Some relatives are grieving; others are dancing on the grave. Fathers make a poor showing, being unemployed couch potatoes or bullies. They'd be better off dead, and several are.

Travellers arriving at Turnhouse airport, with its embarrassing mural of congratulatory quotes on the glories of Edinburgh civilisation, may not recognise Butlin's city, but Ian Rankin will. This is encapsulated as 'a cul-de-sac of uncollected bin bags, broken glass, dogshit and lack of sunlight' where the only tourist

---

[108] *Scottish Review of Books*, vol.3 (3) 2007.

site visited is Calton Hill: 'Big deal. A lumpy stretch of grass with Greek pillars stuck in it.' Innocent lads won't want to hang about with the company up there.

There is also the death-in-life of the meaningless job or marriage, or the alcoholic's insensibility. The town is full of alcoholics: the derelict renting out student lodging; the homeless slumped in doorways; young men staggering across pubs with a skinful of Heavy; a professor with a skinful of malt insulting the wife; an elderly butler drowning in bitterness and the master's claret. The house guests get pished and lob peeled prawns for a bimbo to catch in her mouth: 'She would lean forward, instead, catching them in her cleavage. Purpose-built, it seemed.' The young rot their livers with Black Velvet, meaning here a blend of beer and cider. (I'd always thought Black Velvet was Guinness and Champagne, but there I go with my elitism.) Haute cuisine is wasted on the Edinburgh elite, while the rest of the population subsists on McRubbish, Chinese carry-outs and the fine dining to be had at Giorgio's flop-house: 'slice of bread – 15p butter, 10p marge.'

If the tone of all this seems rather unremitting, it is. Butlin can write very amusingly, but this collection has a bad case of the glums. One looks in vain for much beauty or love or celebration, and after a while the misery can become wearying. So the flashes of light and humour are to be treasured: the kindness of a 'Paki' shopkeeper to an old lady, or that same old lady skewering a road-hog's tyre with an artificial Christmas tree, or the kiss from a girl who had seemed a prize bitch of a tease, but who might just be a genuine sweetie after all.

Some of the best stories are the deft short fables. A nice one features a Tony Blair lookalike, 'who had turned sincerity into a brand-name stamped across his forehead', having an unfortunate encounter with the Delphic oracle. There's also a jab at pretension in art music; when you see Arnold Schoenberg described as 'the great composer and music theorist', you can be sure that Modernism is in for some happy slapping. Sure enough: 'After turning the corner into the glorious future ahead, the engine [goes] slamming into a solid wall.' Schoenberg is soon 'rushing up to complete strangers. 'My twelve-tone system offers real value for money to composer, player and audience alike.' It is neatly done, with a stripped-down, agile humour that RLS would have enjoyed.

Much the most effective and moving story, though, is the longer piece that closes the book, *Alice Kerr went with Older Men.* I am increasingly convinced that the art of the short story (so often said to be in the doldrums) is ill-served by the constraining '3,000-word max' of competitions, radio reading and magazine publication. *Alice Kerr* makes the point. In this tale – sixty pages instead of the routine eight or nine – Butlin shakes off his slightly formulaic horrors and allows his characters to grow, to achieve a complex personal journey. The result is a very superior piece of fiction, a fine story. The world is the same: youth seeking an escape from crushing parents, dead-end prospects and hopeless love, and the route leads through the familiar landscape. But Butlin's young hero comes to life in a way that is varied, funny, convincing, worldly wise but, at the last, hopeful. The story (and the collection) concludes: 'He was so very, very glad' – and this we can genuinely share.

COOKING WITH FERNET BRANCA
by James Hamilton Paterson [109]

I was engaged to a girl in Venice once (it didn't last) and we often amused ourselves by hunting down the most noxious *amaro* (bitters) to be found in the Serenissima's many bars. Fernet Branca is one such *amaro*, tasting like a blend of nettle juice and cough medicine that turns your tongue oddly green. I have to tell you that Fernet Branca is for wimps; indeed, it has a slightly sweet undertaste. The real humdinger is called Amaro de Udine, a beverage compounded of paraquat and aviation fuel (which I suspect hastened the demise of our romance).

The hero of James Hamilton Paterson's new novel is Gerry Samper, an English resident of the Tuscan hills. Gerry, an effete and cynical foodie, cooks with Fernet Branca, all on the basic premise that 'lilies are much improved by gilding'. He has created recipes such as Garlic & Fernet Branca Ice-cream, Otter with Lobster Sauce (with Fernet) and Rabbit in Cep Custard (with Fernet). He actually makes his living by ghost-writing autobiographies of champion skiers ('Downhill All the Way') and racing drivers ('The Absolute Pits') in which he describes 'the Pit Stop Game as played by three Ferrari drivers in a Monaco hotel suite.' Each driver pretends to be a car coming into the pits, and is set upon by a team of girls who have him away ('back in the race') in record time. Gerry's contempt for his subjects is poorly disguised.

Into his idyll crashes a new neighbour, Marta, an eastern European composer of film scores now working for an Italian who

---

[109] *Scotland on Sunday*, June 2004.

specializes in 'R-rated' films (R=*ragazzi*: suitable for boys accompanied by a priest). This director's current project has as its villains a beach-dwelling commune of viciously racist Greens. Gerry's distaste for Marta's clumping vulgarity ('a Bedouin traffic warden') cannot, however, keep her frumpish sexuality at bay, while his pergola is flattened by the down-draft from helicopters piloted either by her movie employers or by her own family of ex-Soviet mafiosi. It's all very bad news for Gerry.

Don't be misled by the publisher's claim that 'the English obsession with Tuscany is mercilessly satirised'. It is, in fact, hardly mentioned. The heart of the novel is Gerry and Marta's relationship. Of the two, Gerry is by far the funnier. Marta's background has a cartoonish quality, rather weighed down by exposition. Gerry, though, is a comic creation of some genius. When not blundering into DIY (pinning himself to a new fence with a nail gun), he is compiling 'The Boys Reformatory Cookbook' which includes, for determined dog-eaters, the advice that 'Jack Russells are absolute buggers to bone'. His singing is excruciating, but in his bottom drawer languishes the libretto for 'a delightful and lubricious operetta' entitled '*Vietato ai Minori*'. Emotionally hamstrung, he has a rubber farting teddybear and has discovered that you can modify the fart with KY Jelly, depending on how wet you want it to sound.

This is a very funny novel, and I have only one cavil. I have actually eaten otter (stewed, in Burma) and I wish to put on record that it is delicate neither in taste nor texture, having the flavour and consistency of boiled brake-linings. However, in that respect at least, I daresay overnight marinading in Fernet Branca would help.

BEFORE I FORGET
by André Brink [110]

André Brink is a prolific writer and a courageous one. His fiction
– fifteen novels in English, many more in Afrikaans – got him
into very hot water with the old apartheid regime in South Africa.
These novels have a number of common themes, among them
retrospection, colonial history, violence and sexual exploitation.
A caricature Brink novel would be the life story of an elderly,
oversexed Boer farmer, related while he pursues a lovely
Hottentot girl across the Kalahari *c*.1930. This new novel shares
too much of that caricature for comfort. It is a first person memoir
by one Chris Minaar, a South African lawyer-turned-writer (aged
78), who is stirred by the violent death of his greatest love (some
decades younger) to contemplate all the women that he has
bedded in the past.

Of whom there has been no lack. Starting with a childhood
encounter with a pretty cousin up a tree, his partners in a seven-
decade career are paraded before us. Their physical attributes are
dwelt on – the shape and colour of their nipples, their delectable
bottoms. All are lovely, some are neurotic, some are artistic, one
is a police spy, but almost all are handmaids of Priapus. The
result, to my mind, is very unappealing.

As Minaar looks back over his life and the 20th century history
of South Africa, he sees how, at every turn in his nation's story,
there was a new woman in his own. Which could not fail to be the
case, given the number he gets through. He muses: 'I have read of
a Frenchman who [said on his deathbed] with a small smile of

---

[110]*Scotland on Sunday*, October 2004. André Brink died in 2015.

contentment, "I have eaten well". When my time comes, I hope I'd be able to say with equal satisfaction and equal conviction, "I have loved well." '

This tone of connoisseurship is maintained throughout. Minaar is a wine buff, and his Uncle Johnny once catechised him: 'A man who cannot taste his wine properly will never understand a thing about women.' So, roll those girls about your tongue, and we get:

'In Pietmaritzburg there was Charmaine, an eager but bland run-of-the-mill Colombard; at a festival in Stavanger there was Astrid, a pleasant Tinto de Barrocas, down-to-earth, ready for drinking on the spot; in Cologne, where I had to collect a prize, there was Gertrude, a rather thin, metallic Zinfandel...'

Meanwhile, as Minaar looks back he also looks at the television, horribly fascinated by the invasion of Iraq, day by day, citing particular *New York Times* correspondents, or the movements of specific US Army formations. Minaar cannot help viewing all this in sexual terms. The invasion, he decides, is George Bush's ultimate orgasm. 'The whole enterprise reminds one of nothing so much as an unscrupulous man intent...on 'getting' a particular woman...All one knows for certain is that somebody is getting fucked.'

Does this tell us anything about war, or neoconservative ideology, or women, or South Africa or even sex? The latter is described in words that are mostly cliché 2-D fantasy: for instance, 'explosive' (an unfortunate term in the context). As he holds his dying love's hand, he concludes: 'We betray those we love by loving them... We transform the one we love into the one we should love to love. That denies the reality of one we love.'

So, we put our lovers on a pedestal. Not an original thought, and offered without irony. Out of respect for Brink's dauntless career, one would like to be kinder. But feminists will hate this book, and I didn't much warm to it either.

PRAYING MANTIS
by André Brink [111]

Reviewing André Brink's previous novel [*Before I Forget*], I suggested that the archetypal Brink tale would be the life story of an oversexed white farmer recalled as he pursued a Hottentot woman across the South African veldt, *circa* 1930. I got it slightly wrong: the new book is the life story of an oversexed Hottentot man pursuing women and the white man's religion across the veldt *circa* 1800.

It is also a fine novel. The story (largely true) is simple, concerning the remarkable Cupido Cockroach, a Hottentot (or Khoi) who, born on a back country farm, becomes a roaring boy, drinking and leching until he falls under the spell of Dr van Kemp of the London Missionary Society. Cupido shuns his native beliefs and turns to Jesus with a violent passion; he's not averse to literally beating the hell out of sinners until they repent. A preacher of epic gifts, he is ordained as the first Hottentot missionary of the LMS, while conducting a personal correspondence with God: 'Dear God, I know you are a very busy man, but this situation is crushing my balls...'

But these are violent times in the Cape as expanding European colonies collide with incursions of Xhosa people from the north,

---

[111] *Scotland on Sunday,* 2005.

with Hottentots and missions caught in between. Brink evokes all the tension and drama, as 'commandos' of tough farmers threaten to raze townships to the ground if the authorities and the missions don't support them. The missionaries' plight is powerfully drawn. Desperately poor, struggling with a drought-stricken, unforgiving landscape, they are dependent on cooperation and goodwill, yet their attempts to 'save' the Bushmen and to curb the abusive violence of the white farmers towards their slaves set them all at loggerheads.

This is a driving theme of the story; the missionaries' failure to procure justice is very poignant. We failed (one Brother concludes) not only the Hottentots, whom finally we could not protect, but also the colonists themselves: 'We did not look beyond their reign of terror... they were human too, suffering too, ignorant too, filled with ungodly fear.'

Praying Mantis is full of vivid scenes and of comedy. Cupido encounters a travelling trader whose wares include nails, pails and gunpowder and also 'a small skull of St Peter as a child.' When a new missionary, Brother Read, takes a new wife, his wedding night is marred by Cupido who stays outside the bedroom window singing hallelujahs at the top of his voice. The prose is clean and strong. Only very occasionally does Brink falter: I don't, for instance, believe that anyone in 1800 would have thought an 18-year-old wife 'very young'.

Cupido's own first wife is the splendidly long-suffering Anna Vigilant, who boils the best soap in the Cape (there's an intriguing description of how to do it). But as Cupido himself is exploited by the missions, Anna reminds him of his own gods that he has deserted, but who never quite leave him. The novel's finest section is the ending, in which Cupido – having been sent as a lone missionary to a distant region – is progressively abandoned by his LMS patrons. Sliding into destitution, he is at last deserted by his tiny native congregation also, to preach his gospel to the stones.

MINARET
by Leila Aboulela [112]

Leila Aboulela has found an unusual literary niche. Many African male writers have sought their fortunes in Europe. A Sudanese, Tayeb Salih,[113] came to London where he became a leading novelist of the Arab world. But for a Sudanese woman to move to Aberdeen and then win literary repute is something special. Aboulela, winner of the Caine Prize for African fiction, has had work read on BBC radio and has gone from publishing in Edinburgh to Bloomsbury in London. She is courted by book festivals and literary events. She has arrived by a most unusual route.

What does she offer? Essentially, her own experience: that of an educated Muslim woman no longer able to live in Khartoum, but unwilling to renounce her identity. Her 'Caine' winning story, *The Museum*, focussed on such a woman meeting a Scottish male student at university in Aberdeen. Her fine first novel, *The Translator*, concerned a Sudanese woman in Aberdeen falling in love with her Scottish academic boss who converts to Islam to be

---

[112] *Scotland on Sunday,* June 2005
[113] Author of two favourite books of mine, *The Wedding of Zein* (1968) and *The Season of Migration to the North* (1980)

193

with her. Her new book, *Minaret*, concerns a wealthy, westernised Khartoum girl whose father falls foul of a political coup, and who finds herself 'come down in the world' in London, finally reduced to working as a maid servant.

In this situation are many tensions. There is the love-hate relationship of an African colony for its former master. Among the Sudanese-in-exile in London there are victims of other coups, with little sympathy for Najwa's father executed for corruption. There are modernists and Marxists, but none of these speak to her particular distress. At first she seems carefree, enjoying shopping and the sights. But as the family fortune dwindles and the news from Khartoum gets worse, Najwa feels rootless, becoming more Sudanese in London than she was in Khartoum.

Only when she comes into contact with the women of the local mosque does she feel touched: the *azan* calls to a hollow in her, she says. *Minaret* is a profoundly Muslim story. Islam comforts and heals Najwa, and it is the Islam of women, relishing situations (without men) when the mood can be 'silky, tousled, non-linear.' The consolations are those of submissiveness that is quasi-erotic – she day-dreams of being a concubine – but which is based on renunciation, 'when we respect the boundaries of Allah,' of wearing the hijab, and of turning down love with a younger man to set him free.

Some readers may be irritated by the deliberately narrow emotional range, a new-found innocence that can seem simplistic, and the willingness to admit – indeed, to enjoy – naïveté and personal limitation. Aboulela offers these as strengths. Her prose moves with the steady pace of someone who knows her faith, and knows she must not falter. She occasionally falters in her English idiom (she takes the chicken from the freezer to 'melt'; an uncle

194

'immigrates' to Canada) but it is often delicate and evocative, as when she describes girls praying and the faint sound of 'the fall of polyester on the grass.'

Minaret will enhance Aboulela's reputation as an exponent of religion in fiction, a faith that brings 'new gentleness...[as] all the frisson, all the sparks died away.'

THE SEA ROAD
by Margaret Elphinstone [114]

Historical novels are not easy to get right. If they are under-researched, they don't ring true. If they are over-researched, they groan under a burden of detail that the author was delighted to discover but which may have no place in the story, or were not made new by the imagination.

Nor is it enough to get material facts correct – what Edmund White recently called 'brand name history'. Littering the text with period nuggets without going deeper into the culture and mores of an earlier society is as bad as any other anachronism. You cannot evoke the 1960s by mentioning Ford Cortinas if you fail to master the different attitudes to, say, race or sexuality that prevailed.

The Sea Road, derived from three Norse sagas, largely avoids these pitfalls; Margaret Elphinstone manages to be physically most evocative, while convincing me, at least, that she has striven to imagine how an 11th century Viking might have thought and felt. She wears her research lightly but well.

---

[114] *The List*, 'Scotland's 100 Best Books', 2006

The novel concerns early Norse journeys to Greenland and then Vinland – that's to say, America. Her principal character is Gudrid, a woman who once sailed with her menfolk to the chilly shores across the Atlantic, and who in her old age fetches up in Rome and there relates her adventures to a young Icelandic monk.

There are many fine passages in this book. In one, Gudrid, her husband, their longship and crew are trapped in a settlement in Greenland for a terrible, hard winter. As if the freezing conditions aren't enough, a killing sickness strikes them. One by one, the crew die. The hardships are described with chilly power, but Elphinstone also manages the considerable feat of introducing ghosts from which Gudrid must free herself, and does this believably because she has managed to get inside her characters. Similarly, in the tragic first encounters between the Norsemen (and women) and the natives of North America, she avoids fashionable blame and brutality but depicts two warrior societies colliding with predictable results.

The Sea Road is a short, terse novel, an excellent example of 'less is more'. The prose is often luminous, and the whole a most satisfying read.

LOS DE ABAJO (UNDERDOGS)
by Mariano Azuela [115]

It has been said that in this century there have been only four
significant Latin American revolutions: Mexico (1910),
Guatemala (1944), Bolivia (1952) and Cuba (1958). Today one
would certainly add Nicaragua.[116] This history suggests that a
mere putsch, one clique ousting another, is of no consequence:
there must be aspirations to radical change in the People's lot to
create a revolutionary uprising. Demetrio, the guerrilla leader at
the centre of Mariano Azuela's *Underdogs*, has such hopes.
Watching his house burned by Federal troops, it is as though he
and his homeland are on fire. He gathers a band of the rural
oppressed, fights a first heroic fight, is wounded, then recovers to
lead his band into the mainstream uprising. So far, a model of just
revolt.

But *Underdogs* is about a revolution turned sour. We see
Demetrio's men looting, murdering, drinking themselves stupid
because they've lost direction, and finally dying in a pointless
skirmish. The articles of faith are overturned. At first the illiterate
rebels regard literacy with awe. 'It's incredible that we need this
slicker to come and explain things,' they say of Luis Cervantes, a
journalist and glib theorist of revolt who joins them. Later,
however, a typewriter is smashed in bitter frustration. Yet
Demetrio needs Luis to provide names, facts and formulations.
So, inexorably, confused issues and in-fighting blur the rebels'
clarity of purpose. Watching clouds of smoke and dust rise over

---

[115] *New Internationalist*, July 1985. 'Classic book'. Original published 1916.
[116] Although in 2021 one might not be in such a hurry.

the battlefield, an insurrectionary struggles with disillusion:

'We must try to hope a little; that there'll be no more bloodshed, that the minds of the people – formed now of only two words, rob and kill – will shine with the clarity of a water drop once more. What a mockery, if our enthusiasm should depose one murderer only to erect a pedestal on which we place a thousand identical monsters.'

Mariano Azuela knew whereof he wrote. A doctor who believed passionately in literature and the Revolution, he fought with and healed revolutionaries, undertook public office out of a sense of duty rather than natural inclination, and wrote *Underdogs* on the run. Like his characters he saw his ideals betrayed, idols like Pancho Villa fallen, factionalism and megalomania displacing any thought of the social justice they'd suffered for. The novel he produced is deeply pessimistic. Only a blind compulsion drives Demetrio on. He smiles as a friend shouts:

'I love the Revolution as I love an erupting volcano; the volcano because it's a volcano, the Revolution because it's a revolution. Who cares who ends up on top of the heap?'

With historical hindsight, he might have cared more. Mexico today is an unhappy country; 60% of the population are undernourished, the rural economy chronically depressed, the foreign debt effectively infinite. Mexico City is a purgatory where, it is said, you can catch hepatitis just by breathing, while the Republic is governed by a system of patronage that has led to gross corruption, electoral fraud and riots. 70 years after the Revolution, a recent study remarked, 'Mexico's social profile is barely distinguishable from countries of the region that have had no revolution.' Azuela's underdogs are now fleeing to

California.[117]

After initial hardships, his own fortunes improved. He continued working as a doctor and writing, won a steady income and a national literary prize, and – in spite of his continued jibes – no government ever attempted to muzzle him. He died in 1952, a thoroughly bourgeois success. The poor were as poor as ever.

But who would have told Demetrio that he should never have embarked on his battle, but should have watched placidly as his house burned? It is one of the book's limitations not to discuss other courses of action. Azuela's view is, after all, only partial. The great revolutionary Emiliano Zapata is never mentioned, and Azuela ignores the large part the Mexican bourgeoisie played in the revolt. His guerrillas are utterly contemptuous of the industrial wealth owners, saying: 'It's the city slickers who betray revolutions.' The novel avoids any attempt to examine what went wrong; it is finally no more than a sequence of events that could have been otherwise.

Nonetheless, the uncomfortable partial truths of *Underdogs* ring true. As we anxiously watch developments in and around Nicaragua we may have to live with the unpalatable, and we might have to abandon doctrinaire selectivity. But we need not be disheartened for all that, since anyone who believes in simple purgation by incorruptible revolution is mistakenly thinking that justice can be achieved without altering the ways in which power and authority are exercised. Demetrio is not wrong to rebel and not wrong to despair – but that need not prevent those who come after making their revolution better.[118]

---

[117] At the time of writing this review (1985), I did not think of the predominant images of Mexico in the 2000s: the interminable feuds of the drug cartels, and the migrant caravans heading for the USA.

[118] I apparently still believed in revolutions, and the following year (1986)

ARTS

LOVE & RECONQUEST
Spanish music of the *Reconquista* [119]

THE RECONQUEST OF GRANADA

In 1492 the last Moorish city in Spain – Granada – was recaptured after a near-800 year struggle, the kingdom's Jewish population was expelled and America was 'discovered'; by any measure, it was a year of unusual significance. It may be regarded as ushering the High Renaissance into the Peninsular. But the concept of a Golden Age – often used to describe the decades that followed – is a slippery and poignant one. It is slippery because, while the best Spanish secular music dates from *c.*1490 to 1570, the 'golden' epoch of literature, theatre and painting comes later, *c.*1600 and after, when Cervantes, Lope de Vega and Calderon, and Velasquez were in their prime. It is poignant because the defeat of the Moors and the Jewish expulsions turned an intellectually vivid, Afro-European society into a forcibly homogenous one. The heady optimism of Ferdinand and Isabella (the Catholic Monarchs who completed the Reconquest) was soon crushed by the Imperial burden weighing on their successors Charles V and Philip II. In little more than one hundred years, Spain acquired an American empire and lost a European one, and the country rose to and then fell from its position as a superpower with a speed which astonished all observers, none more so than

---

travelled to Nicaragua to have a look at theirs.

[119] Essay for the ensemble Fires of Love CD *Love & Reconquest*, Delphian Records (Edinburgh), 2003. This was the first recording by Fires, and only the third in the Delphian catalogue. I sang, and played recorders and 2nd lute.

FIRES OF LOVE

the Spaniards themselves.

In 1500, however, the confidence and excitement in Spain must have been palpable, above all in cities like Granada and especially Seville, crowded with adventurers hopeful of fortunes in the Americas. A history of the time could be written around the texts of its songs. Many of these – some in print, most in manuscript – are preserved in a group of songbooks or *cancioneros*. The most famous is the colossal *Cancionero Musical de Palacio* (CMP), the nucleus of which was probably compiled at Alba de Tormes, the palace of the Dukes of Alba outside Salamanca. It was completed around 1520, rediscovered in 1870 and originally contained more than 500 songs, 90 of which are now lost.

FRONTERIZOS – SONGS OF RECONQUEST

Many songs of the time relate the highlights of the last campaigns on the borders of Granada, a genre known as *fronterizos*. One of the most famous (translated by, amongst others, Lord Byron) is *Paseavase,* possibly a Moorish melody and re-worked by several composers including Luys de Narváez. It tells of the taking of the town of Alhama, the 'gateway to Granada' whose startling capture by the Marques de Cadiz in 1482 was the beginning of the end for Islamic Spain. The song had such an emotional impact for the Moors of Granada that after the Reconquest it was for a time banned because of fears it would provoke riots – as Narváez, born in Granada, would have known.

From the CMP comes *¡Levanta Pascual!* by the composer most often featured in the collection, Juan del Encina. It is a dialogue between two excited shepherds who set off to see a wonder that has come to pass. These bickering pastoralists are not Biblical

Israelites, however; they are guardians of the vast Merino flocks that, with royal license, traversed medieval Spain devouring all greenery in their path. And they go to view not the Infant Jesus but the newly conquered Alhambra, and to marvel at the glories of a Moorish epoch that is about to be terminated. Curiously, this is the only song in the entire CMP that refers specifically to Granada's surrender.

The Christians saw the Reconquest (and then the conquest of the Americas) as a Crusade, and the vaguely Biblical *Israel, mira tus montes* neatly elides the struggles of the Hebrews with those of the Spaniards in its depiction of noble Christian knights dead on the field of battle. In 1541 Charles V had continued the Crusading enterprise by sending his armies into Africa to seize Algiers. But the attacking Spaniards were soundly beaten and Alonso Mudarra's song (published 1546) may allude to the defeat.

Frequently it is the Moorish side of the story that is told, the Moors being portrayed with sympathy, even admiration. This has led some to claim that such texts were composed by *moriscos* or Christianized Moors, while other scholars see them simply as symptomatic of Renaissance humanist tolerance. *De Antequera sale el moro* refers back to the siege of that town in 1410. Antequera was the first Moorish fortress of the Kingdom of Granada to fall to the Reconquest (this being reputedly the first important use of gunpowder in Spain). *¿Qu'es de ti, desconsolado?* by Juan del Encina is a somewhat smug call to the last defeated Moorish king Boabdil to turn from Islam to Christianity. Like many musicians in the royal entourage, Encina witnessed the capture of Granada, and a number of his songs reflect this key event. They are frankly propaganda; as early as

203

1462, the Crown was commissioning *fronterizos* to whip up enthusiasm for the Reconquest.

Love in the Orchards

The surrender of Granada's Alhambra palace was witnessed by Christopher Columbus who was there petitioning the Crown to subsidise a risky and highly speculative sea-voyage that he proposed. His successful Atlantic crossing that same year is echoed in a curious little piece in the CMP. The calabash (gourd) was one of the New World trophies brought back to Europe by Columbus and his followers. It was an instant success, the sun-dried tomato of its epoch, and was cultivated all round the Mediterranean. And it was soon celebrated in music: *Calabaza, no se,* is a love song addressed to a gourd and dates from before 1520. The garden is the preferred sexual arena of the time; we meet it again in *Niña y viña,* where a girl is berated (it would usually be by her mother) for creeping out to dawn assignations. Meanwhile, the knight from Seville who picks lemons in the convent garden in *Gentil cavallero,* and the Prioress who begs him for a kiss, hint at a social problem that the devout Queen Isabella struggled with for much of her reign: the shocking moral laxity of the church. The Queen's reform programmes met with mixed success. Rather than give up their concubines, some four hundred clerics converted to Islam and decamped to North Africa.

Song forms

Calabaza, Niña y viña and other songs are in the short popular verse form known as the *villancico,* or 'peasant song'. The term was first used *c.*1450 but the form probably derives from older Cordoban-Arab models; texts survive from the 11th century using

Arabic for the verses and a southern Spanish dialect for the refrains. Some *villancicos* are religious and with time the form became synonymous with Christmas carols, certain of which are still popular in Spain today. *Virgen digna de honor* and *Ay los maytines era* are typical of the uncomplicated beauty of these pieces; it is not difficult to imagine them sung at a crowded popular festival where strict adherence to the Gospels was perhaps not an issue; *Que bonito niño* introduces two midwives at the Virgin birth. Many simple *villancicos* have an exquisite poise, notably *Ay, luna,* which comes from the extensive and usually amorous repertoire of the *serrania* or 'mountain pastoral'. Others are gloriously trivial; what is one to say of Rodrigo Martines, a handsome young chap who cannot tell the difference between a cow and a goose?

Fata la parte is a joke of a rather different sort. Juan del Encina was for a time employed by the Duke of Alba who was Viceroy at the Kingdom of Naples, a Spanish possession. Encina was a learned and witty man and the song is an example of *chappurado* or 'broken' text, a bizarre mixture of 15th c. Aragonese and Italian, sung by an outraged Neapolitan husband who has in a fury murdered his wife because he has been cuckolded by a crafty and doubtless very macho Spaniard. In other words, it's a Spanish jibe at the expense of the locals. It is also thoroughly theatrical; Encina's fame in his own day was as a dramatist.[120]

Besides the *villancico*, a major verse form was the *romance*, derived from that knightly tradition soon to be mercilessly taken apart by Cervantes in *Don Quixote*. The earlier *romances* were

---

[120] In this song, the title 'Micer' applied to the plaintiff – Micer Cotal – is Spanish for 'm'lord'. It appears in *Don Quixote.* For a while I thought it was Jewish, i.e. that the song was anti-Semitic.

based on fragments of ancient heroic epics, preserved and developed and used repeatedly as the basis for music of a courtly variety. The *romances* frequently dealt with the campaigns against the Moors, although often in a rather muddled fashion. *Durandarte* is a knight sometimes regarded as synonymous with Roland of the Battle of Roncevalles (788 AD). In the great French *Chanson de Roland* what was in reality a fight between Charlemagne's rearguard and the local Basques is depicted as an epic struggle with the Moors. 'Durandal' (the word suggests hardness, endurance) was actually the name of Roland's sword, reputed to have supernatural powers such as the ability to chop an enemy and his horse in half at a single swipe. Here the sword is transmogrified into Durandarte, a knight in his own right. The rival lover could perhaps be Waiferius, Duke of Aquitaine, killed in 769; the name 'Gaiferos' occurs in several poems in which he is usually having a wild time in Paris, leaving his anxious wife in Spain surrounded by Moorish suitors. Courtly verse was never especially fastidious about mere facts, and the elaborate rhymes in *Durandarte* (eight endings in '*ado*') suggest that the poet was more interested in virtuosity than historical reportage. The heroic knight was to reappear in one of the most fantastical but touching passages of *Don Quixote*, the Cave of Montesinos.

MUSICAL CHARACTER OF THE SONG FORMS

Musically, the *villancicos* and the *romances* are markedly different. Many of the former, with their roots in folk tunes, are simple. The vocal range is constrained and the vast majority are in duple time; triple time is rare, though a handful (such as *Con amores*) are quintuple, and mid-stream time changes occur. Melodic phrases are usually short and pithy, with sparing use of

206

imitation. The CMP *villancicos* are mostly in three parts, with some in four parts and a very few duets; the treble almost always leads. Many are bawdy and very lively.

By contrast, the *romances* are more austere as suits the verse form, a quatrain with lines usually of eight syllables. The music generally places a well-defined line of melody against each line of text. The effect can be sombre, and the form was ideal for the more melancholy *fronterizos*.

A BROAD SOCIAL BACKGROUND

Thus, the music in this recording ranges from folk tunes to refined instrumentals and chivalrous amours, from pseudo-popular pre-Lenten gluttony in *Hoy comamos* (actually written by Encina for a palace entertainment) to courtly allegories. Similarly, the composers of 16th century Spain came from a wide spread of social backgrounds. The royal family were themselves great lovers of music, Queen Isabella especially, and certain composers were of noble family. The vihuela master Luis Milán was a cultivated Valencian aristocrat who wrote *El Cortesano*, a handbook of courtly life based on Castiglione's *Il Cortigiano*. His work includes songs of the Reconquest but also of Troy, and settings of Italian poets such as Petrarch.

A minor nobleman of the previous generation was Juan de Anchieta who sang in Isabella's chapel choir and was thus possibly another who, with the Queen, witnessed the fall of Granada. Anchieta was closely related to Ignatius Loyola; in 1514, before acquiring a more saintly disposition, 'Ignatio' beat up his musical cousin in a family financial dispute. Primarily a composer of sacred music, Anchieta wrote a few exquisite *villancicos* such as *Con amores*, with its very condensed and subtle little verse. Composers of humbler background included Juan del Encina – son of a shoemaker – and Luys de Narváez, the supremely professional musician employed by both Charles V and Phillip II. Narvaez was (said his contemporaries) the finest instrumentalist of the age, able to extemporise in four parts over four given parts at sight, such that it was 'a wonder to those that did not understand music, and an even greater wonder to those that did'.

INSTRUMENTAL MUSIC

Many of the lighter or more 'popular' songs are accompanied here on the 4-course Renaissance guitar, a much smaller precursor of the modern instrument. But the chosen instrument of serious composers such as Narváez was the vihuela, superficially like a guitar but in fact a closer relation of the lute, double-strung and similarly tuned. The lute – *al ud* – was of Arab origin and had entered Spain after the original Moorish invasion of 711 AD. With time, Arab plectrum strumming gave way to an elaborate plucked technique. Just one (oversized) actual vihuela has survived; modern versions are reconstructed largely from prints and descriptions in treatises. The vihuela repertoire that we have is contained in seven publications dating from 1536 (Luis Milán) to 1576 (Esteban Daza). Forms range from loose and quasi-improvisatory meditations to variations on strophic *villancicos*, from courtly dances to instrumental renditions of sacred works. Much of this printed music is intended for instruction, as is indicated by the title of Mudarra's *Fantasia de pasos largos para desenbolver las manos* ('with wide steps to loosen the hands'), or that of Luis Milán's volume, *El Maestro*. Works such as Milán's *Fantasias* are of a contemplative refinement that suggests some very sophisticated pupils.

A celebrated and intriguing piece is Mudarra's *Fantasia que contrahaze la harpa en la manera de Ludovico,* 'imitating the harp playing of Ludovico', who was a famous blind musician at the royal court. Perhaps apprehensive of the reception of the dissonances (*falsas*) in the last section, Mudarra writes in the printed score that, 'It will sound good if it is well played'. *Falsas* were a virtuoso effect that allowed musicians to show off their skill in getting out of harmonic difficulties. For their quiet, modest little instrument, the vihuela masters created a repertoire that is among the most perfectly wrought of the Renaissance. It is sophisticated and often technically very demanding music, one reason why the vihuela gave way to the strummable guitar. In North Africa the Arab lute continues to be strummed,[121] and thrives to this day.

FOREIGN MATTER

The vihuela collections show that Spain was increasingly open to the rest of Europe. The earlier *cancioneros* reveal relatively little foreign influence, although a Josquin song, a few Italian *frottole* and even a piece by an Englishman (Robert Morton) sneak into the CMP. But Spanish composers had begun to travel widely: Encina, Mudarra, Anchieta, Ortiz and others all went abroad; Narváez is thought to have reached England with the future Phillip II's wooing of Mary Tudor. The Kingdom of Naples had been seized by the Aragonese prince Alfonso the Magnanimous in 1442, opening an important cultural link with Italy, but it was the arrival of the Hapsburg monarchs in Spain in 1516 that brought the greatest influx of Italian and Netherlandish

---

[121] Or, at least, played with a plectrum.

tastes and musicians to the Peninsular. Narváez's *Cancion del emperador* is an elaboration of a famous chanson by Josquin, *Mille regretz*, apparently a favourite of the Hapsburg Charles V. The Narváez version gives a very different, Spanish feel to the music, but it follows the structure of Josquin's song so closely that they can be performed simultaneously as here.

The collection entitled *Orphénica Lyra* by Miguel de Fuenllana (1554) contains – apart from his own compositions like the *Fantasia de redobles* – many pieces by foreigners such as Claudin de Sermisy and Jacques Arcadelt that Fuenllana has 'spanished' for vihuela. Our example is *Madonna mia* by the Italian Vicenzo Fontana, which was also re-worked by Lassus. *A quand' a quand* is another well-travelled piece. The Italian original is by the Netherlander Adrian Willaert who in 1527 was appointed *maestro di capella* at St Mark's, Venice, and who for many years dominated musical life there. Our version is by Diego Pisador of Salamanca who included it in his *Libro de música* of 1552 alongside sections of a Mass by Josquin entabulated for vihuela. In Naples, Diego Ortiz – brought from Toledo to Italy by the Spanish viceroy – was taking popular music and turning it into *recercadas*, originally for the viol. These were published in 1553 in simultaneous Italian and Spanish editions. His sources included well-known songs by Arcadelt and Pierre Sandrin, and popular Italian dance tunes as in the *Recercada primera*. From simple beginnings, Ortiz created some of the liveliest and most inventive instrumental music of the age.

All this openness makes it doubly sad that, in near-panic at the discovery of nests of Lutherans in Valladolid and Seville in 1558, a new and intolerant policy was instituted. Foreign books were banned, Spaniards barred from studying abroad. The regime attempted to close the doors of the country.

In our own age, a rapidly modernising Spain has been rehabilitated in the eyes of the rest of Europe, and Spanish culture happily restored to favour. The 'Black Legend', the Civil War and political repression suddenly seem dim memories as all things Hispanic have become fashionable, from film to dance to cars. No cultural field has benefited more than music, notably that of the Spanish Renaissance. Twenty-five years ago, recordings were limited to a handful of dry musicological reconstructions:[122] no longer.

For musicians, there are many pleasures in rediscovering the *cancioneros* and the vihuela, not least the challenge to one's own ingenuity. The pages of the CMP, for instance, give perhaps three bare lines of music without any indication of instrumentation or clear instruction as to which of the lines were intended to be sung, and with a highly erratic underlay of text, while there is much scholarly uncertainty as to how much influence Moorish performance styles actually had on the Christian courts. Thus, there are many decisions to be made before one can start to play. The truism that no two performances of music are the same could not be more true than here. Combine that with the charming tunes, the high craftsmanship and the vivid lyrics, and you have a most enjoyable form of music making. We hope we've conveyed something of that enjoyment.

---

[122] Two of these I possess, from the old DG *Arkiv* series. They date from the 1960s, before the movement known as 'HIP' (historically informed performance) had reached this repertoire. The vocal performances by groups such as the Quartet Polifonic de Barcelona are solidly academic, but quite devoid of the lively engagement that would follow a decade or so later.

CHANSONS À PLAISIRS

Music from 16th century France and the circle of Adrian le Roy [123]

Adrian le Roy dominated French musical life in the second half of the 16th century as a virtuoso musician, teacher, composer, arranger, and music publisher. Le Roy collaborated with the older generation of composers – Claudin de Sermisy, Arcadelt *et al* – and with new talents like Claude le Jeune, as well as with imports, notably Lassus, whom he made a star. The firm of Le Roy & Ballard led the field, publishing chansons, sacred works, dance music and instruction books. Le Roy became Royal Printer in 1553, a position he held until his death in 1598 and in which he served three kings.

This extraordinary career came at the height of French Renaissance classicism, during which the Pléiade poets – Ronsard and friends – claimed for French verse a standing alongside Latin and Greek. Ronsard, keen that his poetry be sung, supplied musical scores with his first book of Petrarchan sonnets, the 1552 *Amours*. French high culture might have achieved remarkable unity – had it not been for thirty years of civil war.

Religious persecution started in the 1530s. Fighting commenced in 1562 at the village of Vassy, where a Huguenot (Calvinist) congregation worshipping in a barn were massacred. Huguenots were slaughtered again on St Bartholomew's Day 1572, and conflict only ended in 1598 when the new Protestant king, Henry IV, decided that 'Paris is worth a mass' and converted to Rome, but also decreed tolerance for Calvinists.

---

[123] Essay for the Fires of Love CD, Delphian Records (Edinburgh), 2008.

Meanwhile, France had lost perhaps 4 million people, with plague and famine adding to the misery.

How did music fare? The flood of publications begun in 1529 by Pierre Attaignant (Le Roy's predecessor as Royal Printer) continued unchecked by conflict. Some 4,000 chansons were published in 16th century France, besides numerous sacred and instrumental collections. Stylistically, the 'Parisian chanson' seems so calm and relaxed – quite unlike the expressionist contortions of Italian madrigals of the time – that few commentators make much of the historical context.

But musicians were not immune from danger. The Protestant composer Claude Goudimel died at Lyons in the St Bartholomew killings, while the Catholic Antoine de Bertrand was murdered by Huguenots at Toulouse. Others temporized; Paschal de l'Estocart set poems by the Catholic zealot Guy de Pibrac (author of a verse justification for St Bartholomew's Day). But L'Estocart's chef d'oeuvre was his *Octonaires de la Vanité du Monde,* an essay in Calvinist musical moralising.

Music was known to enflame passions; in 1580 the Parisian authorities forbade musicians to excite people '*par cris et dictz de chansons*'. Music could also, however, heal division and mollify anger – as in the classical story of King Alexander and Timotheus, whose lyre so excited the king that he grabbed for his sword, whereupon Timotheus switched to a different mode, calming him.

The story was a favourite. After the Treaty of Sainte-Germain in 1570, amid fragile hopes for peace, Jean-Antoine de Baïf established in Paris his Academy of Poetry and Music, with the aim of emulating those calming Antique skills. The metres of classical verse would be applied to French poetry, in musical settings following that metrical pattern. Baïf was a Catholic, his Academy was under royal (Catholic) patronage, but he deliberately brought Catholic and Protestant musicians together; his leading composer was Claude le Jeune, a lifelong Huguenot. Baïf's Academy foreshadows today's orchestra established by Daniel Barenboim and Edward Saïd, in which young Israeli and Palestinian musicians play side by side.

The Timotheus tale was updated in a story about Claude le Jeune. At an Academy concert, a gentleman was so impassioned by Le Jeune's playing that he 'swore loudly that he felt absolutely impelled to fight someone'. When Le Jeune switched mode, he became tranquil. But only two years after the founding of the Academy, French cities witnessed the greatest atrocity of the wars, on St Bartholomew's Day.

Yet hope was resilient, that the arts might bring an end to strife. At the Entry of King Charles IX into Paris in 1571, and at the *Joyeuse Magnificences* of 1581, Ronsard and his Catholic friends provided neoclassical verse for which the Huguenot Le Jeune wrote festive settings. The message was clear: a wise French monarch would restore a Golden Age of harmony.

Reality proved different; kings, cardinals and poor folk were murdered, while war, disease and starvation tormented the people. This does not render the aspiration naive, just terribly poignant.

Our recording straddles generations and the onset of war. It illustrates how the music published by Adrian le Roy and his rivals reflects their troubled world in a curiously oblique way, responding with neoclassical civilisation. Classical mythology appears in Le Roy's own *Laissez la verte couleur*, depicting the discovery of the dead Adonis by Venus, who fills the valley with her grief; the blood stains upon the ground remain to teach a terrible lesson. The piece suggests a *tableau vivant*; the links between music and theatre (street and court) were drawing closer.

Fortune, laisse moi la vie likewise invokes a classical god, Cupid. Le Roy recycled material as he saw demand for new formats. This Attaignant tune appears as *Si je m'en vois* in Le Roy's *Premier Livre de Tabulature* (1551), printed as dance music without text. Le Roy then eyes the educational market; our version appears in his *Premier Livre d'Instruction* (1567) as an exercise in 'diminution' (variations by subdivision), but still without the words, which are now lost; we have borrowed other anonymous lyrics from another setting.

Claudin de Sermisy's *Joyssance*, printed by Attaignant in 1529, had many reincarnations, and Le Roy reused much Attaignant material. Attaignant had published numerous dances such as the *Pavane & Galliarde*, played here as a lute duet; Le Roy followed Attaignant's lead, favouring strongly rhythmic regional folk dances such as the *Branle de Poitou* and the *Pimontoyse* (from Piedmont).

J'ay le rebours, with its catchy refrain, shows how composers could make the popular sophisticated. Le Roy had a gift for spotting material and predicting trends, and his books include the first original songs with guitar accompaniment published anywhere. The *voix-de-ville* were 'urban' songs doubling as dance tunes; Le Roy issued a collection in 1555, while Jean Chardavoine gathered 200 *voix-de-ville* with texts described as 'commonly danced and sung in the cities'. *Une jeune fillete*, with its strong narrative element, appears frequently. The storyline is found in 15th century Siena; the tune conquered Europe as 'Monica' (the little nun), and later resurfaced as a Bach chorale (Cantata BWV 107).

215

Le Roy, looking ahead, saw a market for more refined vocal solos, developed from the *voix-de-ville*. In 1571, he used the term '*air*' for the first time in print. Many early *airs de cour* were available as 4-voice chansons, but were now issued as accompanied solo songs '*miz sur le luth par Adrian le Roy*'. The form evolved slowly: our *air de cour* edition of *Qui prestera* dates from 1613, but derives from Le Blanc's 1579 four-part setting of Du Bellay's 1550s poem. Another early composer was Thomas Crequillon (d.1557); although published in both solo and 4-part formats, his *Cessez mes yeulx* is already a soprano '*air*' at heart, its plaintive melody set over lower lines in which, again and again, the grief literally rises up.

French music did not develop in isolation. Crequillon probably never worked in France, nor was French his first language. He was a Fleming, his music printed in Antwerp or Louvain. But his songs are all settings of French verse, and reflect the power of the Parisian music industry. Jacques Arcadelt – also probably Flemish by birth – spent his early career in Italy. He moved to Paris *c.*1551 (to be published by Le Roy), bringing Italian stylistic features and celebrated hits like *Il bianco e dolce cigno*. This would be recast decades later by Orlando Gibbons as 'The Silver Swan'. Whereas the English madrigal uses the dying swan to bemoan a decline in civic wisdom, the Franco-Italian original is about sex.

16th century French lyrics on love's pains can seem formulaic, and some modern editors treat them disparagingly. But in a context of wars and plague, *Fortune, laisse moi la vie* – 'Fortune, leave me my life and love, for you have taken everything else' – seems vividly immediate. And why must the lovers in *O combien est heureuse* conceal their feelings at court? Is she a young

216

Catholic, and he a Huguenot? The danger was real; the factions were assassinating each other.

Le Roy's song publications seldom refer to civil strife; although instrumental evocations of warfare are quite common, 16th century 'battle' pieces (famously, *La Guerre* by Janequin) usually concern victories over the Italians or English. The suffering in most chansons is personal, private, and unrelieved, as in *Qui prestera la parole*: 'Who will lend words for my grief?' Where there is joy, as in *Joyssance vous donneray*, still Death hovers nearby.

There are delightfully upbeat pieces here, and the dances are spirited. But the chansons suggest an effort at self-control. They are restrained in structure, and usually syllabic; the melody moves with the text, syllable by syllable, with one musical phrase to each line of verse; *Il me souffit* is a good early example, *Qui prestera* is typical of later work, a touch more florid. Chromaticism is muted, with little tortured word painting. How, then, can such songs be so beautiful while yet so simple? Not, surely, because their emotional life is formulaic; rather, because they are the product of a society striving to preserve its civilisation.

REMEMBER ME, MY DEIR
Jacobean songs of love and loss [124]

In April 1603, as King James VI of Scotland prepared to depart for London to take up the crown of England, many Scots must have wondered what would become of their cultural traditions, not least of poetry and song. The two countries were part of a wider European picture, but with very different experiences – and for Scottish poets and musicians, the 16th century had been a bruising ride.

Trouble had started 40 years before. The Chapel Royal, founded by James IV in 1501, had run against the rock of Reformation in 1560. When Mary Stuart attempted to have mass sung at Holyrood in 1561 there were outraged protests, with 'broken heads and bloody ears'. In 1571 the great organ at Stirling castle was dismantled by order of the governor. By the 1580s, art music in Scotland was the preserve of consenting adults in private, and the departure of the court for London was another blow.

Yet music had not been impossible. Though French political influence in Scotland fluctuated, French artistic fashions seldom lost their appeal. As a young man in the 1580s, James VI had cultivated both poets and musicians. Much has been made of a 'veritable Academy' at James's court known as the Castalian Band;[125] the king himself was supposedly the epicentre, with a

---

[124] Essay for the Fires of Love CD, Delphian Records (Edinburgh), 2014. The essay and the recording are concerned with secular music, not the church.

[125] The idea of the Castalian Band gained currency through the work of Scottish musicologists Elizabeth Mennie Shire and Kenneth Elliot in the 1960s. It soon became orthodoxy in Scotland, fulfilling as it did the desirable idea of a 'Scottish Renaissance', and it still features in certain websites. But the scholar

gathering of musicians and poets such as Alexander Montgomerie aspiring to revivify Scottish arts much as the neoclassical Pléiade group of Ronsard, du Bellay *et al* had done for France a decade or so earlier. Whether the Castalian Band actually existed is another matter; it has been forcibly argued that the entire notion is a modern myth based on an optimistic misreading of a single line of a poem by King James. Nonetheless, there were authors active in Scotland in the 1580s and 1590s who were alive to the best French models; their love lyrics were being set to music (just as in France), and a discernible style was emerging which resembled the French *air*.

Song settings of Montgomery's poems, such as *Quhat mightie motion,* have uncomplicated but supple and attractive melodic lines, following strophic patterns. The text is important; although the love conceits are conventional – Cupid's darts, the eyes as the entrance to the soul – they are put to elegant use in songs such as *In throu the windoes of myn ees*. Meanwhile, there is poignancy and authenticity in *Remember me, my deir*. The melodies are often related to dances, and settings are largely chordal. They move with a dignified poise reminiscent of the songs of Claudin de Sermisy. Some Scots songs, such as Andrew Blackhall's *Adeu, O desie of delyt,* are re-arrangements of French tunes.

These qualities shared with French *chansons* and *airs* are perhaps typical of songs written by (and for) talented amateurs, the product of a cultivated elite with neoclassical tastes. Lutenists are recorded at the Scottish court from 1474, and there must have been some professional musicians in the great houses and castles, in spite of Reformation strictures. But we know next to nothing about them; perhaps they kept their heads down. One problem

---

Priscilla Bawcutt showed it up as 'a modern Scottish myth' in a paper in 2001.

was the lack of a music publishing industry. Music printing on the Continent dates from before 1500; in England it was underway by the 1520s. But in Scotland the domestic market was tiny and could not support the costs, while Reformation divines frowned upon anything but psalms. Thus the first Scottish printed collection of songs with lyrics only appears in Aberdeen in 1662.

The divines had not been too keen on the theatre either, other than church-sponsored Corpus Christi cycles. There was a visiting company of English actors preparing a show in a close off Edinburgh's Royal Mile just before James made ready to leave, but we know of little else.

So we must make half-informed guesses; fortunately the preserved manuscript repertoire of Scottish instrumental music is both rich (some four hundred pieces) and in many cases based on an enduring folk tradition. On our recording, Gordon Ferries plays some of these on the four-course Renaissance guitar, and some on the lute, an instrument of Arab origin and perhaps originally brought to Scotland by returning Crusaders. The *Scottish Huntsupe* (or 'the hunt is up') is markedly Scottish in character; we perform it as a duet, the second lute emphasising the tune's double-tonic nature, moving up and down between chords one tone apart, just as much Scottish music has always done. Solo reflections such as the *Gypsies Lilt* and *I long for thy virginitie* could hardly be anything but Scottish. Such tunes are 'amateurish' insofar as they are simple, pentatonic, and harmonised often with plain octaves. They are, however, delicate and full of feeling.

Though the Scots inhabited the peripheries of Europe, they were by no means insular. Scots music was spread abroad, sometimes by musical mercenary soldiers such as Tobias Hume.

Our *Huntsupe* appears in the *Jane Pickering Lute Book*, a cosmopolitan collection whose binding is decorated with King James's armorials. A particularly sweet tune is the *Canaries*, a dance form that began in those islands and spread throughout Spain, France and Germany, and also Britain. This example comes from a compilation by Robert Gordon of Straloch in a manuscript dating from *c*.1627. Like many Scottish gentry, Gordon of Straloch was partly educated in France, and he found the *Canaries* in Jean-Baptiste Besard's *Thesaurus Harmonicus*, published in 1603.

In April that year, James and his courtiers headed south, taking a leisurely month to reach London and writing ahead to request their travel expenses. When they arrived, they found a different culture, a world of professional virtuosi like John Dowland; of famous madrigalists like Morley, Weelkes and Wilbye; and of multi-talented church-based composers like William Byrd and Francis Pilkington who wrote our *Rest, sweet nymphs*. Far from keeping their heads down, English composers had a sense of professional community and would dedicate pieces to each other (Dowland to Holborne, Pilkington to Dowland) or would write elegies on each other's deaths (Byrd on his master Tallis). Others such as Thomas Campion and Philip Rosseter would work in collaboration; the latter's *When Laura smiles* comes from their shared volume.

The English published enthusiastically; all the above composers issued collections. Dowland published airs although never his solo lute music, but he was so famous that others spread it throughout Europe; his pieces appear in numerous manuscripts, one favourite being his variations on the song *Go from my window* (played here as a song with two lutes). The subject is not far from the old Scots 'Let me in this ae nicht', but at home the Scots could not get their songs printed at all, while in England Byrd and Tallis published by Royal licence.

The rapid spread of music publishing indicates a vigorous middle-class market without Reformation qualms, the English gentry (like the Scots) often enjoying novel settings of familiar tunes such as an English *Huntsup* which originated with Henry VIII. Many English publications have titles such as 'Introduction', 'Tutor', or 'Lessons'. Thomas Morley wrote for his singing club of 'gentlemen and merchants', and Campion dedicated his *Book of Ayres* to amateur musicians, commending its 'ear-pleasing rimes without Arte'. Dowland and colleagues still chased noble patrons, but others had alternative means: Campion was a doctor; Rosseter was a theatre manager – although a rather unsuccessful one: he failed to get proper permission for his theatre, and it was demolished by the London authorities.

The London theatre must have startled the Scots newcomers; the level of activity was astonishing, the Globe and Rose stages being run by repertory companies putting on different plays throughout the week. Musicians were a component of each company, with popular tunes woven into the plays. The songs in *Hamlet* are sung in snatches by poor mad Ophelia; the First Quarto stage direction reads, 'Enter Orfelia playing on a lute and her hair down singing.' Her songs include *How should I your true love know* ('Walsingham') – the name of the tune referring to the celebrated Norfolk place of pilgrimage – along with *And will he not come again?* (here played on guitar and lute together), and more disreputable numbers such as *St Valentine's Day*. Other plays mention dance tunes such as 'rounds'; *Sellinger's Round* was widely popular and published later in John Playford's *English Dancing Master*. The text sung here is by Thomas Lodge, published in 1593; the verse scheme is unusual but fits *Sellinger's Round* perfectly, suggesting an intended match. We believe we know the song melodies used by Shakespeare because, in the early 1800s, two scholars interviewed actresses at Drury Lane who claimed to be preserving the traditional tunes for the plays.[126]

All this musical activity would have been a source of some excitement for the Scots, and perhaps of some envy also.

But one aspect would have given them pause: musical and poetic tastes in Scotland were still markedly French; in England the fashion was all for Italy. Italian madrigal styles were studied, Italian verses translated and reset, Italian musical tastes imitated but 'Englished'. It was from Italy that English composers derived the lute duet, although with local adaptations; the Italians generally used two lutes tuned apart from each other, playing two interweaving lines; the English preferred a ground bass with a light treble melody. A leading proponent of lute duets was John Johnson, whose *Queen's Treble* is typical.

Few English songwriters employed the French verse manner favoured by the Scots, but one who did was gifted: Thomas Campion was not only a fine musician; his own lyrics are outstanding. Campion was an able theoretician, and his *Observations on the Art of English Poesie* argued for the importation of the French technique of *vers mesuré* which counts the metre of a line by syllables, not by beats (the English norm), while his musical writings foreshadow changes realised later by French composers including Lully. But Campion's own efforts to use *vers mesuré* were not too successful; his English-metre *The*

---

[126] See *Hamlet*, Arden Shakespeare (2nd series) ed.Harold Jenkins, p.359.

cypress curtain of the night is far better. Had he influenced London tastes towards French styles, Campion might have made a space in which the Scots could have flourished. But it was not to be, and soon the Scottish court style of music faded. Any Scottish courtier-musician with James in London after 1603 may have thought regretfully of the north, and of *Remember me, my deir*.

King James revisited Scotland just once, in 1617, when he commanded that choral services be reinstated in the Chapel Royal. By 1630, resources in Edinburgh were so thin that a newly appointed director of music, Edward Kellie, was obliged to travel to London to see how services were run, to buy music, and to engage an organist, cornett and sackbutt players and even singers, so few being available in the north.

So, had the Union of Crowns dealt a fatal blow to Scottish music, after its Reformation wounds? No, for that would be to look in the wrong places. There was, certainly, a vacuum at the centre. But in other cities (Aberdeen, for instance), and among the folk great and small, and in fine houses around the country – less accessible in an age of dire communications, and so more self-reliant in their entertainments – there the traditions continued. Portraits of the Scots nobility show them holding lutes of considerable size and sophistication long into the 1600s, at which time the Scottish lute manuscripts still contained French dance tunes but also pieces in common with popular English collections such as Playford's *English Dancing Master*. Ironically, by the mid-1600s Scottish tunes were all the rage in the south – so much so that after 1700 whole volumes of these were published in London: not the French-born high style of Montgomerie and friends, but the lively dances, the folk songs and the 'huntsupe'.

REKINDLINGS
Early Music in Scotland [127]

One weekend three years ago, with snow threatening, I spent two days in a pretty but icy little church south of Edinburgh, evoking the burning south of Spain in song. We were making a recording, 'we' being Fires of Love, the Early Music quartet I work with.

It was so cold that we sang dressed in coats, woolly hats and mittens, only taking these off when required to play an instrument. To keep my recorders in tune, and to prevent the curling metal mouthpiece of the base recorder from filling with condensed breath and spit faster than a Glenfiddich still, I stood directly over an electric fire, trying to hold the instrument in the warm up-draft as I played. Our lutenist blew onto his fingers, our drummer fretted over his chilly skins, our soprano shrank into her mufflers. Out in the porch, the Delphian Records engineer wailed as a frigid dew settled on his expensive and sensitive DAT machines. Hardly ideal conditions for a programme of music from Andalucía called *Love & Reconquest*. When we'd finished, we got out by the skin of our teeth: a blizzard was blowing, the lanes were filling with snow. Back in Fife two hours later, I drove into a drift and stuck.

Such are the pleasures of Early Music in Scotland. It's an under-developed market. For three years we'd been plying our trade around the country, jammed into my rusting Toyota with a roof-box as long as the car to accommodate drums and an elongated archlute, performing to local music societies from the Borders to the West Coast, earning a professional fee when we

---

[127] *Early Music News*, no.281, July 2003. The recording was made in Crichton collegiate church.

could, covering our costs at least. We refused to wear codpieces, and tried to insist that our repertoire was as mainstream as Bach. We did some awful things to keep afloat, including two gigs for international conferences. One was for a pleasant but bemused bunch of electronics experts in Edinburgh Castle, where we found ourselves in direct competition with a punk bagpipe ensemble and a falconer. The falcon buggered off in disgust, and so did we.

Audiences were, to begin with, apprehensive and sceptical. In one Borders town, we tuned up in a little modern theatre and played a trial song. 'How does that sound?' we called to a committee member lurking at the back. 'All right,' he muttered, 'if you like that sort of thing.'

I have a passion for that sort of thing, for Renaissance secular music, the songs of Josquin and Narváez, Willaert and Dowland, the soundtrack of Shakespeare's plays and the operas of Monteverdi. With two voices, two lutes, and lots of guitars, recorders and drums, there wasn't much we wouldn't tackle. Our touchstone for authenticity was, 'I'm sure at the time they'd have worked with whatever resources were to hand.'

I also adore the texts. Some of my happiest days have been spent in libraries tracking down ancient lyrics. I stumbled on the original of a 17th century Roman lullaby in a Neapolitan song of the early 1400s. I've worked out that 'Durandarte' does *not* refer to the Carolingian hero Roland, but is instead a strange personification of Roland's sword (see me for details). I've come up with many an unsubstantiated theory, and I'm sticking to them all. I've sweated cheerful blood over translations. Some songs are settings of super-refined and virtually impenetrable Petrarch sonnets. Others are anything but refined: occasionally, even I blink at the ribald texts. One Venetian song openly incites youth to beat up old ladies in the piazza, for obstructing young love. The chorus urges, 'Beat them! Beat them with sticks!' It never fails to get a nervous laugh.

We had Lottery money for equipment, we had classy design work done, we had some splendid reviews (well, mostly) and had played abroad (well, England, lodging on the floor of a nursery school). But it all fell apart. In the best rock-and-roll manner, just as we were about to launch our CD, we quarrelled. We patched our differences for the launch night… And that was that. I had to cancel 10 concert engagements.

We've not worked as a quartet for 18 months since, although the rump three of us have kept a small flame alive. Our problem has been replacing our lutenist. As I said, it is a small and under-developed field. England has its National Early Music Centre in York, innumerable ensembles and a score of festivals. Scotland has not one; professional lutenists north of the border may be counted on one hand, all spoken for.

Imagine our excitement on catching wind of a new arrival: an expatriate Scottish lutenist, returned to the country. We've snaffled him for Fires of Love before anyone else can. The Renaissance repertoire ranges from the wacky to the sublime, and it's possible that we have given some pieces their first Scottish performances in hundreds of years. That alone lends a sense of mission.[128]

---

[128] In the event, the replacement lutenist proved even more of a liability, very reluctant to work as a team member and insisting on travelling to all gigs separately, with his wife – rather like the members of the Amadeus Quartet who, I believe, would not travel together. After a year or so we fell out over travel expenses and things looked bleak, until our percussionist effected a reconciliation with the original lutenist and we regrouped, staying together for several more years and making two more recordings, *Chansons à Plaisir* and *Remember me, my Deir*. The latter was a *Gramophone* 'Editor's Choice'.

KARAWITAN SUNDA: TRADITION NEWLY WRIT
A survey of Sundanese (West Java) music since Independence [129]

(I lived and worked in Bandung, West Java, from 1978-80, and studied *kacapi* and singing under Tatang Benjamin and Yuyun Sulastri. The twenty recordings listed at the end of this essay were donated to the British Institute of Recorded Sound. In 1983 the BIRS was absorbed into the British Library and became part of the Sound & Moving Image archive (SAMI) where the recordings can now be found catalogued by title.) Several of the instruments described have been given to the Horniman Museum (London).

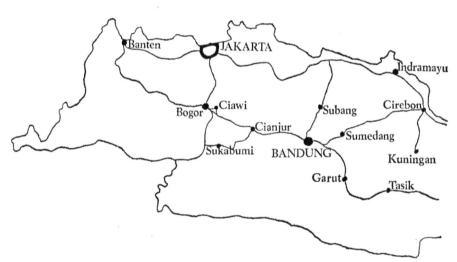

SUNDA (West Java). The provincial capital is the mountain city of Bandung, now a major industrial centre.

---

[129] First printed in *Recorded Sound* – Journal of the British Institute of Recorded Sound – Number 82 (July 1982) pp.19-34.

SUNDA IS TO JAVA much as Scotland is to England: the unfairly neglected, wilder, more mountainous part of the island, persistently disadvantaged in politics, often regarded as the poor relation in culture, but in fact possessed of a proudly independent language and civilisation that is in many ways more vigorous than that of its domineering neighbour. Thomas Stanford Raffles in 1817 referred to the inhabitants as 'rude Sunda mountaineers'[130] and certainly Sundanese and Javanese culture developed along different lines. The Sundanese language differs from Javanese much as Portuguese differs from Spanish. Communications in Sunda were difficult until quite recently and communities lived in relative isolation under local rulers. Court culture had a limited influence and the Sundanese sometimes remark that their civilisation is *rakyat sentris* (centred on the people) as opposed to that of Java which is *kraton sentris* (*kraton* = court/palace). The consequence for the performing arts was a plethora of regional styles changing markedly over distances of only a few dozen kilometres, with highly localised forms such as *Sisingaan* (the 'lion dance') at Subang,[131] and *angklung Bungko*, an ensemble of bamboo instruments found at the village of Bungko, near Cirebon.[132]

The relatively small role played by royal courts may go a little

---

[130] Thomas Stanford Raffles, *The History of Java*, for the East India Company, London, 1817.

[131] The origins of the *Sisingaan* dance are a little murky and odd, if only because there are no lions in Java or anywhere else in East Asia. So why is there a circumcision dance with a young man riding on the back of a lion? It is said to date from the short period of British rule in Java, under Raffles, with the lion signifying the British crown and its emblematic lion as depicted on coinage, and now subdued by the young Sundanese astride its back.

[132] Atik Soepandi and E.Atmadibrata, *Khasanah Kesenian Jawa-Barat* ('treasury of the arts of West Java'). Pelita Masa editions, Bandung 1976. The authors list the regional forms and the areas in which they are to be found.

way towards explaining the contrast between the great vigour of contemporary Sundanese music and the much more conservative, still court-oriented Javanese music, which seems to have been adversely affected by the rapid decline of the great sultanates since independence in 1945. Sundanese music has much in common with Javanese: the metallophone *gamelan* orchestra, bamboo flutes (*suling*), a wide range of bamboo idiophones (*angklung, arumba* etc), and also the elegant *rebab* (bowed spike-lute). There has always been much cross-fertilisation, and the museum at Sumedang (West Java) preserves a *gamelan* which was a gift from the Sultan of Jogjakarta (Central Java) in the 18th century.

There are, however, important differences. In Javanese music the board-zither (*celempung*) takes a minor role. In Sunda the board-zither (*kacapi*) is of major importance as accompaniment and increasingly as a solo instrument, and many of the recordings discussed below are of *kacapian* (*kacapi* songs). A *kacapi* may be light and portable, no small advantage on mountain roads. The pentatonic tone-scales of Sunda differ from those of Java, the Sundanese scales (*salendro, pelog, degung* and their relations) being perhaps more accessible to the Western ear as the intervals are closer to those in the Western diatonic scale. The term *karawitan Sunda* refers specifically to Sundanese pentatonic music. Other musics, for example diatonic *musik melayu* ('Malay music') and *dangdut* (pop music closely related to Indian film scores; the name is an onomatopoeic reference to the tabla-type drums employed) are heard in Sunda and throughout Indonesia but are outside the scope of this study. Descriptions of *karawitan Sunda* may be found in the works of Jaap Kunst (who began his

Playing a *kacapi siter*, the modern, lightweight and readily portable member of the kacapi family. Standard steel guitar strings are used, sometimes doubled like a 12-string guitar. It may also be fitted with an electric pickup. Tuned in a variety of pentatonic scales, it can play either quite elaborate solo instrumentals or a steady four-beat accompaniment.

studies of Indonesian musics in the 1920s) and of EL Heins and Max Harrell,[133] in books in the Indonesian language by Atik Soepandi and in the proceedings of the Asian Traditional Performing Arts (ATPA) seminar held in Tokyo in 1976.[134] The British Institute of Recorded Sound (BIRS), in addition to previous holdings of Sundanese music, has recently acquired my collection of 20 commercial Indonesian cassettes of *karawitan Sunda* representing many of the major genres. These recordings reflect important trends in post-independence Sunda, and it is these aspects that will be considered here.

THE SETTING: MUSIC IN POST-INDEPENDENCE SUNDA

Sundanese cultural life has been greatly affected by the communications revolution of recent decades. New roads, radio, television and cassette recorders have to some extent smoothed out local stylistic variations. There are now scores of small commercial radio stations (over 30 in the city of Bandung alone), some playing little but Western pop, others specialising in *karawitan Sunda.* These stations are heard over wide areas, making common property of previously restricted forms. A national government and the growth of state education have had a similar effect. There are now government organisations such as the Lembaga Kesenian Bandung (Bandung Arts Institute) and

---

[133] Jaap Kunst, *The Music of Java*, Martinus Nijhoff, The Hague, 3rd ed. by EL Heins, 1973; ML Harrell, 'Indonesia: West Java, Classical Music' in *New Grove's Dictionary of Music and Musicians*, 6th ed. by Stanley Sadie, London 1980; EL Heins, *Goong Renteng: aspects of orchestral music in a Sundanese village* (PhD thesis, University of Amsterdam, 1977).

[134] *Asian Musics in an Asian Perspective: Asian Traditional Performing Arts (ATPA) 1976*. The Japan Foundation, Tokyo 1977. It was a source of considerable pride that a Sundanese *kacapi* ensemble represented Indonesia at this major seminar rather than, say, a Javanese *gamelan*.

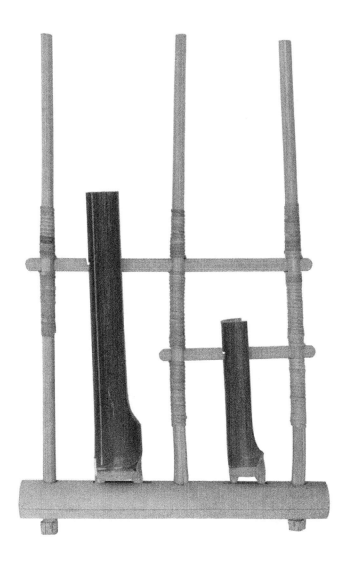

Angklung tuned rattle, made by Daeng Soetigna (Bandung, 1980). Each paired rattle is tuned to an octave. A complete instrument may consist of perhaps 16 of these in a diatonic scale, played by many hands.

private foundations such as the Yayasan Cangkurileung established in 1959 by Mang Koko Koswara to promote knowledge of Sundanese culture among children, which now has dozens of branches throughout Sunda. Even the Scout movement has played a part, being the means by which Daeng Soetigna spread the revival of the *angklung*, the orchestra of tuned bamboo rattles that is now almost a national instrument of Indonesia. The government has given considerable support to the arts[135] and in 1958 created the Konservatori Karawitan – usually known as KOKAR although now officially the Sekolah Menengah [secondary school] Karawitan Indonesia. This was the second of its type in Indonesia, and its staff and directors have included many of the most notable exponents of *karawitan Sunda*, Mang Koko and Daeng Soetigna among them.

As the development of KOKAR illustrates, a general music education has become an end in itself for some of the Sundanese middle classes. In its early years the pupils were usually drawn from musical families. They were intending professionals who were often skilled musicians before entering the conservatory. Recently, however, in line with the other Indonesian conservatories, KOKAR has become a state specialist secondary school, just one of the many types of vocational schools. Students may have little thought of music as a career, or at most only as part of work as a schoolteacher. KOKAR takes students from all over Sunda and indeed beyond,[136] and non-Sundanese forms such

---

[135] In a foreword to a collection of songs (by Nano S, 1975), the head of the Department of Education and Culture develops the theme: 'The notation and texts of songs given in this book are in exact accord with the government's strategy for... strengthening National Moral and Cultural development...'

[136] A conscious policy. The 20th Anniversary celebrations at KOKAR in 1978 included an appeal for funds to build hostels for such 'foreign' students.

Daeng Soetigna (L) and Mang Koko Koswara (with pipe). Closely related by marriage, they represent different streams of Sundanese musical culture. (1978)

as Balinese *gamelan* are taught, all of which further reduce local differences. It is now possible for numbers of people to make a living out of music by combining, for instance, teaching with performance at functions, and by making recordings for the extraordinarily vigorous local cassette industry. There are a number of small recording studios and cassette companies and tapes of *karawitan Sunda* are cheap and widely available. Recording fees are generally fairly modest, though enough to encourage the formation of groups: for example, the Sasaka Domas group received Rp.100,000 (about £70) for making *Mangsa Padeukeut* (Recording 12) in 1979. Instrumental music – e.g. *kacapi suling* (zither and flute) and *gamelan degung* (a particular style of *gamelan*) – is especially popular on cassette for background listening (Recordings 13, 14 and 15).

Basic *gamelan* is not difficult to play and this may partly account for one interesting aspect of the cassette recording boom, which is that pre-recorded music has made little headway as an accompaniment for social dancing (although it is quite common as an accompaniment to both rehearsal and performance of classical dance – a reversal of the situation in the West). *Ketuk tilu* and *jaipongan* pair-dancing are enormously popular. Social dance now carries far less of the dubious moral overtones for women than it did in Raffles' day,[137] although *ketuk tilu* nightclubs with professional dancer-hostesses are still popular in Bandung. *Jaipongan* is to be seen at weddings and other ceremonies and gatherings accompanied by small *gamelan* orchestras which often use cheap iron (instead of bronze) instruments. One sometimes sees a hired *gamelan* with musicians so unskilled that they have numbers chalked on the keys to guide

---

[137] Raffles *op cit*, vol I p.342.

them. They are still, however, quite capable of providing sufficiently vigorous dance music.

Radio and tourism have added to the demand for both recordings and live performance. Yayasan Cangkurileung promotes children's concerts twice a month on Radio Republik Indonesia. One large group of young musicians performs regularly to parties of Dutch tourists, while Pak Udjo's Bamboo Village – where concerts using nearly the whole range of Sundanese bamboo instruments are put on for visitors – is an established money-spinner. On occasion, street musicians have become rich. Braga Stone is a blind *kacapi* player who used to have a pitch on Bandung's smartest shopping street, Jalan Braga. He now charges large fees for private or concert performances. Such concerts, and the money accruing from them, have preserved genres such as *kacapi warung kopi* ('coffee shop' *kacapi*) which would otherwise have died out but are now kept alive by a handful of professionals.[138]

At KOKAR, *karawitan Sunda* has achieved academic respectability. Ida Rosida (Recordings 4, and 7 to 10) was, in 1978, the first woman to receive a BA degree in *karawitan* studies, while pursuing a singing career. Academic attention brought with it a demand for standardisation and theoretical formulations. A bulletin of Sundanese culture[139] was first published by the Lembaga Kesenian Bandung (Bandung Arts

---

[138] 'The *kacapi* and its place in traditional Sundanese music,' by Mang Koko Koswara. Unpublished paper translated by the present author, Bandung 1978. 'The *kacapi warung kopi* flourished in the years before WW2. Sadly, today its function is largely usurped by the transistor radio.'

[139] *Buletin Kebudayaan Jawa-Barat* (bulletin of West Java culture) published by Lembaga Kesenian Bandung. The cultural foundation Yayasan Cangkurileung also publish a bulletin, *Suara Cangkurileung.* Also Soepandi, 1975.

Music for the song 'Krida' in the Sundanese music notation originally devised by RMA Keosoemadinata. This 1962 example, made into a low-relief plaque, hangs in the house of Mang Koko Koswara. *Sekartandak* indicates a regular metrical style. The *Pelog* pentatonic scale (*laras Pelog*) is specified at the top along with other features. Each number refers to a note in the scale. The top line of numbers – the *pangkat* – is an instrumental introduction, while the *lagu* is the main song melody, in four-beat bars.

Institute) in 1974 at about the same time as a number of textbooks, notably a *Basic Theory of Karawitan* by Atik Soepandi. There have also been efforts by Yayasan Cangkurileung to produce reference performances on cassette (Recording 4). Finally, there is a new demand for music reference works and dictionaries which has been partly met by the *Kamus Musik Indonesia* of M.Soeharto.

These attempts at standardising theory have met with certain difficulties. Various features of *karawitan Sunda* are simply not consistent throughout the region. Sundanese musicians sometimes disagree on definitions of some quite basic terms, for example the distinction between *tembang* and *kawih* songs (see Recordings). The Sundanese can hear the difference but formulating it is difficult. None of the distinctions of pitch, metric character, style of accompaniment, or subject matter is watertight. The *Kamus Musik Indonesia* (dictionary) avoids trying to define *kawih* altogether.[140] There are widely differing theories as to the origin and meaning of several other terms and names of instruments.

Attempts to rationalise *karawitan Sunda* date back at least to the various collaborations of Jaap Kunst and RMA Koesoemadinata. But, as Tamura Fumiko argues,[141] their formulations were not ideal. These are, however, widely taught at KOKAR and elsewhere, such is the demand for textbook description and the difficulty of being more precise.

Sundanese tone-scales are extremely complex, partly as a result of their diverse origins. Several of the scales have particular association with certain types of music and, in the case of

---

[140]Also attempted by Soepandi and Atmadibrata (1976). See their attempts to unscramble the terms *calung* (p.15) and *macapat* (p.32).

[141] T.Fumiko, 'The tone and scale system of Sunda' in *ATPA,* 1977.

Cigawiran (a religious style found in the Cigawir area) *tembang* song structure has been combined with Arabic tone-scales. The desire to extend the range of expression has led to the increased use of, for instance, the scale *degung madurasa* in which the *kacapi* is retuned so that the tonic moves down two strings, allowing a song with a wide range to be sung comfortably. The performance of the modern song '*Batik*' (Recording 11) is in *degung madurasa*.

Sundanese tone values are, traditionally, only relative. A *kacapi* is easy to tune and is fairly quickly raised or lowered in pitch for the comfort of the singer. The metallophones in any one *gamelan* orchestra were normally attuned to each other rather than to a precise external standard. This, of course, made it difficult to interchange instruments. Increasing mobility of musicians and their instruments and the new demands of academe are beginning to change this. It is increasingly common for a foundry to be asked to produce a *gamelan* tuned to, say, the Western A-440. This has further consequences. It makes it much easier for musicians to experiment with new combinations of instruments – *gamelan degung* with *angklung*, perhaps, or Indonesian with Western instruments.[142] The latter is most noticeable in pop music – Braga Stone accompanies his diatonic *kacapi* with a shoulder-mounted harmonica in the best Bob Dylan manner. It remains to be seen whether *karawitan* performers will follow suit. The casual ease with which new local forms continue to appear suggests they might – for example, the various re-combinings of instruments, sometimes with words in the modern Indonesian language (instead of Sundanese) and with diatonic tone-scales to be found

---

[142] One popular group combines a *kacapi* with a Lowrey organ. 'Balinese rock' featuring *gamelan*, piano, voices and cockerels also caused a certain stir.

in the Pangelengan-Subang area. Regional specialities in the older forms of music still persist, and sometimes find determined defenders. At the small palace of Cigugur (Kuningan), a local style of *gamelan* performance is being kept alive by regular Saturday evening recitals.[143] Many voice teachers hold onto traditional local song styles in *tembang* performance. This results in occasional problems at the now regular festivals and competitions (Recording 3) when respected older teachers acting as judges are sometimes unable to agree on 'correct' interpretation.

In the 1930s a numerical notation for *karawitan Sunda* was worked out by RMA Koesoemadinata, and in the last decade in particular a number of collections of traditional songs have been published.[144] The notation can cover every note of both the melodic framework and the harmony of a given song; however, the complex Sundanese ornaments are not marked. As with much Baroque music, the performer is expected to elaborate on a sparely indicated frame. Although today most musicians can read the new notation, even Sasaka Domas, a group of young professionals, still learn much of their material by ear.

---

[143] In 1980 I was taken to Cigugur by the American scholar Kathy Foley who was appreciated by the Sultan for her interest in the tradition. We stayed the weekend and heard the performance.

[144] Examples: *Haleuang Tandang* ed.Nano S, Paramaartha Editions, Bandung 1975, a graded singing course for secondary schools; *Sekar Mayang* (for primary schools), ed.Mang Koko Koswara, Yayasan Cangkurileung, Bandung 1976; *Pangajaran Tembang Sunda* (course in classical Sundanese song) ed.Mang Endang, Yayasan Cangkurileung, Bandung 1968, 3rd ed.1976; *Lagu-Lagu Pupuh,* ed.K Koswara and P Nata Prawira, Balebat Editions, Bandung 1975 – this last being scores for the reference collection in Recording 4.

Currently, Western music of many types and also Indian film music clearly influence Sundanese (and most Indonesian) popular music. But traditional *karawitan Sunda* has been affected too. On occasion, Western influence has been merely destructive. According to Daeng Soetigna, the introduction of Dutch brass almost wiped out many Sundanese instruments.[145] By the time he revived it, the *angklung* had been reduced to a beggar's rattle. On the other hand, the *angklung* in its revived form has benefited from being closely tied to the Western diatonic scale, making it broadly useful in education. The development of the lightweight *kacapi siter* in the 1930s arguably owes something to the European zither[146] and to the ubiquitous guitar. The arrival of the guitar (Spanish guitar is now a national obsession) gave rise to the curious phenomenon of *tarling* – gui*tar* + su*ling* (flute*)* – the pentatonic guitar-plus-flute music of Cirebon on the north coast (Recording 20). Indonesians have always been noted for their ability to absorb outside influences. In *karawitan Sunda* the flexibility of musicians has greatly facilitated the synthesis of styles and techniques. Leading instrumentalists such as Tatang Benjamin or singers like Taty Saleh will divide their time between every variety of *karawitan* and pop music without thinking twice about it. Most musicians can play a wide range of instruments – wind, percussion and strings.[147] Only more difficult

---

[145] In conversation with the present writer.

[146] K Taeko, 'Classification and Playing Technique – a study of zithers in Asia' in *Asian Musics (ATPA)* 1977, p.134.

[147] There is, however, some division according to sex. For example, as in some other cultures, it is rare to see a woman playing a flute. See R.Emmert on 'Vertical flutes in South East Asia' in *Asian Musics (ATPA) 1977*. Emmert's remark that sex restrictions apply to all Sundanese instruments is, however, an overstatement. In particular, both the *kacapi* and the *gamelan degung* are

instruments such as the *rebab* (bowed lute) have specialist players.

It is especially interesting to note the subtle changes in *kacapian* (*kacapi* songs, Recording Group B). The structure of some modern compositions bears resemblance to Western models. For example, the verses of the song '*Kembang Tanjung Panineungan*' (Recordings 6 and 8) are varied and contrasted in a manner quite foreign to older patterns of contrast such as the flexible recitative followed by a strictly metrical section (*sekartandak*) as may be heard in the *pupuh* group of songs (Recording 4). Subject matter has been updated – '*Kembang Tanjung Panineungan*' concerns the Darul Islam revolt of the 1950s – and has also shifted in style. Thus the topical comic songs dealing with current events and mores, once the preserve of *jenaka Sunda* and *warung kopi* (chatty, humorous 'coffee shop' performances by humble entertainers) are now made into slick, elaborate recordings which are technically impressive but without the warmly gauche humour of earlier versions. (Compare the two recordings of the song '*Beca*', Recordings 10 and 16.) Similar topical songs are arranged for *gamelan degung,* notably by the young composer Nano S (Recording 12).

Meanwhile, *kacapi* technique has developed remarkably. Koko Koswara's song '*Reumis Bareung Dinah Eurih*' (Red Dew on the Long Grass – Recordings 6 and 9) has a long, elaborate *kacapi* introduction with quite new ideas in scene-setting, new use of damping, complex fingerings, picking and melodic runs to establish the mood for the tragic tale that follows. The verses are accompanied by *dirangeum*, the standard picking technique used

commonly played by both men and women. The musicians on '*Mangsa Padeukeut*' (Recording 12) include two women, Yuyun and Sanni.

for *kawih* songs, but they are interspersed with further passages of word-painting on the *kacapi*. These solo sections have some basis in the instrumental (*gelenyu*) sections of traditional *tembang* and *kawih* songs (for example '*Dermayon*' on Recording 10) and in the ornamental (*pasieupan*) accompaniment to the *pupuh* songs. However, none of this remotely prepares us for the extraordinary introduction to '*Reumis Bareum Dinah Eurih*'.

Modern compositions are often referred to as '*kreasi baru*' (new creations). In *kacapian kreasi baru* the *kacapi* is increasingly an equal partner with the voice in a manner unknown in traditional *tembang*, with rapidly developing exploitation of the dynamic range and varieties of tone colour available. Singers of long *pantun* (narrative) songs have always used the physical contours of the *kacapi* to illustrate points in the story,[148] but it has been the achievement of – above all – Mang Koko Koswara to realise the illustrative and evocative potential of the *kacapi's* music. It is not impossible that there may be some link between the changes noted in *kacapian kreasi baru* and the enormous contemporary interest in the classical guitar in Indonesia.

There have been technical changes as well. One extreme product of the new interest in tone colour is the recording by Yoyoh Supriatin (Recording 5) with heavy electronic resonance added in the studio. For public gatherings the *kacapi siter* (the modern, portable maid-of-all-work of the *kacapi* family) is now almost always given an electric pickup for greater volume. A single *kacapi* can thus provide music for an open-air wedding, or for choral singing (*rampaksekar*) at a student festival – Recording 17 is of *rampaksekar* with *gamelan* backing. A *kacapi* can thus, if necessary, take the place of an entire twelve-player *gamelan*.

---

[148] K Koswara, *loc cit*, 1978.

As mentioned above, some makers produce a *kacapi siter* with double stringing in the manner of a twelve-string guitar. More recently, the *kacapi rincik* – the descant partner of the big traditional *kacapi perahu* ('boat') used for the classical *tembang* songs – has been made in a lightweight, electrified version. This has interesting potential, because it allows performers of modern *kreasi baru* songs to combine a melodic framework played on the large *perahu* with a high descant played on the little *rincik*. This fundamental framework-plus-descant structure was formerly the preserve of the *tembang* songs, and the little *kacapi rincik* can be heard in any of the metrical *sekartandak* sections of songs in Group A. Similar use of a descant *kacapi* can be heard in the most recent of the *kreasi baru* songs on '*Batik*' (Recording 11).

Another technical development holds great promise. A pentatonically-tuned instrument makes for difficulties if performers or composers wish to change tone-scale (including major-minor) or pitch quickly. A partial solution was found in Central Java when a *celempung siter* (a board-zither related to the *kacapi*) was devised with stringing on both sides of the body and with reversible legs. Each side is differently tuned and the instrument may be turned over quite quickly, allowing for switching between scales.

A potentially much better solution, in the collection of Tatang Benjamin, is shown in the next photograph. This *kacapi* can be played in three different tone scales. Turning the knob at the end raises or lowers pegs which act as selective bridges altering the pitch of some of the strings and giving an instantaneous change of scale which allows for many new combinations of song and style.

Traditionally, certain songs have been regarded as 'fitting together' – they can be arranged in pairs having similar or

245

A reversible *celempung siter*. Each side is tuned to a different pentatonic scale. The metal legs may be quickly reversed and the instrument turned over.

The experimental instrument half-turned to show stringing on both sides.

A three-scale re-tuneable *kacapi*. The instrument has potential as a means of changing scale quickly, but this prototype doesn't work very well. The rising pegs tend to miss the strings.

complementary mood, scale or pitch (examples on Recording 10). A newer trend is the arrangement of longer medleys of traditional tunes – for example, '*Potpourri*' (Recording 10). Most of the medleys are rather lightweight, but they have led to the development of the genre *gending karesmen/drama suara* in which Mang Koko Koswara has again been prominent.

Gending karesmen is a form of opera, of which *drama suara* (sound drama) is a shorter, unstaged version. An example is '*Pahlawan Samudra*' (Hero of the Seas – Recording 18). The accompaniment is a full Sundanese *gamelan*. The new libretto is usually based on a traditional story and the music is, essentially, a medley of traditional tunes.

Gending karesmen is elaborate and expensive to stage and performances are not common, although attempts were made to promote it as a tourist attraction.[149] One problem that producers of this genre have encountered is that singing while acting is an unfamiliar exercise for the Sundanese; there is not the strong operatic tradition that one finds in Bali, for instance. Sundanese singers normally perform sitting down and their voices lack great projection. At weddings or public functions they almost invariably use electronic amplification. *Gending karesmen* makes demands on singers (and their teachers) which have yet to be resolved.

Several other new musical genres have emerged in various districts of Sunda; one example is *Mubadah*, a speciality of Banten in the north-west which uses an ensemble of various bamboo instruments. But Atik Soepandi (1976) notes that not all

---

[149] Oejeng Soewargana, *Gending karesmen dalam perkembangan Parawisataan* (*gending karesmen* in the field of tourism development). Bandung, Ganaco, 1971.

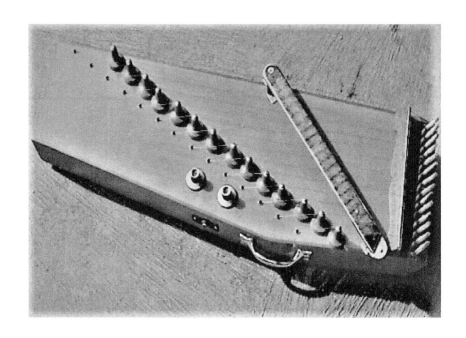

A small *kacapi rincik* (descant) with electric pickup. In the collection of Tatang Benjamin, Bandung.

these new forms have found much acceptance. In some cases, such as the combination of *gamelan degung* and *angklung* attempted in the 1960s, they were expensive and impractical. In others, Soepandi suggests that the 'new creations' failed to find an appropriate social role.[150] New impetuses such as nationalism that might have directly affected *karawitan Sunda* seem to have left hardly any trace. The few famous nationalist songs such as 'Hallo, Bandung' are essentially Western in style, while the *angklung*, supposedly a symbol of Indonesian cultural revival, may be playing Strauss waltzes. In *karawitan Sunda* the drive appears to be for *kreasi baru*, innovation as an end in itself. There is an enormous sense of pride in the vitality and continued development of the tradition,[151] and great store is set by innovation. Final exams at KOKAR include composition in a wide variety of old and new forms.

Sundanese musicians have an enormous range of resources to draw on. Soepandi (1976) lists no fewer than 64 types of instrument, and there is a tradition of making instruments out of tools of work – for example, the *kecrek* derived from creaking baskets, or the *suling kumbang*, a flute that doubles as a defensive weapon for solitary herdsmen – that suggests endless new possibilities. And new social roles: Indonesian villages use a system of drumbeats on a hollow log to warn of thieves, floods and other danger. Recently a new coded signal has been added, reminding the villagers each evening to make proper use of their contraceptives. It is the flexibility, the fluid combining and

---

[150] Soepandi, 1976, pp.43-4 and 64-5.
[151] One symptom of which is the giving out of honours, now a regular event. Presidents Sukarno and Soeharto have both made awards to musicians. In 1971, Mang Koko Koswara was given the title 'Anugerah Seni' (gift from God to the arts), something like the Japanese 'Living Heritage'.

recombining, the inventiveness and the willingness to give anything a fair trial that is impressive. This is not to imply a lack of firm discrimination; the Sundanese persist, for instance, in having no taste for triple time in *karawitan*.[152] There is also a great reverence for the traditional forms. And yet I have heard a *kacapi* player at a wedding insert ornaments derived from Chuck Berry rock-and-roll into the most solemn processional music. No one was the least bit offended.

THE RECORDINGS: The following twenty commercial cassettes were bought by the author in Bandung, West Java, between 1978-80, and given to the British Institute of Recorded Sound in London for dubbing in 1981.

GROUP A: *Tembang*

The classical song repertoire, traditionally performed for the aristocracy. *Tembang* is usually accompanied by a small ensemble consisting of two zithers: a *kacapi indung* (otherwise called a *kacapi prahu* – i.e. 'mother' or 'boat') which is a large instrument providing the base and framework of the song; a *kacapi rincik* (*rincik* = high, little) a small version which plays a descant during the strict rhythm sections; and a *suling* end-blown bamboo flute.

1. *Tembang Sunda*
2. *Sukapura*
3. *Tembang Sunda Timbanganten*
4. *Lagu-Lagu Pupuh*

---

[152] Triple time hardly exists in *karawitan Sunda*, but there are one or two folk songs, probably of distant European origin, which have found their way into the repertoire.

GROUP B: *Kacapian* and *kawih.*

The term *kawih* refers to songs, usually in strict rhythm as opposed to the freer recitative style of *tembang* – although, confusingly, *kawih* is sometimes also used to denote the metrical second half of *tembang* pieces. *Kawih* songs are often accompanied by a solo *kacapi siter* (the modern, portable *kacapi*). Such songs are called *kacapian* and are of very mixed origin, with some old and some new compositions. The acknowledged master of 20th century *kacapian* is Mang Koko Koswara. *Kawih* songs may also be accompanied by a *gamelan* orchestra, and as such are used as light relief during *wayang* (puppet) performances.

5. *Kacapi Abdi*
6. *Swara Euis Komariah G*
7. *Salam Manis*
8. *Panca Usaha Tani*
9. *Tukang Baso Tahu*
10. *Beca* (Koko Koswara)
11. *Kacapi Sunda*

GROUP C: *Gamelan degung.*

The Sundanese *gamelan* is smaller than the Javanese and can be played on its own, or with flutes or voices. It has a large repertoire, both traditional and modern. *Degung* is the name of a tone scale, but also implies a particular ensemble and style of performance.

12. *Mangsa Padeukeut*
13. *Sangkala*

GROUP D: *Kacapi suling*

Haunting instrumental music played on a bamboo flute and one or more *kacapis*.

14. *Pasanggrahan*
15. *Landangan*

GROUP E: various

16. *Badminton* (Koko Koswara)
17. *Kunang-Kunang*
18. *Drama Suara Pahlawan Samudra (gending karesmen)*
19. *Bangbang Sagara (pantun)*
20. *Ngandung Jabang (tarling)*

SMALL IS POOR
Little press poetry in Britain [153]

If poetry is thriving in Britain, much of the credit should go to hundreds of specialist publishing houses which band together as the Association of Little Presses. Unfortunately, while sales are booming, the little presses are not.

The Association was founded by Mr Stuart Montgomery, Mr Bob Cobbing and half a dozen other 'small' publishers ranging from established enterprises like Anvil and Bloodaxe, to short-lived owner-author imprints, some of which have even more bizarre names like Spectacular Diseases, Nothing Doing in London, and Joe Soap's Canoe. Most have long track records in poetry publishing. All need tenacity, humour, and a tolerant bank manager.

Britain's Arts Council – that is, the taxpayer – used to give money to the little presses, but support was reduced in the early 1980s under the Arts Council's former literature director, Mr Charles Osborne. Today, only a handful of presses get government money regularly; many live from hand to mouth, with occasional grants from regional or national bodies. Most of the little presses print only a few hundred copies of each title, and recoup costs only over many years. Distribution is time consuming; bookshops take the titles for sale-or-return; the number of willing outlets is shrinking.

Yet the little presses have given a start to many of the poets who have become mainstays of the established literary publishers.

---

[153] *The Economist, c.*August 1986. Heavily edited in the *Economist* house style, and unsigned.

Mr Tom Paulin, who edited the *Faber Book of Political Verse*, began his career with a pamphlet called *Theoretical Locations* from Honest Ulsterman publications. And they provide an outlet for the many influential figures in British poetry who are ignored by the bigger publishers. Douglas Oliver and J.H.Prynne are poets of international repute, but several of Mr Prynne's works have been published by little presses at his own expense.

The established presses call the little ones 'ivory tower intellectuals'. But what they label obscure often just means influenced by the rest of Europe and America. However discriminating the palate of Mr Craig Raine, Faber's chief poetry editor, it seems unhealthy to leave one third of the British market under the control of one man. The little presses provide necessary diversity.

Museum of Mankind: War Drums on the Amazon [154]

March 20th marks the first anniversary of a British Museum exhibition that has ruffled many feathers. 'Hidden peoples of the Amazon' assembles the best of the Museum's collections of blowpipes, ornaments, weaving and, indeed, an entire communal long-house. Survival International (SI), the organisation that campaigns for the rights of native peoples, immediately objected.

---

[154] *The Economist*, 26 March 1986. The Museum of Mankind, an offshoot of the British Museum sited in the rear half of the Royal Academy, no longer exists, having been reabsorbed into the BM. It had never attracted the visitor numbers hoped for.

It believes that the last section of the exhibition, staged at the Museum of Mankind, trivialises the plight of Amazonian Indians whose lives and environment are daily eroded by prospectors, loggers, road builders and land speculators, who are tearing the rainforest apart. Particularly offensive – says SI – is a large photograph of a Panaré Indian sitting astride a motorcycle. The inference, it is claimed, is that roads bring wealth and freedom rather than disease and destruction.

SI, together with anthropologists and other experts, offered advice and materials to the Museum. The materials were accepted, they say, the advice ignored. A blazing row ensued, with SI accusing the museum of 'falsifying' the situation in the Amazon, and the Museum retorting that 'it would not be proper for the Museum, or consistent with its established scholarly function, to campaign on [the Indians'] behalf.' SI denies that it is asking for a campaign, only accuracy, and has submitted a list of proposed alterations, which the Museum has declined to adopt. 'You misapprehend the situation,' it says, 'if you think you have control over the form and content of the exhibition.'

SI has proved adept at getting press coverage, especially by arranging a visit (paid for by OXFAM) by two established Indian leaders, who expressed their indignation and were photographed in front of the offending photograph. With further money from Christian Aid, a short film was made and a counter-exhibition mounted in the Burlington Arcade, hard by the Museum.

Why so much ill-humour? Behind the specifics lurk other issues. SI has been accused of using the exhibition as a ready means of attracting attention, money and new members in a new style of campaign. This it angrily denies, claiming that it has gained few supporters and spent much time and money that could have gone into projects in the field. The Museum trustees, with the shadow of the Elgin marbles on their shoulders, do not welcome directives from the laity.

The Indians who visited the exhibition are known and seasoned campaigners; their objections caused no surprise in the Museum. But would the Indians want their culture represented at its best or its worst? 'To show these cultures in broken, degenerate states is equally offensive,' says the Museum's Mr Malcolm Macleod. 'Show them at their best and the sense of loss is greater.' SI is unimpressed. Its director, Mr Stephen Corry, remarked, 'It's a bit like an exhibition on the Jews in 1945 that makes no mention of Auschwitz.'

When SI requested a further meeting recently, the Museum's director of public services, Mr Gordon House, refused. 'I know what you're up to... I see no point.' The Museum must see the point a little, however, having in mid-February held a three-day seminar on 'Making an Exhibition of Ourselves'. Meanwhile SI intends to carry the debate abroad. The Museum does not entirely object; admissions are up on last year by 40%.

MADAME MAO IN MANAGUA [155]

Nicaragua is an extreme example of a small, poor country struggling to find its cultural feet. Small and poor undoubtedly: its

[155] *The Economist*, 16 August 1986, an article written at the same time as those on public health in Central America at the top of this volume. This piece was heavily edited to make it critical of any socialist (especially Cuban) involvement, and I realised my brief time writing for *The Economist* was over. The allusions to Mao and Madame Mao, for example, are not mine.

3.3m people have an average annual income of $1,400 each. And extreme for two reasons. First, because the country is, in effect, at war, both literally – against the 'Contras'[156] – and also in words and ideology with the United States. Second because it is, in some ways, a new country.

In 1979, when the Sandinists [157] threw out President Somoza, cultural life was moribund. The cultural establishment had been discredited. Popular culture had been stamped upon. Dance, for instance, had been one of Nicaragua's most vibrant forms of expression; by 1979, traditional dance-theatre such as the *Güegüense* was little more than a memory; other dances, such as the erotic *Palo de Mayo* (maypole) had been commercialised.

The new masters of Nicaragua saw the tasks of reviving the arts and of setting up a new Nicaragua as one and the same. There had been a radical political change. What was needed to reflect it?

Literacy was the key. In 1979, half of adult Nicaraguans were illiterate. Within a month of President Somoza's overthrow, the Sandinists had announced a huge teaching campaign. Sixty thousand volunteers (mostly high-school students and fellow-travellers from all over the world) tramped out into the countryside to teach people to read and write. In only five months, according to UNESCO, they reduced illiteracy to 12%.

If that is true, then Nicaragua had almost overnight become the third most literate country in Latin America (after Argentina and, Cuba, says Cuba). Even if Nicaragua's claim is exaggerated, the contrast with the old days is startling and the benefits have begun to show up.

The literacy programme has provided a new audience, and a

---

[156] See p.14, above.

[157] It was typical of the *Economist* house style that they refused to use the widely known Spanish form 'Sandinista', insisting on anglicising it.

new lease of life, for the country's poets. Nicaragua has a long poetic tradition and has produced one of the best Spanish-language poets of the 20th century, Ruben Dario.

The programme has also revived and preserved the popular verse of rural communities, much of which is published by the Ministry of Culture (and some of which is dreadful). Everybody seems to be writing – even the army and the police force. We fought to restored civilisation to Nicaragua, they say; we should now take part in that civilisation.

Aristotle thought poetics and politics were separate ways of thinking, but the new poetry shows what can happen when politicians try to impose their own ideas on a culture. Mr Ernesto Cardenal argued Maoishly that sonnets, rhyme and traditional poetic forms should be banned – in theory so that peasant writers could create a new poetry. Mr Bayardo Arce, the junta's leading firebrand, railed that 'We don't want to see our new culture sliding back into the decadent forms we had before.' But culture in Nicaragua (as in other states short of totalitarian) has burst the political bounds.

True, bookshops are stuffed with Cuban and Soviet books and censorship is rife. But it does not pass without fierce opposition. Take radio, one of the most important ways of reaching remote parts of the country. The government runs Radio Sandino, but there are a dozen national stations (including Radio Güegüense, broadcasting classical music from dawn to dusk). In the newspaper *El Nuevo Diario*, Mr Augusto Sarmiento recently launched a full blooded attack on Radio Sandino. Lamenting the poor quality of radio broadcasting, he went on to say, 'Silence is preferable to the falsifications, poor analysis and self-aggrandisement... that Radio Sandino transmits daily.'

Or take newspapers. The country's best known newspaper *La Prensa* is censored and its literary editor, the distinguished poet Mr Pablo Antonio Cuadra, says that the Union of Cultural Workers has threatened *La Prensa*'s writers with sanctions. But *La Prensa* is still published and Mr Cuadra has led the attack on Mr Arce. 'Hitler used the word 'decadent' to exile the arts of the avante-garde,' he says. 'Censorship is cowardice.'

Mr Cuadra puts his finger on a problem faced by both government and opposition: 'Since the Discovery, Latin America has been taking its cultural models from elsewhere. This Soviet-Cuban model is just the latest.' The influence of foreign culture – including that of the dreaded Yankee – is everywhere.

The Sandinists' cultural policies have wide-eyed nationalism in them as well as gung-ho Marxism. It is this that has led them to try and get their own version of the cultural revolution presented to the outside world. Gaining access to the world's media has, however, proved a struggle.

Cinema has been a test case. Before 1979, Nicaragua had few technicians and almost no skilled cameramen or directors. To begin with, Cubans and others helped the Nicaraguans to pick up the camera and shoot. Gradually, however, Nicaraguans have taken over the work themselves. They set up a state film institute, INCINE, which made the short film *Alcino and the Condor* in 1983 (it was good enough to be nominated for an Oscar). The first full-length Nicaraguan feature, *Women of the Frontier*, is due to be released on July 19th, the anniversary of the revolution.

Other visual arts – television documentaries, photography, painting – show the same pattern: initial outside domination and increasing Nicaraguan self-confidence. Managua has been called 'the capital of mural art'. It is an imported skill, influenced by the

Mexican muralists of the early 20th century. But the Nicaraguans learn fast: propaganda daubs are becoming refined and expressive. The Videonic documentary studio was set up in 1981 with $120,000 from 14 international aid agencies. Its job is to produce documentaries for use abroad and to train Nicaraguan television journalists. The first spin-off studio is now run by Nicaraguans alone.

It is not in visual arts, however, that the Nicaraguans have most successfully expressed their 'cultural insurrection', but in song. The guitar has become a symbol of the revolution, and the songs which at the beginning included such un-lyrical themes as how to strip and load a machine-gun, have become gentle elegies about reconstruction and hope.

There is little doubt that, for the moment, the arts are flourishing in Nicaragua. But so they did in the early days of Fidel Castro's Cuba. The danger is that what has been achieved by the Sandinists will be ruined, as it has been in Cuba, by the heavy hand of politicians trying to enforce what they have so far had the luck to encourage: a flourishing culture.

WITH MR DICK

The Scottish Branch of the Writers Guild met the head of the Scottish Film Production Fund. [158]

In recent months, the familiar cries of 'Whither the Scottish film industry?' have intensified, culminating in the publication in April of *Scotland on Screen* (*SoS*), a report commissioned by Scottish Enterprise at the request of the Secretary of State and produced by Hydra Associates. It is a measure of the deep involvement of writers in this process that the Scottish Branch of the Writers Guild was entirely unaware of its occurrence until a copy of the report arrived via London. Eddie Dick, fresh from restructuring the Scottish Film Production Fund, was an important adviser to *SoS*, and is in broad agreement with it.

He began our conversation by saying that, in a landscape now being transformed by the Lottery and the revival of cinema viewing, we have got to change dramatically our approach to film-making in Scotland. The nub of the matter is this: although Scotland can claim some successes such as *Taggart, Trainspotting, Small Faces* and others, and although we have some excellent writers and crews and unmatched locations, still our total production output is a small percentage of the UK whole and an almost invisible percentage of world figures, with a

---

[158] *Writers Newsletter* (Writers Guild of GB) August 1996. For a couple of years I was the chair of this Scottish branch. The interview took place in the context of the Edinburgh Film & Television Festival. At the time of writing I was active as a screenwriter, and on the receiving end of some Arts Council largesse such as a week of training with a cohort of others in Inverness, where I was sadly struck by the low level of knowledge and experience in Scottish film aspirants. By this time I had had a year at a Hollywood film school (USC) as a Fulbright Fellow, and had seen what a difference serious training meant.

minuscule market share to match. The networks persistently fight shy of Scottish production; Channel 4, for example, spends far less on making programmes in Scotland than it receives in Scottish revenue, spending twice as much in Liverpool alone. What is needed north of the border is, above all, a boost to production.

SoS compares our fragmented industry – with its insufficient production facilities, uncoordinated public bodies, and inadequate capital – to the disciplined Irish, who captured *Braveheart* from under our feet.

In response, the report recommends a unified Scottish Screen Agency, improved access to finance, new production facilities – located partly in the Highlands – and reorganised marketing achieved by, for instance, transforming the Edinburgh Film Festival into a serious selling forum. The Board of the Scottish Screen Agency would be appointed by the Secretary of State, and would have the muscle to direct resources, grants and tax incentives as required to secure investment in the Irish manner.

SoS is resolute in its industrial emphasis. If the industry is to develop, scripts must not merely be written, developed, and admired, but produced. Making films is the only way to make a film industry. Thus, although there is a relative shortfall in available technical staff – such that crews have had on occasion to be imported from England[159] – the contributors to *SoS* do not see training (e.g. the establishment of a Scottish film school) as a high priority. Rather, the activity of production is itself the stimulus required. 'Talent should be pulled rather than pushed.' And that (argues *SoS*) is above all a commercial matter.

---

[159] Reminiscent of the situation with musicians and the Chapel Royal in Edinburgh in 1630. See p.224, above.

No doubt – though a report in which writers do not feature seems to us a bizarre starting point. In the list of consultant interviews, no writers at all, and no Guild. In the flowcharts of the process of film-making, we see the terms *idea* and *development* but not *writer*. In Eddie Dick's view, those first terms imply a writer's involvement; cold comfort in oblivion, one might feel.

In the report, much is made of the need for developing production facilities, but nothing is said of the development or support in any sense of the writer. Again, Eddie Dick defended the report, pointing out that 'writers get the gigs' – i.e. script development funds – while a producer (let alone a camera operator) sees not a penny until those all too rare moments when pre-production commences.

From our point of view, there are plenty of qualms here. *SoS* asserts that, 'There was some suspicion as to whether the Scottish tradition encouraged commercial writing.' As a result, there are few Scottish writers with any clout at STV. This situation, of course, is hardly helped by an enquiry that does not think writers worth consulting. *SoS* contrasts the Scottish industry with Hollywood's 'well organised response to inherent risk'. For writers the risk is firstly the matter of a livelihood. As *SoS* acknowledges, the European industry as a whole spends less than 1/10th of the money that the US majors put into developing scripts. It's just as frustrating trying to get your script on camera in Hollywood; in my own spell at a leading film school there my (excellent) teacher had never seen one of his scripts filmed. But at least that industry pays writers to keep working, which is surely the *sine qua non* of a continued flow of creativity.

None of us, however, would dispute the need to confront the 'immaturity of Scottish production' (Eddie Dick's phrase) as shown in the exceptional difficulty we face in moving from script to production. Independent producers in Scotland, with so few films actually being shot, are woefully short on experience. For Eddie Dick, it is the 'experience of production' that will transform this situation. Indeed, in the revamped operations of the Production Fund, writers' bursaries do not feature at all – because, of those supported in the past, 'none came close to production.'

The emphasis of the Fund's financing policy will be to support the 'creative producer' and the 'writer/producer core team'. Thus, for example, of a maximum of £15,000 in any first tranche given to a script in development, it is envisaged that a percentage must go to the producer to support their costs. Meanwhile, projects will be examined and funding decisions made by a much broader-based board, thus partly answering the criticism that the fate of every script has seemed to be finally determined by the same two or three people.

Expert panels are to be established on Development, Production and Special Projects (e.g. *Tartan Shorts*). While Catherine Aitken is now responsible for script development, Eddie Dick will head the effort to push productions to completion. On that, our futures may well depend.[160]

---

[160] Just over a year after this interview, Eddie Dick resigned from Scottish Screen and its various permutations, having been accused by film makers of poor judgement and cronyism.

CHAPMAN

Recent paintings at the Galleria delle Ore, Milan [161]

Since his last exhibition in Milan in 1984, Christopher Chapman has taken his painting out of doors. In his previous show, his subjects moved in hothouse interiors, conscious of the space that exists between people even in moments of intimacy.

Now there is access to an outside world: effects of *contrejour* light before windows, people slipping out through doors, luminous exteriors where the figures – some clearly young, human and sybaritic, others only suggestive of human forms – turn away from us, averting their gaze, not speaking.

What has happened? Christopher Chapman dates this line of thought to a visit to the British Museum in 1985. A huge piece of classical statuary – a collosal horse in stone – captivated him, massive, elegant but also brutal. He began to paint a quasi-classical landscape in which the figures possess that same detached gracefulness where the qualities of flesh and stone begin to merge, where the foliage of plants is hard and dense like the columns, where the figures are still, but where there are other forms, lifeless, reminiscent of bones and architectural fragments which are beginning to move, to turn, but always away from us. It is a harshly virile scene painted with a strict sense of design and the discipline of rectilinear composition which the painter has found in Pisanello and the masters of the Japanese print. In spite of their formal elegance, however, these paintings reveal a world beneath the surface, and touch a range of complex emotions.

---

[161] Introductory note for an exhibition catalague, 1987. It was translated into Italian.

Again, from this discipline a tenderness emerges, a love of the playful sensuality between people which transcends the splendid but desolate surroundings which we have invented for ourselves.

These canvases are the work of a painter seduced but not fooled by what he sees; one who is able to give full credit to the beauty which is to be found in a harsh world.

CHRISTOPHER CHAPMAN
MEMORY & REALITY [162]

In probing my childhood (which is the next best to probing one's eternity), I see the awakening of consciousness as a series of spaced flashes, with the intervals between them gradually diminishing until bright blocks of perception are formed, affording memory a slippery hold.

Valdimir Nabokov, *Speak, Memory* (1951)

For the child, the physical qualities of a moment may enshrine or reify a barely understood emotion, to be stored away. The adult, searching back through the deepest layers of their own formation, may find psychological experience preserved in remembered physical perception. Nabokov is trying to recall his own sudden dawning of self-conciousness:

---

[162] Catalogue essay for an exhibition at Sarah Guinan Associates, London, in 1997.

Judging by the strong sunlight that, when I think of that revelation, immediately invades my memory with lobed sun flecks through overlapping patterns of greenery, the occasion may have been my mother's birthday, in late summer, in the country…

Christopher Chapman's work has often dealt with emotional states rendered as encounters with concrete phenomena. One such state is anticipation. In many of his pictures there is a doorway, either bright with a sense of arrival in a bright room or dark with summons to pass through and investigate. What is discovered is never revealed: we are left waiting for the effect of the potential encounter. Much of Chapman's own chldhood was spent in the city of St Albans (north of London), at the margins of which the remains of the Roman town of Verulamium may still be found in amongst thick woods. Faced with a phalanx of trees, with the narrowest of dark openings between, the child's imagination has fed off the encounter: What will I met if I go among them? What is it that now inhabits this place? What forces entice me dangerously forward – or provocatively bar my way?

Chapman's painting has always had a strong architectural aspect, in which people and sculptural forms come together in tightly disciplined classical compositions. Previously these had often been in a Mediterranean setting. The new paintings maintain the discipline but have a much more intimate tone. Paradoxically, now there is no overt human presence – except the observer, who is drawn closer. Many of the paintings evoke the child's intent gaze upon interiors: a door in a corner, an old fireplace, a swag of drapery, with surface patterns compounded of décor and the play of light. The atmosphere is at times claustrophobic; at others, delightful. The artist himself has written:

More than one painting deals with unquiet states of mind, although in others I have tried to capture the wonderful, simple pleasure that gazing at the sunlight on a wall can give, while one's mind is empty of thoughts or feelings.

The infant's unformed intelligence may be simply and directly impressed by luminous spectacle. In adult life we can but rarely recreate a child's intense perception of the immediate world, its physical sensations and its emnotional atmosphere; these are interwoven in the young mind in ways that the adult forgets. Only children appreciate the awesome significance of cracks in the pavement. Yet many of us will dimly recall how acutely we once encountered the roughness of fabric, the sheen of paints, the streaming of dust in a shaft of sunlight. We may vaguely remember how, in quiet moments, tiny patterns or focal points seemed to bulk huge in front of our infant eyes, or how trivial actions – passing through a door, parting a curtain, moving from sun into shadow – took on a frightening or a grand significance. A child in a small room may feel itself to be contained in a cavern of colours and shadows, onto which emotions are projected. A dark corner may be fearful – not fear of something hidden *in* that corner, but the place itself. A sunwarmed surface may constitute safety or pleasure; love and light may be the same thing.

Occasionally the artist recreates these direct correlations – and such is the world of these paintings: not memory as such, but a means of merging subject and emotion that derives from earlier experience. This is a species of metaphor which differs from our usual understanding. For example, the subject of the painting – a pattern, a pace – does not *represent* or *stand* for a certain

270

emotion; rather, in a literal sense, it *is* the artist's emotion. Such literal metaphor is difficult for us, but has been noted in other cultures by anthropologists: Evans-Pritchard quotes the view of the Nuer people of Sudan, that 'a twin is a bird'. Not *like,* but *is.*

For an artist of this turn of mind, painting *is* emotion. An impulse is rendered as a painted surface. The result is something tangible – both the painting that emerges, and the 'subject' that emerges. The subject, the emotion and the painting are identical: they take shape together as the artist carefully applies layers of pigment. The emotion then passes away; the painted scene may never have had any substance at all – but the painting stands.

The style of these works seems to follow readily: they have a tactile but soft-edged quality in which the flash of light or the pattern above the mantel seem almost more solid than the architectural features. Small details are absent, not because they have been excluded but because they never featured in the emotional impulse.

Then again there is that quality of potential and anticipation. It may seem strange to refer to silence in painting – but something like it pertains here. It is a living, expectant silence. The observer is poised, waiting, wondering whether to move or to stay still. The status quo will not last; the enquirer will make a decision to move to one side, losing the symmetry; the door will close, or a cloud pass over the sun. The moment will be remembered only as a screen of warm colours, of living patterns.

LETTERS

In the 1980s in particular I was much involved with nuclear disarmament, having been taken as a small child on one of the very first Aldermaston marches by my parents, and being pictured with a placard in Regent Street on the front of the *Daily Telegraph*. As a student nurse in Oxford (1982-5) I was a member of the Medical Campaign against Nuclear Weapons, and took part in a sit-down demo at Upper Heyford (US Air Force) base, being duly dragged across the road by Thames Valley Police who outnumbered the demonstrators ten to one. For this I was warned by the School of Nursing that I risked disciplinary action for 'bringing the profession into disrepute'. I was also local secretary of the Peace Tax Campaign, a Quaker initiative. To this day I pay £5 a month to Scottish CND, who have long forgotten my address or who I am.

One other letter backfired. I wrote to my mother's parish council in Oxfordshire, demanding in some detail to know what provision had been made for civil defence in the case of nuclear attack, and I attended the next council meeting to hear their reply. They responded politely that they didn't disagree with my position, but that my mother's house was actually just over the boundary, in the next parish.

1. TO *ENCOUNTER* [163]

Lord Chalfont,[164] in his piece on nuclear disarmament (*Encounter*, January) makes several acute and cogently phrased observations, particularly with regard to the psychology of strategic parity. He also uses a number of arguments that are wrong-headed. For example, with reference to the 'inconvenient historical fact' of Hiroshima, would he have us believe that, had the Japanese been able to retaliate with nuclear weapons of their own, the Pacific War would have ended in the subdued rattle of small arms? Such historical speculations are hardly sufficient to allay the perfectly reasonable fear that, in a rapidly escalating European war, any enemy might soon feel obliged to knock out Britain's nuclear armoury before it could be used. Nuclear war is indeed a very different matter from conventional war. But, because the planners increasingly see nuclear weaponry as no more than an extension to the conventional arsenal, the example of Hiroshima is rapidly and sadly losing any force it might once have had.

Lord Chalfont continues: 'Since the British nuclear arsenal is largely submarine-based…it is invulnerable to a pre-emptive strike directed against the United Kingdom.' What sort of smoke-screening is that? Surely he realises that much of CND's current effort is directed against the introduction of land-based cruise missiles? And what of those American missiles sited in the UK that he himself refers to?

What is perhaps more distressing is his use of *ad hominem*

---

[163] *Encounter*, February 1981.

[164] Lord Chalfont was a former soldier who became a Labour minister under Harold Wilson, then a crossbench peer, then a Tory by 1981. He died aged 100 in 2020.

arguments to discredit the Disarmament Campaign. To the characterisation of E.P. Thompson and his allies as the harbingers of the Dark Ages of a Marxist Britain, one can only reply that Lord Chalfont cannot have paid very close attention to the writings of a man whose attachment to fundamental British institutions is passionate and unambiguous. His slur on Thompson's military acumen rests on the [BBC TV] *Panorama* argument over the value of tanks.[165] At the time no doubt many other brows were raised. More recent events on Iranian soil have, if anything, proved Thompson right. Western military observers have (it is widely reported) shown increasing alarm at the ease with which Iran's British-built tanks have been knocked out. Thermal imaging and lasers have done little to save them.

Lord Chalfont's attacks on the integrity of other disarmers are little more than abuse, especially the image of the 'protagonists of Soviet influence in our society [who] ply their trade in many disguises – teachers, professors etc.' This is cheap, and particularly hurtful to the many intelligent, indeed distinguished people who have had to wrestle hard in order to reconcile themselves to the full implications of an anti-nuclear position. He certainly can't have sampled the heartbreaking business of door-to-door campaigning.

There are 'mindless fanatics' on both sides of the argument. Does Lord Chalfont feel his own position to be in any way

---

[165] E P Thompson had been a tank commander in WW2, and had emphasised tank vulnerability. Other speakers in the debate had accused him of being out of date, of not knowing about modern laser-guided weaponry etc. However, during the Iran-Iraq War of 1980-88, Iran's British-made Chieftain tanks had suffered numerous casualties, as did hundreds of Iraqi tanks then and during the two Gulf Wars. A consignment of British tanks bought by Iran in 1976, paid for but never delivered, remain in dispute today. In modern military thinking, tanks are of diminishing importance.

discredited by the antics of the British Movement, or his own opinions irredeemably soiled by the coincidental utterances of Mr Martin Webster? [166]

2) TO THE *WITNEY GAZETTE* on 'HISTORICAL PARALLELS'. [167]

I would like to reply to various points raised by Mr Charles Hornsby in his letter 'In Defence of Defence.'

Surely the tossing about of statistics – 200 million tons of TNT here, 16,000 million tons there – only illustrates the lunacy of the situation we are now in? Never fear, Mr Hornsby, there will be enough to go round. But, for the moment, I am more interested in the problem of historical example. Like many other advocates of deterrence, Mr Hornsby asks us to consider the 'parallels with 1939.'

What are these parallels, exactly? Do they not rest on the assumption that history repeats itself, and that we can predict events in 1985 by examining those of 1945? Suppose I was to draw a different lesson from history, and argue that I know of no single case in which the circumstances of war have even remotely repeated themselves?

Or suppose I was to extrapolate statistics and say that, in the war of 1939-45, 20 millions or more died, and that we should multiply this figure by some unimaginable factor to account for

---

[166] Leader of the National Front (UK). The following year (1982), 'rumours of his homosexuality led to his being vilified in right-wing circles.' (Wikipedia)

[167] *Witney Gazette* (Oxfordshire), 14 January 1981. My mother's local paper. Witney is a solidly conservative market town, and was David Cameron's constituency until 2016.

the power of nuclear weaponry in the next war. And suppose I was to wonder whether our traditional liberties are actually worth 20 million dead (times factor X)?

And then, further lessons from history press for consideration. I don't wish to be overrun by Russians. But what are the 'historical parallels'? Britain has been seriously invaded twice within our written history – by the Romans and by the Normans. The results? The revivifying of a sagging culture and great long-term benefits all round. Just think what it might do for British Leyland.[168] Is there no lesson there? But Mr Hornsby would have us be more selective about our parallels.

I trust Mr Hornsby will not take me seriously. We are not answerable to history, we are answerable only to the future. A nuclear war will be like nothing we have ever known. There is only one relevant lesson from history, which is that arms races, arms parity and 'balances of power' are as old as mankind. And so are wars.

---

[168] BL's headquarters factory was at Cowley, Oxford, and was forever in the doldrums. The plant is now owned by foreigners (BMW) and doing much better.

LETTERS TO THE *TIMES LITERARY SUPPLEMENT*

Not all my letters to the *TLS* have been published, sadly. Other topics I tried included the confusion of the playwright John Ford with the film director; the translation of Proust; the 'tight boot' philosophy of Machado de Assis; the poor public reading technique of the poet John Ashberry compared to Basil Bunting; the riverside monuments of Torgau; the neglect (by the *TLS*) of Cambridge poetry; the titles of Steig Larsson thrillers; and the 'Castalian Band' of Renaissance Scotland. The latter was at least cited in an editorial column. Here are others they have accepted:

1. BURNING HOUSES

Reviewing *House of Fiction: From Pemberley to Brideshead, great British houses in literature and life*, Paula Byrne chides Phyllis Richardson for not giving due mention to the Anglo-Irish tradition. But Byrne's own choice of an example – Molly Keane's *Good Behaviour* – itself misses a notable feature of houses in fiction: their propensity to go up in flames at the end of the story. Think, rather, of Keane's *Two Days in Aragon*, where the IRA set fire to the old home. Think, too, of Elizabeth Bowen's *Last September* in which not one but two Irish houses are burned by the rebels in the last pages.

In fact, burning houses are a recurrent feature of storytelling. Henry James (*Spoils of Poynton*), Charlotte Brontë (*Jane Eyre*) and of course Jean Rhys (*Wide Sargasso Sea*), likewise Daphne du Maurier (*Rebecca*) all finish by burning a house. So do I, in fact (*The White Porcupine*). So do modern crime writers such as Belinda Bauer (*Darkside*) and Barbara Vine (*The Minotaur*), while Vine's denouement in a burning library recalls Umberto Eco's *Name of the Rose*. Drama is flammable too: Tom

Stoppard's *Arcadia* consumes a stately home in an inferno. Other houses that combust in films started out by burning in a novel first, for instance *What's Eating Gilbert Grape* (by Peter Hedges), while at the end of *The Dressmaker* (novel by Rosalie Ham) the whole town burns down, as of course does Margaret Mitchell's Atlanta (*Gone with the Wind*), these two taking a hint from the Gawain Poet who burns down Troy in line 2 of the poem.[169]

TLS readers can I'm sure think of many other examples. It is a truism of Creative Writing courses that, by the end of the story, 'the world will have changed' – and nothing changes a character's world so conclusively as arson.

2. TRILINGUAL MALAYSIA

Thomas Meaney takes George Steiner to task for the embarrassing 'inaccuracy' of saying that in Malaysia 'one grows up speaking three languages'. I wonder what the inaccuracy would be? My father, Robert Le Page, was a sociolinguist who worked in Malaysia and Singapore among other multilingual societies, and by his account three languages would be very common for children. Exactly which languages would depend on the social and ethnic groups, but a middle-class Chinese child might speak Hokkien to the family servant and/or their parents, perhaps Mandarin to their grandparents, Malay at school, and English as they advanced in education or became commercially active. Other families would be speaking Tamil, Malay, English... The permutations were many. Steiner – always a gifted linguist – no doubt recognized kindred spirits.

---

[169] One letter in reply thought that I should have given this credit to Homer.

3. ELENA FERRANTE

Ruth Scurr is only the latest commentator to savage the Italian Journalist Claudio Gatti for his 'shabby' outing of Elena Ferrante. I find this bluster unfair and unconvincing. Before I was ever aware of the debate, I read two of the Neapolitan novels with enjoyment, but this began to flag, as did my belief in the world I was being offered. I was intrigued by the tussle over the novels' authenticity, however that is understood. Scurr says that there will be no applause for Gatti 'in the vital literary world'. Maybe not – but I'm sure readers currently keeping quiet are interested, too. [170]

Commentators would have me ashamed of my interest in the 'tittle tattle' of Ferrante's own life. I'm not ashamed, any more than I am ashamed of my mild interest in the personality behind George Eliot, Baron Corvo, Barbara Vine or any other pseudonym. I am a novelist myself, and an academic, and a private reader too. From each point of view, and as Scurr's review itself illustrates, the relationship with her readers that Ferrante has constructed is of interest. She did not have to do this; plenty of writers have politely declined interviews without jeopardizing their home life. Scurr elaborates on other reasons Ferrante may have for detaching herself from her writing, but why should the author call every shot? Claudio Gatti outsmarted her in a game which she herself initiated. *Vis-à-vis* the readership that pays for her books, Ferrante has taken up a position – and one need not insult readers who take one back.

---

[170] Dr Ruth Scurr is a biographer of that supreme literary gossip, John Aubrey.

4. PLAIN ENGLISH

Nicholas Murray writes of his tribulations teaching plain English to rather resistant students at London universities. I had one of those Royal Literary Fund fellowships at Dundee University, trying to encourage fourth years and postgraduates to write clearly and simply. One MA student brought me her thesis in which she repeatedly mentioned 'individuals operating in the commercial environment'; it took me a little while to realize what she meant, and to ask why she didn't just call them 'people shopping'?

'I can't,' she wailed, 'I have to sound like an economist!'

5. FRONTERIZOS

James Fenton yearns for a new edition of the fine old Spanish ballads of the *Romanceros*. I agree, but if Fenton would go a little further back in Spanish poetry he'd find a corpus of poems of perhaps even greater interest: the *fronterizos*. These were shorter lyrics portraying the final years of the Reconquest, the Christian defeat of the Moors, and their final expulsion from Spain in 1492.

Quite apart from making lovely songs (by composers such as Narváez, Encina and Fuenllana), what is remarkable about the *fronterizos* is their sympathy for the opposition, even though many would have been written at a Christian court. Several tell the story of the Reconquest from the point of view of the defeated Moors, for example the grief of the King of Granada on hearing of the imminent fall of his citadel at Antequera to a Christian army.

As frontiers harden against migrants across Europe, and as President Trump's battalions march towards Mexico to confront a caravan of half-starved families, how good it is to be reminded that one does not have to despise people on the far side of a frontier.

6. BURIED SPITFIRES

Mark Burman considers the story of the 'buried Spitfires of Burma', which were supposedly hidden on Mountbatten's orders to aid Britain's allies, the Karen people, in an uprising against the Burmese that eventually broke out in 1948. The story is ludicrous, but when I worked (in village healthcare) with the Karen in the 1980s, some villagers still recounted it. This was not the only instance of their being duped. My Karen counterpart showed me traces of an airstrip he had helped hack out of the forest in 1953, because two foreigners – British or possibly French – had come promising to deliver arms if the rebels gave them money and cleared a strip. The Karen handed over money, but no plane ever arrived. In the 1970s, the Karen downed a Burmese aircraft, and an American appeared saying he was a mechanic who could fix it, but he needed to purchase spares in Bangkok. They gave him the money...

The episodes are related in my *True Love and Bartholomew: Rebels on the Burmese border* (1991). Karen often characterized themselves to me – not without a wry pride – as honest and gullible. It's perhaps the way with outnumbered, outgunned insurgents, desperate for help.

7. THE OSTRICH INSTRUCTION

N J Enfield writes of the 'Ostrich Instruction', a principle in US law established by the case 'United States *v.* Jewell' (1976) in which Mr Jewell, having accepted $100 from a stranger to drive a car laden with marijuana across the border from Mexico, was caught and prosecuted, and whose defence – that he didn't know what was stashed in the car – was deemed inadequate. He must have had a pretty good idea (the prosecution claimed) and his wilful ignorance was tantamount to knowledge. The court agreed.

A similar situation arises at the beginning of Raymond Chandler's *The Long Goodbye* (1953). Philip Marlowe agrees to drive Terry Lennox south to Mexico, in spite of it being obvious that Lennox is a fugitive from imminent arrest. Marlowe refuses to let Lennox speak about what he has done. On Marlowe's return to Los Angeles, it is to the news that Lennox's wife is dead. The police insist that Marlowe must have known; Marlowe, in spite of a beating up in custody, insists that he did not – and after an uncomfortable day or so, gets away with it.

Much as I love *The Long Goodbye,* I can't be the only reader to wonder if Marlowe's escape is plausible. Did 'US *v.* Jewell' really change matters so radically?

8. STRICT FORM

Katherine Duncan-Jones says that, apart from the sonnet, the strict verse forms of early Languedoc and Sicily have little currency today. With respect, she is quite wrong. The sestina, villanelle and pantoum[171] are the stock-in-trade of writing groups across the land, and also of undergraduate creative writing courses. The reason is not far to seek: they are easy to teach and easier to mark.

---

[171] KD-J replied, correctly of course, that the pantoum is a Malay form, not European. This doesn't alter the point, though; these verse forms are part of the Open University course I teach, and I think many other courses also. KD-J was also unnecessarily disdainful on the subject of writing groups.

It is curious to think that modern students are more familiar with verse as practised at the court of Palermo $c.1200$ than they are with the work of, for instance, Ezra Pound at Pisa $c.1945$. It's as though art students were being taught to paint in the manner of Cimabue and Giotto.

Printed in Great Britain
by Amazon

76656203R00163